India and China

Professor Prabodh Chandra Bagchi
(November 18, 1898 – January 19, 1956)

India and China

Interactions through Buddhism and Diplomacy

A Collection of Essays by
Professor Prabodh Chandra Bagchi

Compiled by
Bangwei Wang and Tansen Sen

ANTHEM PRESS
LONDON · NEW YORK · DELHI

Anthem Press India
An imprint of Wimbledon Publishing Company India Private Limited (WPCIPL)
WPCIPL is a subsidiary of Wimbledon Publishing Company Limited (UK)

This edition first published in India 2011
by ANTHEM PRESS INDIA
www.anthempress.co.in

Cover illustration: Travelling Monk, from Cave 17, Mogao, near Dunhuang, Gansu province, China. Five Dynasties or Northern Song Dynasty, 10th century AD. Courtesy of the British Museum.

ISBN-13: 978 93 80601 37 3 (Pbk)
ISBN-10: 93 80601 37 9 (Pbk)

FOR SALE IN SOUTH ASIA ONLY

CONTENTS

COMPILERS' NOTE

It has been our honour to assemble some of Professor Prabodh Chandra Bagchi's (1898–1956) important articles on the interactions between ancient India and ancient China. The idea emerged during our discussions at a conference commemorating the scholarly contributions of Professor Bagchi and Tan Yunshan (1898–1983) to Sino-Indian studies held in Beijing, China, on 23–24 November 2008. The conference marked the 110th birth anniversaries of these two leading figures in the field of Sino-Indology.

We immediately contacted Professor Rajat Kanta Ray, Vice Chancellor of Visva-Bharati University in Santiniketan, India, for permission to use Professor Bagchi's essays, especially those that were reprinted in the volume entitled *Indological Studies: A Collection of Essays*. Professor Ray quickly responded to our email and allowed us to use the relevant essays from the volume. We also contacted the Monumenta Serica Institute seeking permission to publish Professor Bagchi's insightful essay on the names for ancient India found in Chinese sources. Professor Akira Yuyama kindly agreed to let us include his article on the contributions of Professor Bagchi to Sino-Indology. Mrs. Ratna Sinha, one of the daughters of Professor Bagchi, supplied some of the short articles and translated those that were written in Bengali. Readers familiar with Professor Bagchi's seminal work *India and China: A Thousand Years of Cultural Relations* will recognise these writings.

We appreciate the enthusiastic support and encouragement we received from the individuals and institutions responsible for copyright permissions. We would especially like to thank Mrs. Ratna Sinha for her continuous encouragement and support during this project. She was also instrumental in putting together a centenary volume dedicated to Bagchi, where a list of all his publications is appended. The volume is called *India and Asia: P. C. Bagchi Centenary Volume*. It was edited by B. N. Mukherjee and published in 2009 by Progressive Publishers.

The next step of composing this volume turned out to be a tedious process, even though we decided not to make any major changes or corrections to the text. Scanning the articles, reformatting them, and re-inserting diacritical marks and Chinese characters took more time than we expected. Here the team at Anthem Press was most helpful. Indranil Mitra and Anindita Ganguly worked overtime formatting the scanned documents. The Anthem team in England did the final typesetting for the book. The fact that we could eventually put together this volume owes much to their dedication and tremendous work ethic.

While both of us have been greatly influenced by Professor Bagchi's scholarship, we decided not to summarise his life and scholarship here in this brief note. A key reason for this is the detailed biographical sketch by the late Professor Suniti Kumar Chatterji that has been included in this volume as one of the appendices. Additionally, the essay by Professor Akira Yuyama provides an in-depth analysis of Professor Bagchi's scholarship. All we can say is that as students of cross-cultural interactions between India and China, we are in awe of Professor Bagchi's broad knowledge and understanding of Buddhist and diplomatic exchanges between the two regions. We hope the essays by Professor Prabodh Chandra Bagchi collected here will be inspiration, as they have been to us, to a new generation of scholars dedicated to the study of the historical interactions between India and China.

Tansen Sen and Bangwei Wang
30 August 2010

Introduction

IN MEMORY OF PROFESSOR P. C. BAGCHI

Bangwei Wang

The 2,000 years history of interaction between India and China has been an outcome of the immense contributions made by a number of prominent personalities. Among them, from the Chinese side, we know the names of Faxian, Xuanzang and Yijing. From the Indian side, the names of Kumārajīva, Buddhabhadra, Pāramārtha should be mentioned. Of these renowned monks, Kumārajīva was perhaps the most remarkable. Kumārajīva's father was an Indian and his mother was a princess from the ancient kingdom of Kucha. Since Kucha is now within the territory of China, we may say Kumārajīva was half-Chinese or a Chinese Indian. The various accounts of the life and work of these great historical figures have left deep impressions on our minds.

In modern times, the name that requires special mention in the development of Sino-Indian rapport is Gurudev Rabindranath Tagore. His visit to China in 1924 was an important event in the interface between modern China and India. It rekindled the mutual exchanges between these two nations and propelled the development of a new genre of literary writing in China.

It is noteworthy, at this point, that all these personalities, who tried to bring the two countries closer, were extraordinary scholars with great knowledge and wisdom. Their intellectual acumen and academic achievements played a crucial role in shaping Chinese and Indian cultures and their subsequent intermingling.

In this context, we should never forget Professor Probodh Chandra Bagchi, an Indian scholar of Bengali origin. He was a well-known figure in the field of Sino-Indian studies within India as well as in the international arena. As one of the appendices of this book outlines his biography, I think it would be unnecessary to say more on his life here. During the nineteenth and twentieth centuries, the social and cultural environments of China and India underwent significant changes and greater academic pursuits increased the mutual exchange between these two countries. In 1921, Gurudev Rabindranath Tagore established the Visva-Bharati University at Santiniketan in West Bengal. With the help of Professor Tan Yunshan in 1937, he founded Cheena Bhavana to encourage the study of Chinese culture. Probodh Chandra Bagchi learned the Chinese language at Cheena Bhavana, Visva-Bharati, and more than 20 years later he became professor at the same place and eventually was appointed Vice Chancellor of the university. During that time, Probodh Chandra Bagchi established the journal called *Sino-Indian Studies* and published a number of his research papers as well as that of other scholars in it. The prime focus of the journal was India-China interactions and it once played an important role in the related fields. Unfortunately, the publication stopped soon after his death. Some of the essays in this book first appeared in the journal.

Professor Probodh Chandra Bagchi also enjoyed a very special connection with Peking University. He was the first Indian scholar who spent two years as a guest professor at the campus. The then-president of Peking University, Dr Hu Shih – one of the greatest scholars of modern China – extended a warm welcome to him. He wrote, 'To promote the mutual understanding and cooperation between China and India, the government of India has established a Chair of Indology at Peking University. Dr Probodh Chandra Bagchi has been appointed the first professor of it. His job will be to build a steady base for friendship and academic cooperation between our two countries'. These words immediately bring to my mind the story of Master Xuanzang, who was also offered a position as teaching chair at Nalanda, the great Buddhist University, nearly one thousand and four hundred years ago in India. Xuanzang's achievement was appreciated greatly by his Indian colleagues and friends. Similarly, Probodh Chandra Bagchi's teaching experience at Peking University is a memorable chapter in the history of Sino-Indian relations.

I was born much later and did not have the opportunity to meet Professor Bagchi. However, in the Department of Eastern Languages of Peking University, Professor Ji Xianlin and Professor Jin Kemu were his friends. They were my teachers from the end of the 1970s to the beginning of the 1980s when I was a graduate student. I heard the name 'Probodh Chandra Bagchi' more than once from them. They used to praise the academic merits of Professor Bagchi. The university library also has a collection of some of his works, though not all can be found. His books and papers have been important for my research for many years. We are all grateful to him for his pioneering publications in the field of Sino-Indian studies.

From the viewpoint of academic research, Professor Bagchi's essays are already well-known. However, these were groundbreaking when they were first published. Some of his conclusions are still valid and frequently used by modern scholars of Sino-Indian studies. At the same time, some of the topics he touched upon are not well-researched by present-day Chinese and Indian scholars. The research area of Probodh Chandra Bagchi was quite broad. We may say that he was a Sinologist, an Indologist and at the same time a Buddhologist. But these areas are not all he studied. A review of all his works makes us use one term to indicate his area of research: Sino-Indology. This may cover all his achievements; he set an example that we should all follow today in this innovative field of study.

The year 2008 marked the 110th birth anniversary of Professor Probodh Chandra Bagchi. Both in India and China some events were held to commemorate him and his scholarship. For this reason, Professor Tansen Sen of the City University of New York advised me to compile a new collection of Bagchi's papers. I certainly agreed with him on this good idea. Tansen started the job very quickly and all things went quite smoothly. Tansen completed most of the job, and I am grateful to him for his efforts.

Tansen is also from West Bengal State in India. He arrived in Beijing while he was a high school student. We have known each other over twenty years. After he graduated from Beijing Languages University, he joined our master's degree program at Peking University; thereafter he went to the University of Pennsylvania and obtained his PhD degree. His area of research interest is Sino-Indian cultural relations. In this field he has published one academic book and a number of scholarly articles. His research has won high praise from the scholastic community. I am happy to see that young promising people such as Tansen are now carrying forward the cause started by Probodh Chandra Bagchi more than half a century ago. The situation is becoming more and more encouraging with the publication of new studies on India-China relations, albeit mostly on the contemporary interactions.

Recently, I had the opportunity to participate several times in the Nalanda Mentor Group (now the Governing Board of the Nalanda University) meetings where we discussed the plan to re-establish a new university at Nalanda, which will follow the brilliant educational tradition of ancient India. Professor Amartya Sen, a well-known scholar and Nobel laureate in economics in 1998, is heading our group. As a friend of Chinese people, he showed much interest in Chinese culture. In his book *The Argumentative Indian*, he discussed and compared at length the characteristics of our two cultures. We appreciate his remarks. Professor Sen also hails from West Bengal; he was born in Santiniketan and spent his teenage years there. So, in our conversation we mentioned Probodh Chandra Bagchi and he admired this great scholar. Bengal is really a wonderful place to connect our two civilizations.

Therefore, the significance of editing and publishing this book will not be confined to the memory to Professor Probodh Chandra Bagchi and/or the retrospection of his academic achievements. Through this book, we hope to reflect back on the history of friendly exchanges between China and India and the history of academic research on Sino-Indian culture. We hope that following the footsteps of our predecessors, we will also be able to promote understanding and exchange between the scholars and common people of our two countries.

August 30, 2010 at Peking University

纪念师觉月教授

王邦维

在中国和印度两千年密切交往的历史上，曾经出现过许多杰出的人物。在中国方面，法显、玄奘、义净这些名字当然不用说，在印度方面，不可以不提到鸠摩罗什、觉贤、真谛这些名字。尤其是鸠摩罗什，父亲是印度人，母亲是古代龟兹国王的妹妹。龟兹在今天中国新疆的境内，鸠摩罗什因此也算是半个中国人了。中印两国历史上这些了不起的人物，他们的名字和一生的经历，都给我们留下了深刻的印象。

进入近代，到过中国，最有名的，最值得提到的是师尊泰戈尔。1924年泰戈尔对中国的访问，是近代中印文化交流史上的一件大事，中印两个伟大国家的交往就此重新开始。泰戈尔的作品对中国近代新文学的发展也发生过重要的影响。

中印历史上所有这些伟大的人物，有一个特点，不知被人注意到没有，那就是，他们大多都是有学问的人，而且不是一般地有学问，往往都是饱学之士。他们为中印文化互相的交往和品格的形成所做的贡献，很大一部分，就在于他们学术上取得的成就。

说到学问之事，近代与中国有关的印度学者，就不能不提到师觉月教授。

师觉月教授是印度孟加拉人，是上个世纪印度，也是国际上研究中印文化和文化交流史一位著名的学者。关于他的生平和学术成就，收入本书作为附录的文章中已经有详细的介绍，无需我在这里多说。我想强调的只是，十九、二十世纪以来，中印两国的社会和文化环境发生了极大的变化，两个国家的文化交流，更多地加入了学术的成分。二十世纪的二十年代，泰戈尔在西孟加拉邦的“和平之乡”创立国际大学（Visva-Bharati）。1937年，泰翁又在中国去的谭云山先生的协助下，在国际大学里专门设立中国学院（Cheena Bhavana），推动对中国文化的研究。师觉月最早开始学习中文，正是在国际大学。二十多年后，他在国际大学的中国学院任教，后来还作了国际大学的校长。在这期间，他在国际大学创办了《中印学刊》（Sino-Indian Studies），集中发表有关的研究成果。这是世界上唯一一份以中印文化研究作为主题的学术刊物，出版后在国际上颇有影响，可惜他去世以后，没有能继续办下去。本书中选编的文章，有一些最初就发表在《中印学刊》上。

对于北京大学而言，师觉月教授则更有特别的一份因缘，那就是，他是近代历史上第一位到北京大学担任讲座教授的印度学者。他在北京大学的时候，学校的校长是胡适之先生。胡适之先生是中国近代最伟大的学者之一，他对师觉月的到来，十分欢迎。胡适之先生曾经这样写道："印度政府为了增进中印两个民族之间的了解和合作，特在北京大学设立一个印度学的讲座，第一任教授就是师觉月博士。他在北大的工作是给中印友谊与学术合作建立了一个有力量的基础。"这段话不禁使我们想到，一千三百多年前，中国的玄奘，也曾经在印度的佛教大学那烂陀担任过教职，也得到了印度的同行和朋友们极高的赞扬。师觉月在北京大学任教的经历，与他一千多年的许多前辈一样，是中印友好交往中一段新的佳话。

我生也晚，没有能见到师觉月教授，但北京大学东语系的季羡林先生和金克木先生当年都与他是朋友。七十年代末，我到北大念研究生，跟随两位先生学习，两位先生不止一次地跟我讲起过师觉月。他们对师觉月都很称赞。北大的图书馆里，师觉月的著作，书和文章，能找到一些，不过不全。北大图书馆有的，我大多读过，但还有一些是我一直没有机会读到的。他的书和文章，曾经是我做研究时重要的参考资料。我们所有的人，都感激师觉月在中印文化方面所做的很多开拓性的工作。

就学术研究的角度而言，师觉月的学术论文，已经有相当的影响。其中一些在发表的当时，曾经有着创新的意义。论文中一些结论，至今仍具有说服力，甚至可以说至今仍然还处在研究的前沿，被从事中印研究的学者们所引用。但在此同时，我们也要看到，他文章中涉及的一些题目，在今天的中国和印度，还需要有人去做更多的研究。师觉月研究的范围很广，如果要对他的研究做一个全面的评价，可以看到，他不仅仅是一位"汉学家"，也不仅仅是"印度学家"，他也不仅仅是研究佛教，而是跨越于多个方面，只有一个词，"中印文化研究"，大概可以概括他研究的领域。他在这方面研究的特点，其实值得我们仿效和学习。

2008年是师觉月诞辰的110周年，在印度和中国都举行了一些活动来纪念他和他的学术成就。为此美国纽约城市大学的沈丹森（Tansen Sen）教授向我建议，重新编辑一部师觉月的学术论文集，我当然很赞成。丹森很快行动起来，搜集文章，编排次第，联系出版，承担了大部分的工作。为此我很感谢丹森。

丹森也是印度孟加拉人，读中学时来到中国，我们认识已经有二十多年。他先是在北京语言大学学习，后来进入北京大学，在北京大学获得硕士学位。再后来他到了美国，在宾夕法尼亚大学获得博士学位。丹森的研究兴趣和领域，就是中印文化关系。他在这方面已经出版了一部学术著作和发表了不少学术论文。他的研究，成绩斐然，得到学术界广泛的肯定和称赞。我很高兴地看到，大半个世纪以前师觉月开始的中印文化研究，现在有了像丹森这样的年轻学者继续地做下去。而且，近年来有兴趣研究中印文化的人渐渐多了起来，这样的形势使人鼓舞。

2007年以来，我有机会数次参加为重建那烂陀大学而成立的顾问小组（Nalanda Mentor Group）的会议，我们小组的主持人，是著名的经济学家，1998年诺贝尔经济学奖的获得者阿马蒂亚•沈（Amartya Sen）教授。阿马蒂亚•沈也是印度孟加拉人，他在国际上被称作“为穷人说话的有良心的经济学家”，这样的经济学家当今并不多见，因此非常伟大。阿马蒂亚•沈对中国十分友好，对中印文化也非常关注。他写过一本书，书名是《惯于争鸣的印度人》（The Argumentative Indian），他在书中讨论到中国和印度的文化，意见非常精辟。他的青少年时代，就在“和平之乡”度过。我们因此也谈到过师觉月，他也认为，师觉月是一位非常杰出的学者。孟加拉真是一个了不起的地方，不仅历史上与中国有许多联系，而且人才辈出，这不能不说是一种因缘。

因此，我的看法，我们编辑出版这本书，其意义其实不仅仅限于纪念师觉月教授以及讨论他一生的学术成就，我们还希望，通过这部书，重新回顾中印友好交往的历史，回顾中印文化研究的学术史。我们要把包括师觉月在内的所有前辈学者开创的工作进一步发展下去，让中印两国人民、两国学者之间有更多的了解，更多的交流，相互学习，永远友好。这是我们今后还会长期努力的一项工作。

2010年8月30日于北京大学

Part One

Chapter 1

ANCIENT CHINESE NAMES OF INDIA*

India is at present known in China under the name *Yin-tu* (印度). This is not a modern adaptation. It goes back at least to the T'ang period. It seems to have been current slightly earlier, but the great Chinese pilgrim Hsüan-chuang was the first to baptise it. In his *Hsi-yü Chi*,[1] while discussing the various Chinese names for India, he says:

> "We find that different counsels have confused the designations of Tien-chu (India); the old names were Shen-tu and Sien (or Hien)-tou;[2] now we must conform to the correct pronunciation and call it Yin-tu. The people of Yin-tu use local appellations for their respective countries; the various districts having different customs; adopting a general designation and one which the people like, we call the country Yin-tu which means the Moon".

It is clear from the statement that the Indians themselves had no popular general designation for the country as a whole[3] and *Yin-tu* was a name used by the Chinese for the country. Hsüan-chuang as a great Sanskritist was keen on explaining the etymology of the names and hence explained the name *Yin-tu* (*ien-duo>indu) as "moon". In fact, as a Sanskrit word it (*indu) can mean only "moon". Hsüan-chuang also justified his explanation in an ingenious way:[4]

> "The unceasing revolutions of mortals' existence are a dark long night; were there not a warden of the dawn they would be like the night with its lights which succeeds the setting of the sun; although the night has the light of the stars, that is not to be compared to the light of the clear moon. Hence India probably was likened to the moon as (since the sun of Buddha set) it has had a succession of holy and wise men to teach the people and exercise rules as the moon sheds its bright influence – on this account the country has been called Yin-tu".

---

* *Monumenta Serica* 13 (1948): 366–375. Reprinted with permission of Monumenta Serica Institute", (c) Institut Monumenta Serica, Sankt Augustin.

Not quite satisfied with his spiritual explanation the pilgrim was anxious to find an objective confirmation of his thesis. Thus he says that on enquiring from the people of India he came to learn that India had the shape of a half-moon.[5]

Since the explanation was given by Hsüan-chuang, later writers[6] began to consider the old Chinese names for India, such as *Shen-tu, T'ien-chu,* etc. as wrong and *Yin-tu* as the correct form of the name. Even the most popular name *T'ien-chu,* although it persisted in Buddhist texts, had to yield place to the new name *Yin-tu* in historical records.

China came in contact with India since the time of the former Han dynasty. From that time till about the T'ang period various names were used to designate India. Let us examine the most important of them in chronological order.[7]

The oldest form of the name, *Shen-tu* (身毒), as is well known, occurs in the *Shih-chi* (chüan 116, 西南夷列傳 56) in connection with the mission of Chang Ch'ien to Ta-hsia. In his report on the western kingdoms, which was submitted to the Emperor in 122 B.C., Chang Ch'ien says that "while living in Ta-hsia he saw the woven stuff and bamboo goods of Shu (Szechwan) which he heard had come there from the country of *Shen-tu* which was to the south-east". On the basis of this report the *Shih-chi* says later (chüan 123, 大宛列傳 63): "Shen-tu is several thousands of li to the south-east of Ta-hsia. Its customs and natural products are like those of Ta-hsia. The country is low, humid and hot. The people fight from the back of elephants. A large river flows by it".

The *Hou-Han shu* (chüan 118, 西域傳 78) for the first time uses the name *T'ien-chu* (天竺) for India and since then it became the almost universally accepted name for India in China. The name of Indians who came to China were qualified with a *chu* (竺), the second part of the country's name. The text of the *Hou-Han shu* runs as follows: "T'ien-chu country – it is another name of Shen-tu (身毒). It is several thousands of li to the south-east of the Yüeh-chih country... From the 2nd year to the 4th year *yen-hsi* (159–161 A.D.) of Huan-ti, this country sent tributes several times from beyond the border of Jih-nan. Ming-ti dreamt of a golden man very tall and with a halo around his head. He asked his ministers about it and they replied: 'In western country there is a holy man named Fo (Buddha), he is 16 feet tall and his colour is of yellow gold.' The emperor then sent ambassadors to T'ien-chu to make enquiries about the law of Buddha".

The *Hou-Han shu* (chüan 110, 上, 杜篤傳 78) probably records another form of the name of India as T'ien-tu (天督): "To the south-east of the headquarters of the Governor-General there are the countries of Huang-chih (黄支), Huan-erh (緩耳), Tiao-t'i (雕提) and T'ien-tu (天督)". Yen Shih-ku (567–645) in his commentary says that this country is the same as T'ien-chu.[8]

The name Hsien-tou (賢豆) is recorded in the T'ang period first by Hsüan-chuang and later on by Tao-hsüan. We have already quoted the passage of the *Hsi-yü Chi* which mentions it. Tao-hsüan mentions the name in various places. In the *Hsü kao-seng chuan* (chüan 2),[9] while dealing with the biography of the Indian monk Dharmagupta, he says that Dharmagupta was a native of the country of Lo-to (Lāṭa) in south Hsien-tou (i.e. South India). He further says in the same biography that the city of Kānyakubja (Kanoj) was in central Hsien-tou (i.e. Mid India). The T'ang catalogue of the Buddhist Tripitaka, the *K'ai-yuan shih-chiao lu* (chüan 7), reproduces the same biographical notes but replaces the name Hsien-tou by Yin-tu (印度) in both places. It may be noted that in other places of the *Hsü kao-seng chuan*, wherever there is a reference to India, Tao-hsüan mentions the country as T'ien-chu and not as Hsien-tou. For the biography of Dharmagupta Tao-hsüan was evidently using some old material. Dharmagupta, as we know, came to China towards the close of the Sui period. He had travelled much and, besides translating Sanskrit texts into Chinese, had written a book of travels called *Ta Sui hsi-yü chuan* (大隋西域傳). This book was subsequently lost. It is likely that Tao-hsüan used this book in writing his biography. In fact, this biography is essentially a summary of the description of various countries visited by Dharmagupta in the course of his travels from India to China. So it is possible that Hsien-tou (賢豆) was the name as used by Dharmagupta himself for his own country.[10]

There are two other names used in early Chinese literature which were probably connected with the name of India. These are *Yüan-tu* (捐毒)and *Hsüan-tu* (懸毒). Yüan-tu is mentioned in the *Han-shu* (chüan 96上, 西域傳 66上) in connection with the movement of the Sakas: "Yüan-tu is in the north and Ta yüeh-chih in the West" and again "The Saka race were originally scattered in different countries to the west and north of Su-le such as Hsiu-hsün, Yüan-tu..". and further, "Yüan-tu is 9860 li from Ch'ang-an". In the text Yüan-tu figures as a small country in the neighbourhood of Su-lê (i.e. Kashgar).[11] The commentator Yen Shih-ku says that Yüan-tu is the same as Shen-tu (身毒) and T'ien-tu (天篤).[12] Quite likely. Chi-pin (罽賓) of the Han period, which was Kashmir, was occupied by the Sakas in the second century B.C., after they had been driven out of Ta-hsia by the Yüeh-chih. It was this part of India which probably was in view of the compiler of the Han-shu. Chi-pin bordered on Su-lê.[13]

Hsüan-tu (懸度) originally means "hanging bridge", and it was mentioned in this sense by the Chinese travellers in the course of their passage from the Ts'ung-ling (Pamir) region to the upper Indus valley.[14] Some authors either through confusion or on account of the similarity of the names used it to mean the country. This is fully explained by Kuo Yi-kung as quoted by Li Tao-yüan in the *Shui-ching chu* (chüan 1): "To the west of Wu-ch'a [or yana] (烏秅)

there is the country of Hsüan-tu (懸度). The river in the hills cannot be crossed except with rope bridges. Hence the name of the country".[15] Li Tao-yüan says that the region in question is Chi-pin (Kashmir).[16] This is confirmed by the account of Fa-hsien.

Therefore the most important forms of the name of India as used by the Chinese writers since the time of Chang Ch'ien are: Shen-tu (身毒). T'ien-chu (天竺), T'ien-tu (天督), Hsien-tou (賢豆), Yüan-tu (捐毒) and Hsüan-tu (懸度). Since the T'ang period the name Yin-tu (印度) came in use, and this is the form that has come down to the present times.

The sources of these Chinese names for India have not so far been clearly explained. Watters[17] was probably the first to make some critical observations on them, but as the study of Chinese phonology had not yet started in his times, he was not in a position to solve the problems connected with the names.

Prof. Wu Ch'i-ch'ang, in his article already referred to, takes into consideration the ancient pronunciations as reconstructed by Karlgren but works too much under the influence of Watters' suggestions to reach a satisfactory conclusion. We will therefore re-examine the old pronunciations from a new point of view.[18]

The ancient pronunciation of Shen-tu (身毒) was *śiĕn-d'uok which would give a Śindhuk or Śinduk. This was regarded by all previous scholars as a transcription of the name of Sindhu – the name of the westernmost kingdom of India (modern Sind), as well as that of the Indus valley. In fact, foreigners looking at India from the west would naturally call the country by this name in the absence of a general designation of the country. Chang Ch'ien in all appearance did the same.

It is, however, forgotten that Chang Ch'ien had no direct contact with India or with the Indians. He gathered the name from the people of Ta-hsia which was a pure Iranian zone then under the occupation of the Yüeh-chih. So he had heard the name as pronounced either by the Iranians or by the Yüeh-chih. We have no record of the Yüeh-chih version of the name. But the Iranian version is well known. The Iranian form of the name Sindhu was *Hindava, Hind-*, and this is also the name which was adopted by the ancient Greeks as *'Indoi, 'Indos*. So Chang Ch'ien was expected to hear a name like Hind- in Ta-hsia.

There is again another more serious difficulty in accepting the explanation till now given of the name mentioned by Chang Ch'ien. It is impossible to argue that he had heard the name directly from the Indians. In that case it should have been a *Sindhu, Sindhu* (ka), commencing with a clear dental sibilant. There was no dearth of dental sibilants in Chinese. The ancient writers who had either gone to India or had a direct knowledge of the country use it while rendering the name of the river Indus (Sindhu). Cf. Hsin-t'ou (新頭) – in the *Shui-ching chu*; Hsin-t'ao (新陶) – Kuo Yi-kung as quoted in the *Shui-ching chu* ;

Hsin-t'ou (辛頭)–Chih-mêng; Hsin-tu (信度) – *Yi-ching*. All the three characters 新, 辛, 信 were pronounced in early si̯ĕn with a dental sibilant. But *shen* 身 according to the old pronunciation was a śiĕn, starting with a palatal. We must therefore assume that the character *shen*身 had another dialectal pronunciation. In fact, Watters had already suspected it.[19]

The ancient Chinese writers suggested too that *Shen* of Shen-tu 身毒 had a different pronunciation. Thus Yen Shih-ku in his commentary to the *Han-shu* [Vol. 96 上, 西域傳 66 上] says: "Yüan-tu (捐度), Shen-tu (身毒), and T'ien-tu (天篤) are originally the same name pronounced either lightly or with emphasis (語有輕重耳)".[20] Hsü Kuang (352–425) in his commentary to the *Shih-chi* (chuan 116, 西南夷列傳 56) notes first of all that for Shen-tu another text of the *Shih-chi* had the reading 乾毒.[21] He then says that *shen* 身had the pronunciation of either 齕 or 訖.[22]

According to Hsü Kuang, therefore, shen身 in the present case could be pronounced in three different ways: 乾, 齕, 訖. In ancient pronunciation chieh or ho齕 was a γuət and chi 訖 was a kiət, but alternatively also χi̯ət. In these two cases, therefore, Shen-tu would be pronounced as γuət-d'uok and χi̯ət-d'uok leading to an original form like Hinduk(a). So far as 乾, various readings from another text of the *Shih-chi*, is concerned, it is possible that it is a graphical mistake arising out of the abbreviated form 軋 for both 乾 and 韓. 乾 *chien* was pronounced g'i̯än but 韓 *han* γân. In the latter case Shen-tu身毒 would give a Händuk(a), Hinduk(a).

Yen Shih-ku suggests that *yüan* 捐 and *shen* 身were pronounced in the same way. In this case Shen-tu, 身毒 would give a i̯ωän-d'uok leading to an original form like *Induk*(a). Which of the two pronunciations of Shen-tu, *Hinduk* (a) and *Induk* (a), was then correct so far as Chang Ch'ien's use of the name is concerned?

It seems that Yen Shih-ku suggests the more correct pronunciation of the name in the present case. Watters had probably this suggestion in view when he wrote: "Then accepting the character now read as Shen as the genuine text of Cheng's report we are told that in this name it is to be pronounced like *in* or *yin*. This does not seem very improbable".[23] We may therefore assume that Shen-tu stands for an original Induk(a), and that was the name heard by Chang Ch'ien in Ta-hsia. He did not pick up the Iranian form *Hinduka*, but in all likelihood its Yüeh-chih version.

In the latter Han period when the Chinese had more direct contact with India through the arrival of Buddhist missionaries their country began to be described as T'ien-chu (天竺). In this case it should be noted that most of the first Buddhist missionaries were either Iranian or Sogdian (cf. the names of An Shih-kao 安世高, An Hsüan 安玄, K'ang Chü 康巨, K'ang Meng-hsiang 康孟詳, etc., appearing in the *Kao-seng Chuan*, chüan 1).

The Sogdians, who belonged to the Iranian stock, were the intermediaries between the various people in this period in their capacity as merchants. So it is likely that the Iranian form of the name was carried to China by this people. But how far do the names beginning with *t'ien* (天) represent the Iranian form of the name?

In regard to the pronunciation of *T'ien* in T'ien-chu, Watters made the following suggestion: "Then as to the first part of the name there seems to have been an old and perhaps dialectal pronunciation of the character as *Hien* or *Hin.* This pronunciation is found at present in the dialect of Shao-wu-foo in the province of Fuhkeen in which it is read Hien-tu".[24] This is amply supported by an old authority like Liu Hsi (died 126 A.D.) in his *Shih-ming* (釋名). He says: *"T'ien* has a lingual pronunciation like *hsien* (以舌腹言之天顯也)".[25] Therefore T'ien-chu (天竺) was pronounced in the Han period as Hsien-chu (顯竺) – *χi̯en-t'i̯uk > Hinduk (a). It is clear that this was the correct Iranian pronunciation of the name of India. All the subsidiary forms of the name such as: 天篤 *χien-tuok, 天督 *χien-tuok, 天毒 *χien-d'uok, 賢豆 *χien-d'əu as well as 懸度 γien-d'ak (d'uo'), all similarly go back to the same Iranian form, either purely as *Hindu* or with a suffix *-ka* as *Hinduka.*

We have not so far discussed the origin of the form *Yin-tu* (印度) which in old pronunciation was either in-d'ak or ind'uo from Indak or Indu. The name as pronounced in Hsüan-chuang's time was evidently Indu (final consonant probably being dropped in some of the dialects in the T'ang period), otherwise he would not have explained it as "moon". These forms of the name: *Induk - Indu* could not have been derived from T'ien-chu. Then again the intermediate links between them and Shen-tu of Chang Ch'ien are so uncertain that it is impossible to suggest any connection between them. What was then the origin of these forms of the name?

In Hui-li's biography of Hsüan-chuang we find another form of the name of India as used by the T'u-chüeh (Turks). While the pilgrim was in the country of the T'u-chüeh (near Tashkend) he had an audience with the Khan. The Khan told him: "The master need not go to the Yin-t'e-ka (印特伽) country, that land is very hot".[26] Hsüan-chuang was evidently quoting the name as pronounced by the Khan himself. The Turks, as we know, had overrun a highly civilised country and derived their culture and religion from the people of the northern part of Eastern Turkestan such as Kuchi, Karasahr, etc. Their information of India as well as the form of the name seem to have been derived from the same source.

In connection with the biography of a monk named Man-yüeh (滿月 Purṇacandra), who came to China in the T'ang period, the author of the *Sung kao-seng chuan (*chüan 3) observes: "The people of Ch'iu-tzu (Kuchi) do not understand the language of T'ien-chu (India). They call T'ien-chu

'Yin-t'e-ka' (印特伽)". The *Sung kao-seng chuan* was compiled by Tsan-ning in 988. Kuchi had ceased to play any part in the Buddhist propagandism in that period. The author was evidently using some old material, the source of which is not known. We may therefore accept the information as correct and suppose that the Kuchean (-Tokharian) form of the name of India was Yin-t'e-ka (印特伽) *in-d'əkka > Indäk(a). This is quite in consonance with the characteristic of the Kuchean (-Tokharian) language, which did not possess an *h* or an aspirate. The Turkish Indäk(a) was in all appearance borrowed from the same Kuchean (-Tokharian) source. A later borrowing from the same source is found in Uigur in which the name of India appears as Änätkäk (cf. also Mongolian Änädgäk).

This Kuchean (-Tokharian) Indäk(a) is in my opinion the source of the Chinese *Induk – Indu.*[27] Does this Kuchean (-Tokharian) Indäk(a) go back to the Yüeh-chih *Indukas* recorded by Chang Ch'ien? Although a possible connection between the two cannot be suggested for the present for want of further facts, it is clear that the language of the Yüeh-chih, like the Kuchean (-Tokharian) lacked an aspirate and could not render an *h* of the original Iranian name of India — *Hind-*.[28]

The connections between the various names for India in Chinese therefore may be suggested as follows:

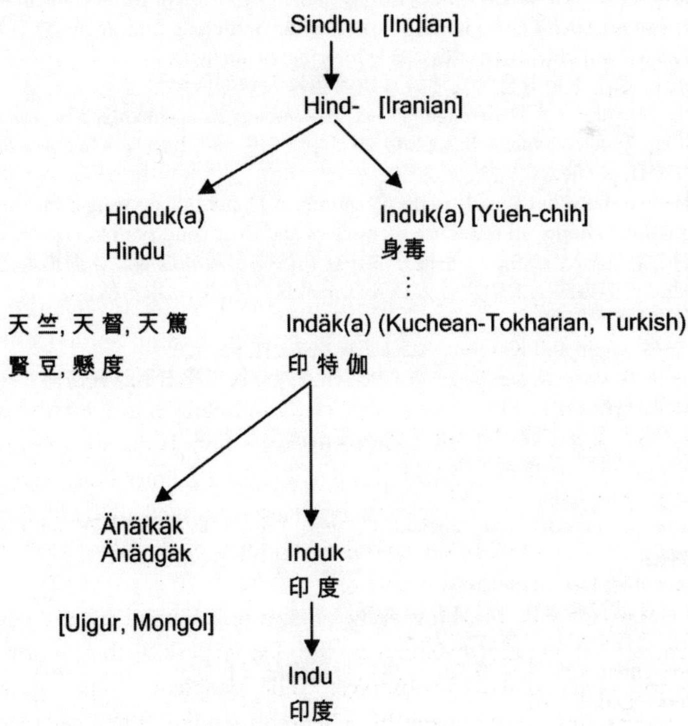

Notes

1 *Hsi-yu Chi*, chüan 2: Watters – *On Yuan Chwang*, I, p. 131: the original text runs as follows: 詳夫天竺之稱異議糾紛舊云身毒或曰賢豆今從正音宜云印度印度之人隨地稱國殊方異俗遙總名語其所美謂之印度印度者唐言月.

2 Sien (or Hien)-tou 賢豆 is in the present paper transcribed as Hsien-tou. – Ed.

3 This does not mean that there was no general designation for India. Hsüan-chuang himself says that India was known as the "Brāhmana country" on account of the high reputation of its highest caste – the Brahmins – Watters, ibid. p. 140. In the Buddhist texts the name of India is mentioned as Jambudvîpa and this is the name by which Aśoka also mentions the country in his inscriptions. In the Purâṇic literature Jambudvīpa has a larger geographical significance. India proper is called in these texts Bhāratavarṣa and this is the name that has come down to our times. Among the high class people, northern India was also known as Āryāvarta or Āryadeśa – "the country of the Āryas". The overseas Indians used to mention India as Āryadeśa – CF. Cœdès, *Histoire ancienne des états hindouisés d'Extrême Orient*, p. 274.

4 Watters – ibid. I, p. 188, *Hsi-yü Chi*, chüan 2: 言諸群生輪迴不思無明長夜莫有司晨其猶日既隱宵燭斯繼雖有星光之照豈如朗月至明苟緣斯致因而譬月良以其土聖賢繼軌導凡御物如月照臨由是義故謂之印度.

5 Watters — ibid, I, p. 140, *Hsi-yü Chi*, chüan 2: 形 如 半 月.

6 Tao-hsüan – *Shih-chia fang-chih* (釋加方志); Hui-lin — *I-ch'ieh-ching yin-i*, chüan 26, chüan 58: 身毒即天竺之訛語也. Tao-hsüan mentions 印度 as the correct form of the name.

7 Some of these texts have been extensively quoted by Prof. Wu Ch'i-ch'ang in his article *Yin-tu shih-ming* (印度釋名) in the Journal of the Yen-ching University (燕京學報) IV, pp. 717 ff. I am indebted to this article for some of the texts.

8 The text: 都尉東南兼有黃支連緩耳瑣雕題摧天督即天竺國也.

9 For the biography of Dharmagupta – cf. *Hsü kao-seng chuan* chüan 2, *K'ai-yüan shih-chiao lu*, chüan 7; Chavannes – B.E.F.E.O 1903, pp. 439–440; Bagchi – *Le Canon Bouddhique en Chine*, II, p. 464.

10 This would show that as early as the 6th century A.D. the Indians were using the Iranian designation "Hindu" to introduce themselves and their country to foreigners.

11 北與捐毒西與大月氏接 ... 塞種分散往往為數國自疏勒以西北休循捐毒之屬皆故塞種也 ... 捐毒國王治衍敦谷去長安九千八百六十里 ... 本塞種也.

12 捐毒即身毒天篤也.

13 Bagchi — ki-pin and Kashmir, *Sino-Indian Studies* II, pp. 42ff.

14 Legge —*Travels of Fa-hien*, p. 26, 法顯傳, ch. 7: "昔人有鑿石通路施傍梯者凡度七百度梯已躡懸絙過河 ..."

15 烏秅之西有懸度之國山溪不通引繩而度故國得其名也.

16 余診諸史傳即所謂罽賓之境.

17 Watters – ibid. I, pp. 132–138.

18 For the pronunciation of ancient Chinese I have followed Karlgren's *Analytical Dictionary*.

19 Watters, ibid, I, p. 133.

20 捐毒即身毒天篤本皆一名語有輕重耳.

21 漢書直云身毒史記一本作乾毒.

22 *Shih-chi* (chüan 123, 大宛傳 63): 徐廣曰身或作齔又作訖.

23 Watters – ibid. I, 134.

24 Watters – ibid. I, p. 135.

25 I am indebted to my friend Prof. Wu Hsiao-ling for having drawn my attention to this text; 釋名ch. I, "釋天第一".

26 Watters – ibid. I, p. 75 大唐大慈恩寺三藏法師傳 (pub. by 東方文化學院京都研究所 chüan 2, fol. 6a). A late text, the *Hsü I-ch'ieh-ching yin-i* (chüan 8) which is a supplement to *Hui-lin's I-ch'ieh-ching yin-i* makes a very curious use of this name. It says that all the old names of India 天竺，天篤，身毒, 賢豆，印度 are incorrect and that the correct name is印特伽羅, which means "moon". The text ten refers to the *Hsi-yü Chi* to justify the explanation of the name as "moon". The author however forgets that Yin-tu 印度 as pointed out by Hsüan-chuang was good enough to give the sense of "moon". He was evidently trying to improve upon the name **Yin-t'e-ka** by adding a lo. **Yin-t'e-ka-lo** might have been suggested by Sanskrit Indukalā which however does not mean "moon" but a "digit of the moon".

27 There are numerous evidences of Kuchean serving as intermediary through which Indian words passed into Chinese. Sylvain Lévi was the first to point it out. Such Buddhist words in Chinese as Sha-men (紗門), Sha-mi (沙彌), Po-i-t'i (波逸提) are according to him transcriptions not of Indian words but of their Kuchean forms – samāne, sanmir, payti – *J. As.* 1913, p. 379. Recently Dr. Dschi Hiän-lin has tried to prove that the Chinese word Fo (佛) for Buddha was derived from the same source – 'Origin of the Chinese words for Buddha', *Sino-Indian Studies, III*, pp. 1 ff.

28 There is at least one example to show that the name Shen-tu (Induk) had been adopted in Kuchean very early. About the middle of the 1st century A.D. the Hsiung-nu appointed a nobleman of Kucha named Shen-tu (身毒) as king of the country in preference to the Chinese nominee; – *Hou-Han shu* (chuan 118, 西域傳 78); Chavannes – *T'oung Pao* 1907, p. 198. The coincidence of the name with the Yüeh-chih name of India is certainly not accidental. Shen-tu (Induk) was probably a nobleman of Indian origin.

Chapter 2

THE BEGINNINGS OF BUDDHISM IN CHINA*

Although during the first few centuries of Buddhist missionary activities in China the lead was generally given by the Buddhist scholars of Iran and of countries in Central Asia, Indian Buddhist scholars did not fail to make their presence felt in the various centres of Buddhism in China and create amongst the Chinese an interest in Buddhism and Indian culture in general which would not have been otherwise possible. The first two Indian scholars who came to China in 68 A.D. during the reign of Ming ti, Kāśyapa Mātaṅga and Dharmarakṣa, translated five Buddhist texts into Chinese. These were resumés of the legends of the birth and childhood of Buddha, a resumé of his predication, a short treatise on the main principles of Buddhism, a *sūtra* on the purity of monastic life and a sūtra on the principles of ascetic life for those who wanted to follow the way of spiritual perfection. Four of these works were judicious selection. The "Sūtra of 42 sections" which has been preserved up till now is clearly a catechism for the use of missionaries intending to preach the Buddhist religion in foreign countries. The original text did not belong to the Buddhist Canon. It had been compiled in order to give a general idea of the religion and its practices. The first Buddhist monastery in China *Po ma sse*, the "White Horse Monastery" was built at Lo-yang for these two Indian missionaries.

For about seventy years after this first contact was made we do not hear of any other missionary activity in China. The reason for this is not far to seek. The communications between the Western countries and China were still very uncertain on account of the political condition in Eastern Turkestan. In order to command the routes of Central Asia better, General Pan-ch'ao continued military operations for twenty years from 74 to 102 A.D. These operations were renewed in 124 A.D. by his son Pan-yong. As a result of these operations communication between China and the West became more secure and regular. The Hiung-nus, the eternal enemies of China, who were responsible for this

---

* *Sino-Indian Studies* 1.1 (1944): 1–17.

insecurity in communication between China and the West, were brought under such complete submission as not to raise their heads again.

From this time onwards we hear of regular arrival of Buddhist missionaries in the capital of China. The first among them who came from Persia was Ngan She-kao, an Arsacidan prince. He came to Lo-yang in 144 A.D. and was the first to receive the traditions of the "White Horse Monastery". He was well versed in the Buddhist Canon and had a great personality. It is not known whether he had gone to India to study Buddhist texts before coming to China or had been directly inspired by Indian scholars. Buddhism seems to have been already known to the Persian world in this period. The Indo-Scythian empire was the connecting link between India and Persia.

One hundred and seventy nine translations of Buddhist texts are ascribed to Ngan She-kao. His translations were intended to meet the great need of the period. Buddhism was not yet well known amongst the Chinese people. Thus instead of presenting to them faithful translations of Buddhist tests which were apt to unintelligible to a foreign people he made a selection of small texts from the Canon for translation into Chinese. These were meant to give a general idea of the Buddhist religion in its various aspects, pious legends philosophy, discourse of Buddha, etc. Thus a large number of the texts translated by him are extracts of more extensive Sūtras belonging to the four principal Āgamas of the Sūtrapiṭaka. He was a good translator and a clever organiser. Apart from the translations which he had made of Buddhist texts into Chinese he founded a school of translators at Lo-yang which came to be described as "unrivalled" by the Chinese. The members of this school continued the work of translation upto the end of the Han dynasty (220 A.D.).

We find amongst the collaborators of Ngan She-kao an Indo-Scythian monk named Lokakṣema. He came to Lo-yang shortly after Ngan She-kao had settled there and took part in the work of translation so well begun by the latter. Amongst other members of the school of Ngan She-kao there was a comapatriot of his, named Ngan Hiuan who came to Lo-yang as a merchant but gave up his business and became a Buddhist monk. There were also two Sogdian monks, Kiu Mong Siang, and three Indians. Buddhadeva (?), Mahābala (?) and Dharmasatya (?). The number of translations made in this period was considerable. The religion had already begun to attract the Chinese. For the first time we find a Chinese Buddhist scholar named Yen Fo-t'ao amongst the translators of the "White Horse Monastery". He had received his ordination towards the middle of the 2nd century, after the arrival of Ngan She-kao and Lokakṣema, studied Buddhism under them and translated two Buddhist texts into Chinese. One of these works is a Prātimokṣa or the rules of ordination for the monks.

On the fall of the Han dynasty the country was divided amongst three powers. The Wei rulers had their capital at Lo-yang, the Wu dynasty was established in the south and the legitimate successors of the Hans were driven to Sse-ch'uan. Under the Wei rulers (220–265 A.D.) the church of Lo-yang continued its work of propagation and translation. In spite of the indifference of the Wei rulers towards this foreign religion, the work of translation continued systematically and the Chinese people grew more interested in Buddhism. At the request of the Chinese monks the Indian scholars who had come to China in this period prepared a number of translations which have come down to us. Dharmakāla, Saṅghavarman and Dharmasatya were all Indian monks. They translated a number of Vinaya works towards the middle of the 3rd century A.D. Their works show that the Chinese monks were then feeling a great need for Vinaya works in order to know exactly the Buddhist monastic discipline. Besides the three Indian scholars, whom we have just mentioned there were at Lo-yang in this period a Kuchean monk named Po-yen and a Parthian monk Ngan Fa-hien both of whom translated a number of Buddhist texts into Chinese.

In the South, Buddhism seems to have been introduced and developed in an independent manner. Tche K'ien the first translator of the South at first belonged to the Lo-yang school. But missionary activities had been going on in the South before his arrival. We now know that the land-route through Burma and Yun-nan was already in use before the 1st century A.D. and the sea-route between China and India was probably opened up in the 2nd century A.D. South China in this period included Kiao-che (Tonkin) which had come into contact with India in the 2nd century A.D.

An authentic source of information leads us to believe that already in 65 A.D. a Prince of the Imperial family who had settled in the valley of the Blue River, was surrounded by Buddhist monks. At the time when the school of Ngan She-kao was flourishing at Lo-yang the propagation of Buddhism was being actively pursued in Kiang-su and had reached Shan-tong. The Chinese biographer of Ngan She-kao tells us that Ngan She-kao had himself gone to Kiang-su which indirectly proves that Buddhism had been already introduced in that region. The famous Chinese scholar Mou-tseu who had written in the defence of Buddhism was born between 165 and 170 A.D. He retired to Tonkin in 189 A.D. and it was there that he was converted to Buddhism and composed his famous treatise. Shortly after, in the beginning of the third century Seng-hui, the son of a Sogdian merchant who had come to Tonkin, got himself initiated to Buddhism there and afterwards proceeded to Nanking. Thus it is amply clear that Buddhism was well known in South China long before the accession of the Wu dynasty (222 A.D.) and the arrival of Tche K'ien at Nanking.

Tche K'ien was at Lo-yang but the political troubles in the North compelled him to leave the country and go to Nanking where the Wu rulers had established their capital. His merits were recognised by the Wus and he was appointed preceptor of the Princes. As he was a layman and had no authority to give ordination the only work which he could do for the propagation of Buddhism was the work of translation. He translated into Chinese a large number of Buddhist texts which he had brought with him.

The Sogdian, Seng-hui who came to Nanking in 241 A.D. contributed more to the propagation of Buddhism. He was the first monk to come to the Wu capital and had powers to give ordination to the new converts. He founded the first monastery at Nanking called *Kien-Ch'u sse*. He translated only Buddhist avadanas into Chinese. This was significant. He wanted to carry the religion to the man in the street and for this the stories of the great acts of the Master were more useful than the philosophical disquisitions. He had thus succeeded in converting the people but had not founded a school of Buddhist erudites like Ngan She-kao.

Buddhism does not seem to have made any progress in Sse-ch'uan where the Hans had taken refuge. Lo-yang continued to be a great centre of Buddhist activities in North. Nanking also rose to be another important centre in the 3rd century A.D.

The Tsin dynasty which conquered the Wu in the South in 286 A.D. succeeded for a while in unifying the three kingdoms. During the short reign of this dynasty (280–317 A.D.), Buddhism became a very important factor in Chinese life. The Emperor Wu-ti (265–290 A.D.) showed a great interest in the Buddhist religion and a large number of monasteries were built in different parts of the country by his order. The Emperor Min-ti (313–316 A.D.) also had two monasteries built: these were the *T'ong hiu sse* and the *Po ma sse* at Ch'ang-ngan. The Chinese historians tell us that during the reigns of these two monarchs about 180 religious establishments were built in the two cities, Nanking and Ch'ang-ngan. Thirteen translators worked there during their reigns and translated 73 volumes of Buddhist texts into Chinese. The total number of Buddhist monks in China was 3700 in this period.

This account does not seem to be exaggerated. The Northern capital, Ch'ang-ngan, was an important centre of Buddhist activities as Lo-yang under the Han and the Wei before it was abandoned on account of continual revolts of the barbarians settled in the Province of Shan-si. It was at the time of this unification of the three kingdoms under the Tsin that a famous Buddhist monk named Dharmarakṣa (Fa-hu) came to Ch'ang-ngan from the West. He was of Indo-Scythian parentage, born at Tun-huang which we know was the meeting place of the two worlds, the Chinese and the Western. Dharmarakṣa was a true type of scholar, issue of the contact between the two great civilisations. He had studied the sacred lore under an Indian teacher, had travelled in various countries in Central Asia and probably also in India, was well versed in Sanskrit and knew besides 36 different languages. He was a scholar of exceptional ability and had begun translating Buddhist texts while at Tun-huang. Having learnt that Ch'ang-ngan had risen to be a great centre of Buddhist activities he went there with his own collection of Buddhist texts and settled down to dedicate his life to the work of a pious missionary. The large number of texts translated by him shows his vast knowledge of the Buddhist literature. Dharmarakṣa had assembled round him a number of Buddhist scholars from different parts of Asia, Ngan Fa-kin of Parthia, Mokṣala of Khotan, Po Fa-tsin of Kucha, Dharmaśira and his son Shu-ian (Śuklaratna) who were Indians long settled in China, Fa-tsin the Indo-Scythian and a few others. Almost all the Buddhist countries were represented on his school.

Dharmarakṣa also inspired the Chinese scholars with enthusiasm for the Buddhist faith. Amongst the Chinese Buddhist scholars Nie Cheng-yuan and his son Nie Tao-chen were able collaborators of Dharmarakṣa in the work of translation. Chu She-hing, a Chinese Buddhist monk had started a few years earlier in 260 A.D. for Khotan where he went to study at first-hand and make a search for Buddhist texts. He was the first to complete a Catalogue of Buddhist texts in Chinese translation on his return home. A few years late another Chinese scholar Che Min-tu, an able compiler of Buddhist texts prepared a second Catalogue of the Canon.

In 310 A.D. the Hun chief, Liu-yuan, the king of the Han, attacked the Empire and soon made himself absolute master of the entire country upto the north of the Blue River. The two ancient capitals Lo-yang and Ch'ang-ngan were occupied in 316 A.D. On the death of Liu-yuan and his successor, the kingdom was divided by his generals into two parts under the common name of Shao. Of one, the capital was Ch'ang-ngan and of the other Siang-kuo (Shun-to fu in Che-li). The establishment of these two foreign dynasties in North China was specially favourable for the propagation of Buddhism.

A Buddhist monk named Buddhadāna (? Fo-tu-teng) who was most probably of Kuchean origin arrived in this period at the court of the Northern Chao in Che-li. He exercised a preponderating influence on the Chao ruler-She-lei. All the texts describe Buddhadāna as a great magician. He reached Lo-yang in 310 A.D. After the occupation of this town by the Huns Buddhadāna was introduced to She-lei who greatly respected the monk and began to follow his counsel in all matters. The succsssor of the Chao ruler, She-hu continued to have the same respect for Buddhadāna. She-hu promulgated in 335 A.D. an edict which recommended Buddhism as the best religion to his people.

Buddhadāna lived at Ye (Chang-to in Ho-nan) where She-hu had transferred his capital. During his stay at Ye, Buddhadāna had succeeded in making Ye an important centre of Buddhism with the help of the Indian Fo-tiao and two other monks She-yu and Tao-k'ai who had come from Tun-huang. A Chinese monk named Tao-ngan who was later on to play a very important part in the history of Chinese Buddhism, came to Ye to study Buddhist literature with them. Political troubles broke out in 349 A.D. which led to the destruction of the Chao kingdom. Tao-ngan was compelled to leave Ye with his own students. Although the history of Buddhist community founded at Ye is missing we find references to a catalogue of Buddhist texts compiled most probably at Ye under the title of Chao-lu. This catalogue is also lost.

After the accession of Fu-kien of the Yao Ts'in dynasty in 350 A.D. Buddhist activities received a new impetus. Fu-kien invited the famous Buddhist scholar Tao-ngan to Ch'ang-ngan and encouraged the work of translation and propagation. Tao-ngan inaugurated a new epoch in the history of Chinese Buddhism. He was a Buddhist scholar of the first order and a rigorous critic. He was the first to critically examine the ancient Chinese translations of Buddhist texts. It has been said about him: "Before his time many Buddhist texts had been translated. But the ancient scholars paid attention to the general sense of the texts. But Tao-ngan examined the Sūtras closely and brought out their inner meaning". He composed a series of commentaries and compiled the first comprehensive Catalogue of the translation made upto his days. Tao-ngan invited the foreign monks Gautama Saṅghadeva, Dharmanandī and Saṅghabhūti. These scholars translated a large number of texts between 381 and 385 A.D.

The disciples of Tao-ngan were found in this period in almost all parts of China. One of the most illustrious among them, Hui-yuan, founded the famous monastery of Lu-shan. Ha carried on a vigorous propaganda in favour of Buddhism in China. Another Fa-ho went to Sse-chuan and was probably the first to preach Buddhism in that region. Through Tao-ngan's services, the Buddhist Community at Ch'ang-ngan soon became flourishing. Tao-ngan had heard about Kumārajīva and invited him to come to China. Tao-ngan died in 385 A.D. and it was only 16 years after his death in 401 A.D. that Kumārajīva reached Ch'ang-ngan.

Fu-kien was assassinated in 385 A.D. and the Ts'in succeeded him. But Buddhism did not at all suffer on account of this political change. Yao-ch'ang (385–395) and his successor Yao-hing (395–416) remained faithful to the Buddhist religion and their reign constituted one of the most beautiful periods of the history of Buddhism in China. Tao-ngan was dead but his work at Ch'ang-ngan was continued by another Chinese monk, Chu Fo-nien. He was not only an able interpreter of Buddhism but also a clever translator. He was often invited to help translators of foreign nationalities who did not know the Chinese language well. He also translated a number of texts which have been preserved up till now. It was due to his efforts that the Buddhist community of Ch'ang-ngan continued to flourish as before till the arrival of Kumārajīva in 401 A.D.

Kumārajīva was living in China in Leang-chou since 385 A.D. where he had been brought by General Liu-kuang after his conquest of Kucha. Kumārajīva now came to Ch'ang-ngan on an invitation from Yao-hing. It is said that he was born of a Kuchean Princess and an Indian father and was educated in Kashmir. He was a man of rare genius and during 12 years of his stay in China performed the most important work in the cause of Buddhism. He was the first to introduce in a systematic manner the Mahāyāna in China. In order to facilitate this work he translated some of the fundamental texts of Mahāyāna: The *Sūtrālaṃkāra-Śāstra* of Aśvaghoṣa, *Daśabhūmivibhāṣāśāstra* of Nāgārjuna, *Śataśāstra* of Āryedeva, *Satyasiddhi-Śāstra* of Harivarman and in order to make these philosophical systems well understood he also translated the biographies of these teachers. Amongst the 98 works which are attributed to him, there is also a work of special importance. It is the Brahmajāla-sūtra, a Mahāyāna Vinaya code for the use of those who wanted to follow the path of the Bodhisattvas. This text was one of the most popular in China.

Kumārajīva was the first to introduce in China a more profound knowledge of Indian Buddhism. He found out that the texts translated earlier into Chinese were more or less diffused and full of mistakes. His translations were made in good Chinese. His works are sometimes condensed and abridged in regard to the form but their meaning is very explicit. It is admitted by all that he was one of the best translators.

Kumārajīva died in 413 A.D. but his school continued to do great work upto 417 A.D. when fresh political troubles broke out in North China. To Kumārajīva's school belonged a number of Kashmirian monks such as *Puṇyatirāta, Buddhayaśas, Dharmyaśas* and two Chinese monks Seng-Jui and Seng-Chao.

After the downfall of Yao-hing in 417 A.D. political powers passed into other hands. But before we take up the history of Buddhism under the small rulers who wrested the political power in the North we should turn our eyes to the South and see what the Buddhist Church of Nanking had been doing all this time.

The Tsin rulers who had been driven to the south of the Blue River in 316 A.D. by the Huns ruled in Nanking quite peacefully till 420 A.D. when they were supplanted by the Song dynasty. The Tsin are regarded as the legitimate rulers of China by the Chinese historians. During the one hundred years of their reign in the South, Buddhism continued to prosper at Nanking. The Official history gives us the following details: Yuan ti (317–322) had two famous monasteries built. These were the *Wu kuan sse* and *Long kuan sse* which regularly accommodated one thousand monks. Ming ti (322–325) built the two monasteries *Ming hing sse* and *Tao ch'ang sse* and assembled there more than one hundred Buddhist scholars. Ch'eng-ti founded the monasteries of

Chong hing sse and *Lu ye sse* which also accommodated more than a thousand monks. Kien Wen ti (371–372) erected numerous statutes for the worship of the Buddhists and founded monasteries for accommodating the monks. Hiao Wu ti (373–396) founded the monasteries of *Huang t'ai sse* and *Pen ki sse* and Ngan ti (397–417) the monastery of *Ta-she sse.* During 104 years of their rule 17068 Buddhist temples were built throughout the Empire and 263 volumes of sacred texts were translated by 27 translators in the Southern capital. We do not know how far the figures given above are correct but so far as the number of translations is concerned it is almost exact.

A large portion of translations consists of *Dhāraṇīs* or mystic formulae. *Śrīmitra,* the Kuchean, and the Indian T'an-wu-lan (*Dharmaratna* ?) were probably the first to introduce with a certain amount of success the practice of *Dhāraṇī* amongst the Chinese Buddhists. South China was then Taoist and it was probably necessary to introduce the mystic practice of *Dhāraṇī* in order to satisfy the curiosity of the Taoists who had formed a mystic bent of mind. But the Buddhists of Nanking produced also other things in this period. Gautama Saṅghadeva who left Ch'ang-ngan and came to Nanking in 397 A.D. translated the whole of *Madhyamāgama* of the Sūtrapiṭaka. He also translated an Abhidharma work, the *Abhidharmaḥrdyasāśatra.* He seems to have helped in the translation of the Ekottarāgama which was published under the name of *Dharmanandi.* Vimalākṣa the teacher of Kumārajīva, came to China after the death of his illustrious disciple and came to Nanking where he translated a portion of the *Sarvāstivāda-vinaya.* The famous Chinese pilgrim Fa-hien returned to Nanking from India in 414 A.D. and brought with him a number of Sanskrit texts. Some of these texts were translated into Chinese by Buddhabhadra; the most important of these was the *Mahāsāṅghika-vinaya.*

The monastery of Lu-shan, a new Buddhist institution had risen into importance in the South in this period. It was founded by a disciple of Tao-ngan, Hui-yuan.

In the North-West, Leang-chou, which is the western part of the province of Kan-su had become a centre of Buddhist activities since the end of the 4th century A.D. We have seen that even in earlier times Buddhist scholars while coming from the West used to stop at a place called Tun-huang which was also in Leang-chou. Scholars like Ngan She-kao, Dharmarakṣa, and a few others had actually worked at Tun-huang and some of their translations bear the mark of that place. Since the end of the 4th century A.D. the capital of Leang-chou, Wu-wei-hien became a centre of Buddhist activities. An Indo-Scythian scholar, She-lun translated there a number of Buddhist texts in 373 A.D. in collaboration with a Kuchean monk Po Yen. The prefect of Leang-chou personally took part in the work of translation.

Liu-kuang, the Governor of Leang-chou was entrusted with a military expedition against Kucha in 385 A.D. He had gained a certain military importance in these campaigns and so on his return to Leang-chou he proclaimed himself as independent king. Leang-chou remained independent till 401 A.D. when it was annexed to the T'sin kingdom by Yao-hing. But when Leang-chou passed into the hands of the Northern Leang family it reasserted its independence for a time and its capital became a centre of Buddhist activities. It was finally annexed in 433 A.D. by the Northern Wei rulers (Toba).

The Tsiu-k'iu family of the Northern Leang had special leaning towards Buddhism. One of its rulers Mong-sun (401–433) invited an Indian scholar *Dharmakṣema* to the capital of Leang-chou. *Dharmakṣema* organised a school with the help of a number of Chinese scholars. He carried on the work of translation for about 25 years and translated amongst other things a very important Mahāyāna text named *Mahāparinirvāṇaśutra*, the complete manuscript of which could be then found only at Khotan. One of the nobles of the Tsiu-k'iu family, King-sheng, was a disciple of *Dharmakṣema* and a fervent Buddhist. He had himself translated a number of works at Leang-chou and on the fall of his dynasty went to the South where also he continued his work.

The Wei (Toba) kingdom was at first founded in 386 A.D. and its capital was Ta-t'ong. After the downfall of the Ts'in the Wei occupied almost the whole of North China upto Blue River, annexed Leang-chou and transferred their capital to Lo-yang. The Wei reigned in North China almost uninterruptedly till 550 A.D. The Wei period was one of the greatest epochs in the history of Buddhist art. It was during their reign that the work of excavation of the grottoes of Long-men and Yun-kang were commenced. These are the master-pieces of Buddhist art in China. The official history gives the following information of Buddhism during the Wei region:

"Wu ti (386–407) founded 15 caityas and two monasteries called *K'ai-t'ai sse* and *Ting kuo sse* and personally copied sacred texts. He also erected a thousand statues in gold and every month entertained 3000 Buddhists in a religious convocation. Cheng ti (453–465) encouraged the study of Buddhism in various ways. During his reign the number of monks and nuns had risen to 30,000. Hien Wen ti (465–476) built the monastery of *chao yin sse* solely for the use of monks who practised dhyāna. Hiao Wen ti (476–479) built the *Ngan yang sse* and took a personal interest in the Buddhist religion. The number of Buddhist monks and nuns rose upto 40,000 during his reign. Siuan Wu ti (499–515) himself explained the *Vimalakirtinirdeśa-sūtra* in his palace and founded four monasteries *P'u sse, T'ong sse*, *Ta sse* and *Ting sse* and constantly entertained 1000 monks. Hiao Ming ti (515–528) founded at Ye the *Ta kio sse* and his succsssor Hiao Chuang ti built 5 vihāras and ten thousand statues in stone. Wu ti (532–534) built in Ch'ang-ngan the monastery of *Che k'i sse* in order to accommodate 200 monks. Wen ti (534–551) built the *Pan jo sse* to accommodate the poor and the old and himself recited sacred texts such as *Saddharma-puṇḍarīka-sūtra* and *Prātimokṣa-sūtra.*

"Thus during 170 years of the Wei rule 47 large monasteries were built in Lo-yang, Ch'ang-ngan and Ye by Imperial orders. Grottoes were excavated in the northern hills near Ta-t'ong-fu over a distance of 30 li. The smaller princes built in this period 839 temples and the private families more than 30,000 such temples. The number of monks and nuns in China were in this period more than two million. 49 volumes of texts were translated into Chinese in the Wei period".

Although the Wei were great builders their interest in scholarly work was not in any remarkable. The work of translation was not of the same importance. A foreign monk T'an-yao translated at Ta-t'ong-fu a number of Avadānas. One of his collaborators in the task was Ki-kia-ye (Kekaya?). Towards the end of the Wei rule, Bodhiruci a famous Indian monk came to Lo-yang to continue the work of translation. He also worked at Ye where the wei capital was transferred for a short while (508–536). He translated in all 36 volumes. During the Wei period the Chinese Buddhist monks felt so much need of coming into contact with India directly that a number of Chinese monks had gone upto India. The most famous amongst them were Fa-hien and Song-yun.

The Northern Ts'i succeeded the Wei in 550 A.D. and reigned till 577 A.D. Buddhist literary activity was not very intensive in this period. We get the name of one Indian scholar Narendrayaśas who translated a number of texts into Chinese. The rulers of the Ts'i dynasty however were great patrons of Buddhism. The official history tells us: "Hiao Chao ti (560–561) copied with his own hand 12 Buddhist texts and regularly maintained 3000 monks. Ch'eng ti (561–568) erected a caitya in gold. During 28 years of their reign 43 Buddhist temples were built, imperial collections of Buddhist texts were made and 14 volumes of texts translated". What is more important is that Buddhism was introduced in this period amongst the Turks by the Chinese Buddhists.

During the reign of T'o-po Kaghan (572–581) the Chief of the Western Turks, Buddhism was introduced amongst the Turks. The story of the introduction of Buddhism is given as follows: "In the Ts'i period a Chinese monk named Hui-Lin took courage to go to the country of the Turks (T'sukiu). He approached the Kaghan and told him that China was prosperous and mighty for having favoured the Buddhist law. He then taught him the fundamental Buddhist doctrines and the Kaghan soon became a believer in Buddhism. He built a Saṅghārāma and sent an ambassador to the Ts'i Emperor with a request to send him some Buddhist texts specially the *Vimalakīrti-nirdeśa, Mahāparinirvāṇa-sūtra, Avataṃsaka-sūtra* and the *Sarvāstivāda-vinaya.* The Kaghan took so much to Buddhism that he practised abstinence, observed the Buddhist rules of conduct and made regularly the pradakṣiṇa of the stupas". During the reign of Hou-chu of the Ts'i dynasty (570–575) the *Mahāparinirvāṇa-sūtra* was translated into Turkish by a Chinese scholar named Lieu She-ts'ing at the request of the Kaghan. During the reign of Ts'i dynasty in 575 A.D, a Buddhist mission was sent to the Western countries in search of Sanskrit texts but the members of the mission could not return before the Sui period. The number of texts collected by them was 260.

The Chou dynasty succeeded the Wei in 557 A.D. They do not seem to have been quite well disposed towards Buddhism. Some able Indian scholars like *Jñanabhadra, Jinagupta*, etc. came to China in this period but they were not much encouraged by the Chou rulers in their work.

We have not so far followed the history of the Nanking church since 420 A.D. Four dynasties followed one another during this period in the South. These were the Song (428–479), the Ts'i (479–502) the Leang (502–556), and the Ch'en (557–589). The condition of Buddhism in the South during the reign of these dynasties was very flourishing.

The Song rulers were great patrons of Buddhism. The official history gives the following account of their pro-Buddhistic activities: "Wu-ti (454–465) used to recite Sanskrit texts and copy them with his own hand. He founded four monasteries – the *Ling sse*, the *Yen sse*, the *Fa sse* and the *Wang sse* in which generally one thousand monks were maintained. Wen ti (424–453) used to practise the Buddhist rules of conduct and founded the monastery of *Ch'an ling sse* in order to accommodate one thousand monks. Ming ti (465–472) erected statues in gold and founded the monastery of *Hong p'u ch'ong sse*. During their reign 210 volumes of texts were translated into Chinese and in all 1913 Buddhists temples were built throughout the empire. Amongst those who conducted the work of translation there were some famous Indian scholars *Dharmamitra, Guṇabhadra, Guṇavarman*, etc. Under the Ts'i dynasty Buddhism continued to flourish as before. Of the Imperial patronage the following account is given: "Kao-ti (479–482) copied the *Saddharma-puṇḍarīka-Sūtra* with his own hand and was able to recite the *Prajñāpāramitā Sūtra*. During 4 months and a half he used to arrange the statues in gold and during the rest of the year he used to entertain regularly 300 monks in the monastery of *Po p'u sse*. He built two monasteries for the use of the monks: *Che k'i sse* and *Cheng kuang sse*. Wu ti (483–493) founded *Shao hiuan sse* and *Yu hien sse* and invited 300 Buddhist scholars to lecture on the Tripiṭaka during four successive years. Ming ti (494–498) copied Sūtras with his own hand, erected statues in gold and used to recite the *Prajñāpāramitā* and the *Saddharmapuṇḍarīka Sūtras*. He founded the monastery of *Kui yi sse*. It is said that altogether 2015 Buddhist temples were built in various places of the Empire and 72 volumes were translated into Chinese. The number of Buddhists in this period in the South was 32,000".

Under the Leang dynasty (502–556) Buddhist activities continued with equal success. Indian scholars were coming to South China by the sea route. The most famous amongst them was Paramārtha who was a native of Ujjayinī. He was at first educated in the Brahmanical schools and was afterwards converted to Buddhism. He translated a large number of texts into Chinese and amongst them there were also texts of Brahmanical philosophy in which the Chinese Buddhists were getting interested. About the patronage accorded to Buddhism by the Leang rulers the following account is given by. the official history: "Wu ti (502–549) founded four monasteries viz. the *Kuang sse*, the *Chou sse*, the *Tung sse* and the *T'ai sse* and about one thousand monks used to be entertained in those monasteries. By an Imperial decree in 517, Wu ti prohibited the killing of animals either for sacrifice or for food and recommended vegetarian diet. He lived like a monk. Kien Wen ti (550–551) built two monasteries the *P'in king sse* and the *Pao ngen sse* and studied the *Prajñāpāramitā*. Yuan ti (552–554) built the *T'ien kin sse* and *T'ien kuan sse*. In all 2846 temples were built in this period throughout the Empire and 248 volumes were translated into Chinese. The number of Buddhists in this period was 82000". During the reign of the short-lived Ch'en dynasty (557–589) the progress of Buddhism was hampered to some extent and the religion does not seem to have received any royal patronage.

The accession of the Sui dynasty (581–589) after the suppression of small kingdoms marks a new era not only in the history of China but also in the history of Chinese Buddhism. China was once more united after a long period of internecine quarrels and foreign inroads and the Chinese Imperial traditions were restored once again. With the foundation of this Empire begins a new era in the history of Buddhism, an era of assimilation. The Chinese, with the revival of their own literary traditions, began to see what use they could make of this foreign religion in building up their national life which had been disturbed so much since the fall of the Hans.[1]

Note

1 For references to the sources see *Le Canon Buddhique an Chine*, pp. vii, ff.

Chapter 3

INDIAN INFLUENCE ON CHINESE THOUGHT*

The first contact of China with India goes back to the second century B.C. when certain scientific and cosmological notions infiltrated into China probably through the nomadic agencies of Eastern Turkestan. One of the most renowned Taoists of this period, Prince Lieu-ngan (Huai Nan-tseu), introduced for the first time a cosmology according to which the universe is divided into nine regions spread around a central mountain upon which are arranged the heavenly-worlds. This cosmology is of Indian origin and specially developed in the Buddhist literature.

China received Buddhism from the same nomadic sources, towards the end of the first century B.C. and within a century it was officially recognized as a religion worthy of toleration. Buddhist scholars began coming to China from the end of the first century after Christ and their activities were more and more intensified. But throughout the Han period (65–220), although a number of scholars had come to China, worked among the Chinese and translated a fairly large number of texts into Chinese, Buddhism had a hard struggle with the indigenous systems. Confucianism with its traditional prestige in the court and its hold on the nobility looked down on Buddhism as a barbarian religion. The Chinese, like the Greeks, looked upon all foreigners as barbarians and Indians were no exception to the rule. In the Han period attempts were made to transform Confucianism into a religion but its religious character was much less developed than Buddhism. Taoism was more established as a religion but its religious character was much less developed than Buddhism. Taoism was more established as a religion but its philosophical background was much weaker than Buddhism. This gave Buddhism certain advantages over the indigenous systems.

As Buddhism was a much richer religion than Confucianism and as it possessed a much deeper philosophy than Taoism it soon attracted the Chinese. The Chinese literati themselves started pleading for Buddhism.

---

* *History of Philosophy, Eastern and Western* 1 (1952): 573–589.

Thus Mou-tseu who lived towards the closing years of the Han period (170–225) wrote a treatise in which he compared the doctrines of Buddhism with the teachings of Confucius and Lao-tseu and tried to establish the superiority of the former.

> "The five classics", he says, "are the five tastes while the doctrines of the Buddha are the five kinds of grains. Since I heard the doctrines, I see the fully resplendent sun across the hanging clouds, I enter darkness with a torch. To live a family life, to have worldly connexions, to take advantage of all occasions, to take interest all the time in present things, these are the ways of the common literati which are given up by the really learned one. The saints, however, follow the way of immense perfection (Buddhism). It is mysterious like the sky and deep like the sea".

The writings of such people as Mou-tseu succeeded gradually in creating confidence in the minds of the educated Chinese about Buddhism. Besides, the life of purity followed by the Indian Buddhists who had come to China and by their Chinese disciples did not fail to attract the Chinese to this new faith. The patronage of the foreign dynasties in China also helped the cause of the new religion. The Wei dynasty which came in power in the fourth century was of foreign origin. They were great patrons of Buddhism and the beginnings of all great works of Buddhist art were made by them. The first Emperor of the dynasty made Buddhism a State religion. The edict of toleration which he promulgated in A.D. 335 ran as follows:

> "The Buddha is a god worshipped in the foreign countries. He may not be worthy of receiving offerings from the Emperors of China and from the Chinese. But I who was born in the frontier province, have the good fortune to be ruler of China. In regard to religious duties I must abide by the customs of my people. As the Buddha is a foreign God it is in the fitness of things that I should worship him. It is a pity that the same old laws of ancient times should be followed even now. When a thing is found perfect and faultless why should they still stick to the customs of the ancient dynasties. My people are called barbarian. I grant them the privilege to worship the Buddha and adopt the Buddhist faith if they like to do so".

Since then Buddhism went on prospering in China till about the eleventh century. Successions of Indian teachers coming from India kept the torch burning. From the fourth century onwards the Chinese monks themselves started going to India and making a deep study of Buddhism with Indian teachers. A vast literature of Buddhism, translated from Indian sources by the Indian as well as by the Chinese scholars, helped the Chinese to read Buddhism in translations. Some of the translations also had great literary value and came to be considered classics in Chinese literature.

The influence of Buddhism on Chinese life and thought was tremendous. Dr. Hu Shih, the leader of the Chinese intellectual renaissance, says: "When China was brought face to face with India, China was overwhelmed, dazzled, and dumbfounded by the vast output of the religious zeal and genius of the Indian nation. China acknowledged its defeat and was completely conquered".

*

Indian influence on Chinese thought first manifested itself in attempts at its approximation to Chinese ways of thinking. The pioneer in this attempt was Seng-chao who lived towards the beginning of the fifth century and was a disciple of the famous Kūmarajīva. Kūmarajīva, a scholar of rare genius, born in Eastern Turkestan and educated in Kasmira, came to China in 401. He worked in China till his death in 413 and translated a large number of texts into Chinese, many of which are still considered to be classics in Chinese literature. He was a scholar of deep insight and profound understanding of Buddhist philosophy, especially that of Nāgārjuna which he was the first to introduce in China. He did not fail to notice that the system of Nāgārjuna and the philosophy of Lao-tseu had many things in common. So he was not against interpreting the philosophy of Nāgārjuna in the language of Taoism. He is even believed to have written a commentary on the *Tao-te-king* which is lost. It was probably an interpretation of the Taoist philosophy from the Buddhist point of view. Among his disciples there were many illustrious Chinese scholars and Seng-chao was one of them. It was probably at the dictates of his master that he interpreted the philosophy of Nāgārjuna or rather attempted to synthesize it with Taoism for the first time.

Buddhist thought presented the antithesis between the immutable reality *(bhūta-tathatā)* and the temporal *(utpādanirodha)*, between permance and change and between *nīrvāna* and rebirth *(samsāra)*. These were very much similar to the Taoist contrast between non-being and being, immutability and mutability and *wu-wei (non-existence)* and *yu-wei (existence)*. On the question of mutability and immutability, Seng-chao says:

> "Most men's idea of mutability is that, things in the past have not come down to the present. The result is that they say that there is mutability and no immutability. That things of the past do not come down to the

> present is my idea of immutability; and the result is that I say that there is immutability and no mutability. That there is mutability and immutability is because the things of the past do not come down to the present; that there is immutability and no mutability is because things of the past do not vanish away".

This reminds one of the famous example of the burning lamp cited in the *Milindapañha*. The lamp is burning throughout the night, but the lamp of the first part of the night is not the same as that of the midnight or the last part. From one point of view it is the same lamp whereas from another point of view it is not the same but is changing every moment. On the question of reality Seng-chao says:

> "All things have that in them which makes them not be something, have that in them which makes them not be nothing. Because of the first characteristic, the result is that although they seem to be something, yet actually they are nothing; because of the second characteristic, the result is that they seem to be nothing".

The theory of causation *(pratitya-samutpāda)* is the corner-stone of Seng-chao's synsthesis. Everything is the product of causation. The effect is something new but that does not mean that it is not an effect, of a particular cause.

Seng-chao tries to solve another problem, the problem of the *prajñā*, the highest knowledge. Knowledge has an object and an object has a character. It is not qualityless and hence not the Absolute truth. If that be so, how can *prajñā* lead to the attainment of the Absolute truth? Seng-chao says that it is not knowledge in the ordinary sense. He compares it to a mirror which "though vacant reflects (the Universe) but though it reflects, it is vacant (i.e. it is not affected by the impressions it receives)". So from his point of view this knowledge "has a complete purview of essentials and yet is not knowledge". This does not mean that the Absolute truth exists apart from the relative.

> "Although it is outside the sphere of things yet at no time does it fail to deal with things. Although his spirit is in the beyond, yet it is all the time in the world....Hence in illuminating the qualityless, the sage does not lose the power of dealing with things yet at no time does he fail to deal with things. In his observation of change he is not in opposition to the qualityless....He thus lives in the realm of change and utility and yet abides in the sphere of *wu-wei*".

This synthesis of the Absolute and the Relative, although borrowed from the system of Nāgārjuna, was taken as a Chinese contribution because it was expressed in Taoist phraseology. It was attractive to the Chinese thinkers and they came to regard Seng-chao more as a Chinese philosopher than as a Buddhist thinker. Seng-chao had a great influence on later Chinese thought by showing how Buddhism could be assimilated to Chinese philosophy. It was no more possible to discard Buddhism. It had come to stay and lost its exotic character. Various attempts were made during the next few centuries to create something new out of Buddhism and Buddhist philosophy which would be acceptable to and easily understood by the Chinese who generally abhorred complicated metaphysical speculations. They wanted something simpler, more of a short-cut. While the Chinese monks educated in the Orthodox Buddhist tradition went on strictly following the hard life of a Buddhist monk as prescribed by the canonical works, others continued their attempt at evolving some simpler course.

A contemporary of Seng-chao, Hui-yuan, who though not a disciple of Kūmarajīva was working under his influence, laid stress on certain religious aspects of Buddhism. He was, like Seng-chao, well versed in Confucian and Taoist classics and as a student of Taoism it was the contemplative aspect of Buddhism which attracted him most. He created a new centre of Buddhist studies at a place called Lu-shan, collected a number of followers who gradually formed a School which came to be known as the Lu-shan school. This School, also known as the "Pure-Land School", introduced the cult of Amitābha in China. It was a new type of theism in which the object of worship was Amitābha and the goal was the Paradise of Amitābha – a land of infinite light: longevity and bliss. Faith and meditation alone could lead one to this Promised land. Hui-yuan himself emphasizes meditation (dhyāna) when he says:

> "Of the three phases of Buddhistic Life (i.e. moral discipline, meditation and insight) *dhyāna* and insight are of fundamemental importance. Without insight, meditation cannot attain the highest state of quietude. Without meditation, wisdom cannot achieve its profundity of insight... I regret very much that since the introduction of the Great Religion into the East so little is known of the practices of *dhyāna* that the whole structure is in danger of collapse because of the lack of the solid foundation of meditation".

Tao-sheng, a disciple of Hui-yuan and also of Kūmarajīva, developed a philosophy of *dhyāna* and laid the foundation of the famous *dhyāna* School of Buddhism which had a tremendous influence on Chinese life and thought. The School was known in China as Ch'an and in Japan as Zen, which are only transcriptions of the Indian word *dhyāna* (Prākrta, Jhāna). In common with all mystics, Tao-sheng was against attaching any importance to the Scriptures. They do not help in the realization of the truth. They are a means to the end but it is insight alone which helps to reach the truth. Thus he says:

> "The symbol is to express an idea and is to be discarded when the idea is understood. Words are to explain thoughts and ought to be silenced when the thoughts are already absorbed. Ever since the introduction of Buddhist Scriptures to the East, the translators have met with great impediments, and the people have clung to the dead letter and few have grasped the all-comprehensive meaning. It is only those who can grasp the fish and discard the fishing net that are qualified to seek the truth".

Tao-sheng was responsible for two theories which are considered to be revolutionary by the Chinese scholars and interpreted by them as a sort of Chinese revolt against the foreign religion. Revolt or not, they certainly represent an attempt to evolve a Chinese way of thinking. The doctrines are not new and can be traced to Buddhist sources but the emphasis on them was really Chinese. The two doctrines formulated by Tao-sheng were "good action requires no return" and "Sudden Enlightenment". When Tao-sheng speaks of "goodness requiring no reward", he speaks not from the relative point of view but from the absolute. He is speaking of those who are emancipated. He is in the world but is also above it. Reward and retribution are only true from a relative point of view. But they do not exist for one who has attained the *utpāda-nirodha* or cut through the chain of causation. This doctrine also is a necessary corollary of the Buddhist view of life. The theory of Sudden Enlightenment leading to the attainment of Buddhahood means that this enlightenment is not a gradual process. It dawns all on a sudden. This theory is also not new to Buddhism. It does not do away with all the preparatory stages, the moral discipline, the holy life, etc. Enlightenment, when it comes, comes all of a sudden. Later development of this theory in China brought in certain aberrations of the real view of life. But so far as Tao-sheng is concerned, there is nothing to show that he was raising a standard of revolt against the Indian view of life. He was emphasizing certain aspects of spiritual life with a view to warn his fellow Buddhists against confusion of the ultimate and relative views of truth.

Although Tao-sheng's theories provoked the thought of the Buddhist scholars of his times, his followers did not seem to have formed a school immediately. The origin of something like a School of *dhyāna* goes back to an Indian mystic who, in spite of the fact that a good number of myths had grown around his personality, was a historical personage. This was Bodhidharma who came to

China in the first quarter of the sixth century. He was in China between 486 and 536. An almost contemporaneous account written in 534 testifies to his presence in the newly-built temple of Yong ning sse at Lo-yang.

The teachings of Bodhidharma in China decidedly marked a departure from the old. He emphasized the practice of meditation as a religious means for the attainment of enlightenment. The philosophy which he preached was only a new interpretation of the system of Nāgārjuna. It looks like a Vijñāna-vāda interpretation. According to him everybody possesses the Buddhanature and real enlightenment means the awakening of this Buddhanature. He discredits the study of Scriptures, practice of all monastic rules, and too much attention to the formal aspects of religion as useless for the realization of the Buddha-nature. It is meditation alone, a looking inward and not outward, that helps in the realization. He said:

> "The heart of every man is in communion with all that was in all times and in all spaces. This heart is the Buddha. There is no Buddha outside the heart. Enlightenment and *nirvāna* are also in the heart. Outside the reality of the heart, everything is imaginary. To search for something outside the heart is to try to seize emptiness. The heart is Buddha and the Buddha is the heart. To imagine a Buddha outside the heart is madness. So it is necessary to turn one's looks not outside but inside. It is necessary to concentrate on self and to contemplate on the Buddha-nature of the self".

His philosophy is further elaborated on the same line. When everybody has the Buddha-nature and when there is no Buddha outside the heart, there is no question of saving another or being saved by another. There is no need of praying or offering worship to anybody. As the Buddha is the heart, it is the heart – the real self which is knower of everything. It is useless to go to anybody else or to read the scriptures with a view to acquiring knowledge of the reality. There is no need of asceticism, praying, begging, worshipping and the like for that purpose. If one sees the Buddha in one's own self that brings about deliverance and that only constitutes *nirvāna*. There is then nothing good or bad, meritorious or sinful in his acts. Some scholars would like to discover in the philosophy of Bodhidharma the Vedānta philosophy of India. In fact, by substituting a "Brahman" or "Ātman" for the Buddha we get something like a system of Vedanta. But a *Vijñāna-vāda* version of the philosophy of Nāgārjuna would also look like it. Although Bodhidharma went from South India he lived much earlier than Śamkara who was responsible for the new Vedanta in which the doctrine of māyā plays an important part. It was the Buddhists, the Sautrāntikas and the Mādhyamikas who preached something like a doctrine of māyā before Śamkara.

The reported conversation between Bodhidharma and the Emperor Wu clearly shows that it was the Buddhist philosophy which Bodhidharma was interpreting.

> "The Emperor asked him: Since the time of my accession to the throne I have been incessantly building temples, transcribing sacred books and admitting new monks to take the vows. How much merit may I be supposed to have accumulated? The reply was: None. The Emperor: And why? Bodhidharma: All this is but the insignificant effect of an imperfect cause not complete in itself. It is the shadow that follows the substance and is without real existence. The Emperor: Then what is true merit? Bodhidharma: It consists in purity and enlightenment, depth and completeness and in being wrapped in thought while surrounded by emptiness and calm. Merit such as this cannot be sought by worldly means. The Emperor: Which is the most important of holy doctrines? Bodhidharma: Where all is emptiness nothing can be called holy. The Emperor: Who is that thus replies to me? Bodhidharma: I do not know".

The teachings of Bodhidharma helped the Dhyāna School to be firmly established on the Chinese soil. Although the movement had started earlier with Tao-sheng, Bodhidharma's visit to China and advocacy of the same philosophy gave it a sanction that was much needed. This is why all later Dhyāna teachers trace their lineage from Bodhidharma. The School had a great success in China and later in Japan. During the subsequent centuries a number of sects sprang from it. There were two tendencies among them distinguished respectively by the emphasis they put on the positive and the negative aspects of the Dhyāna philosophy. According to one, the reality is all emptiness, without any quality whatever and cannot be defined as something. The mind as well as the Buddha-nature are also this emptiness. This doctrine was characterized as the doctrine of "not mind and not the Buddha". According to the other, it is the mind that realizes the emptiness. Without mind nothing would come into existence. It is the mind again that attains enlightenment or *nirvāna.* So it is the mind that is the real nature or Buddha-nature. This doctrine came to be characterized as "the doctrine of being mind, being the Buddha". These two tendencies again are not quite Chinese. They represent the two old aspects of the Mahāyāna philosophy as represented by the Śūnyavāda and Vijñāna-vāda. But the origins of the two tendencies were forgotton and they were looked upon as real Chinese interpretations of Buddhist philosophy, something really Chinese and acceptable even to those who had a dislike for the foreign religion.

*

The Dhyāna School by its challenge to Buddhist scholasticism created great confusion in the minds of the Chinese Buddhists. There were numerous monks and nuns in China in this period. Large monasteries had been built in important Buddhist centres. Through the activities of the Indian and Chinese scholars a vast Buddhist literature had come into existence in translation. It contained, according to tradition, "the words of the Buddha". Besides, the works of the great masters had also been translated. The followers of the Dhyāna School would attach no importance to this sacred literature. Besides there was a growing tendency among them to describe the current religious practices: the observance of the rules of monastic discipline, the worship of the Buddha and other divinities, praying to the Buddha, living on alms, etc., which are prescribed by the holy texts as futile.

One of the most illustrious Chinese thinkers of the sixth century attempted a bold synthesis of the conflicting views in order to evolve a system out of the confusion. This was Chi-k'ai who was born in 531. He was a follower of the Dhyāna School and though not a direct disciple of Bodhidharma must have been familiar with his teachings. He founded a monastery at a place called T'ien-t'ai and hence the name of the School. Chi-k'ai evolved a very comprehensive system of his own which was developed by his disciple Tu-shun who died in 640. Although Chi-k'ai was a follower of the Dhyāna School, he could not completely agree with other masters. He admitted that all beings possess the Buddha-nature but maintained that its realization depends on one's own exertion. So there is need of instruction as well as of striving to remove the error and arrive at true ideas. This was the corner-stone of Chi-k'ai's new system. A deep study of the Buddhist literature soon convinced him that in spite of the apparent diversities and contradictions in the teachings of the Buddha, there is an underlying unity of purpose in them. There are numerous philosophical theories but the ultimate end is the same. It is to get over the evils, and to attain the truth and the ultimate good. It does not matter by which method that goal is attained. It was in this light that Chi-k'ai attempted an ordered classification of the literature and a synthesis of the doctrines. The system evolved by him was so rational that it was accepted by all Buddhist Schools of China and other countries in the Far East and has come down to us. This was the real contribution of the Chinese genius to the systematization and rationalization of Buddhism.

In regard to the teachings of the Buddha as embodied in the literature, Chi-k'ai proposed that they were to be classified in a chronological order. He divided the Buddha's active career into five periods and classified his predications accordingly. The first period is represented by the *Āvatam-saka-sūtra.* The Buddha just after the attainment of *bodhi* passed twentyone days under the tree, dazed by the light of Illumination. During these days he taught only to the gods who had come down to congratulate him, and the teachings of this period, which contain the most sublime truths of Buddhism, not intelligible to the ordinary man, constitute the *Āvatam-saka-sūtra.* This is Mahāyāna. The second period starts as soon as he leaves the place underneath the *bodhi* tree and begins his career of a popular religious teacher. His teachings of this period are included in the *Āgamas (sūtra-pitaka)* which are purely Hinayāna. The teachings are destined for the novices and do not contain any sublime truths. This period continued for twelve years.

In the third period the Buddha embarked upon an attack on the various religious and philosophical texts which preached doctrines at variance with his own profession. The preachings of this period are in the form of controversies which are embodied in the *Vaipulya-sūtra* which has the character of both Mahāyāna and Hinayāna. This was a period of eight years. The fourth period was a period during which the attacks of other philosophical schools became so intense that the Buddha had to reveal to his disciples the deeper metaphysical truths. His teachings of this period are embodied in the *Prajñā-pāramitā* which is purely Mahāyāna. It was a period of twentytwo years.

The fifth period was the period of culmination. The adversaries had been silenced and Buddhism had been established on a firm footing. The Buddha's teachings in this period were mainly confined to an exposition of the way of the Bodhisattva, regulation of the life of those who want to attain Buddhahood. The teachings of this period are contained in such Mahāyāna works as the *Sad-dharma-pundarīka*, *Nirvāna-sūtra* etc. It was a period of eight years ending with his nirvāna. So from Chi-k'ai's point of view, the teachings of the Buddha followed a particular order and none of them was without its importance. They fulfil the religious needs of all grades in a progressive order. Hence the contradictions in the teachings are only apparent; seen in the proper context there is nothing contradictory, The Indian teachers also, specially those of the idealist school looked at some of the teachings of the Buddha in the same light in order to explain away the contradictions. Those teachings of the Buddha which did not fit in with their interpretation were described by them as meant for ordinary students incapable of understanding the profound metaphysics of the Mahāyāna. Although the viewpoint was not quite new, it was left to Chi-k'ai to develop into a comprehensive system.

Chi-k'ai regarded the *Āvatamsaka-sūtra* as the highest and the noblest product of Buddhism. He took it as the basis of his exposition of Buddhism. His exposition is, however, not a slavish imitation of the Indian exposition but an original one. It has a syncretic character inasmuch as it does not discredit any part of the teachings of the Buddha. According to him Buddhism is concerned with three faculties of the mind – intelligence, feeling and will. "Intelligence" helps one to know the real nature of life, "feeling" supplies a strong faith in the ultimate goal and "will" leads one to act with a view to attain the goal. Chi-k'ai does not take the Buddha to be an extraordinary being but a simple man who attained enlightenment through the exercise of those virtues. Everyone has that Buddha-nature in him. This Buddha-nature is the universal reality. Everything in nature has a share of this reality. It has a three-fold character – the true, the beautiful and the good. So the beauty of nature, the greenness of the leaves, the colours of the flowers, the songs of the birds and such other things are only manifestations of the same universal reality, the Buddha-nature. It is this latent Buddha-nature in us that has to be awakened. The Buddha succeeded in doing that. That is enlightenment. Chi-k'ai does not distinguish between the phenomenal and the noumenal – he takes them to be two aspects of the same reality. In this he follows the philosophy of the Dhyāna School and through it that of Nāgārjuna. He does not apparently believe in the theory of "Sudden Enlightenment".

Chi-k'ai accepts the Buddhist theory of eternal causality. The causality has no beginning and no end. Every effect is cause of other effects and that goes on in an infinite chain. The essence of the universe is eternal and the ephemeral beings who owe their individuality to the causality are only small waves which are instantaneous *(ksanika)* on the surface of this unique permanence. They are transitory phenomena and do not either add to or diminish the permanent reality.

The individuality is characterized as instantaneous, transitory and phenomenal. The existence is a succession of the instants (*santāna)* which are mutually related as cause and effect of *karman*. There is therefore no soul in an individual. His body is composed of the four elements – earth, water, fire and wind which are united at the time of birth and dissolved at the time of death through the effect of *karman*. Chi-k'ai takes into account two kinds of causes, the material cause *(yuan-yin)* and the efficient cause *(yin-yuan)*. Thus the seeds are the material cause, but it is the efficient cause which leads to their sowing and producing.

In regard to ultimate reality, Chi-k'ai accepts also the Mādhya-mika-Vijñāna-vāda view. This reality is not the impermanent phenomenal world. It is hidden under the multitude of appearance. It is the sole permanent reality, true essence of the world, and the substratum of all the forms. The universal reality has no birth and no death, no increase and no decrease, and no beginning and no end. The phenomenal world has a beginning and an end, increase and decrease, birth and death. It does not end in annihilation but in the beginning of a new series of phenomena. The cosmic reality is absolute, one, infinite, independent and unique. The phenomenal world is relative, distinctive, finite, dependent and multiple.

We have seen that according to Chi-k'ai the relation between the noumenon and the phenomenon is that of the ocean to its waves. As the two are identical so also are the *nirvāna* and *samsāra*. *Nirvāna* is "the being" and "Buddha-nature" in their permanent aspects whereas the *samsāra* constitutes their transitory aspect. In the permanent ocean of *nirvāna*, the individuals are the impermanent waves.

Three articles of faith are important to a Buddhist from the T'ien-t'ai point of view; (i) the cosmic reality fills up the whole space and time and has no beginning and no end. It is eternal and infinite: (ii) This cosmic reality produces the phenomenal world under the influence of causality; (iii) the phenomenal world is also real as it rests in the cosmic reality. The diversity is also unity. The unity becomes diversity under the influence of causality.

This is in short the philosophy of Chi-k'ai. In fact it is an adaptation of the system of Nāgārjuna, but the systematization of the entire Buddhist literature and thought from this angle of vision was Chi-k'ai's own contribution. His system had a tremendous success in his own times and during the subsequent centuries. It gave to the Chinese an extremely rational system free from the absurdities and contradictions caused by the growth of petty sectarianism. It also helps the Chinese philosophers of later times in evolving a new synthesis of Buddhist and Chinese thought in the eleventh century, but about that we will speak later.

*

While Seng-chao Hui-yuan and Chi-k'ai and their followers were striving hard to interpret the Buddhist thought in their own light, conservative Buddhist scholars of the type of Hiuan-tsang, Tao-siuan, etc., were ceaseless in their efforts to impose Buddhist scholasticism of India on their countrymen. They succeeded in introducing some of the Buddhist philosophical Schools of India in China. These Schools also had a fairly prosperous career in China. Some of them still exist in China and Japan.

Hiuan-tsang himself was responsible for founding the YogācāraVijñāna-vāda school. He himself belonged to it and studied its philosophy in India with Śīlabhadra of Nālandā, one of the greatest exponents of the School. He translated the fundamental texts of the School and published in Chinese an exposition of the philosophy of Vijñāna-vāda, documented with copious illustrations from commentaries of nine different teachers of the School. He had a deep understanding of this philosophy and not only his own works but also those of his famous disciple Kui-ki amply testify to it.

This School is known in China as Fa-hsiang (Dharma-laksana) and in Japan as Hosso. The name *Dharma-laksana* was given to the School as its philosophy mainly deals with the true nature of the *dharmas* which constitute the phenomenal world. This school is a true interpretation of the idealist philosophy of Buddhism. According to it *vijñāna*, consciousness is the only reality; the world of phenomena is a projection of this consciousness. In the analysis of the *vijñāna*, the masters of the School establish that the highest kind of *vijñāna* is the *Ālaya-vijñāna*, a sort of sub-consciousness which contains the seeds of all creations. The phenomena *(dharmas)* are all illusory, consciousness alone is real. After Hiuan-tsang, the principal teacher of this philosophy was his disciple Kui-ki who is regarded as the best exponent of this philosophy in China and Japan. The School is the only one of the scholastic type that has survived in China till now.

The origin of another Buddhist School of China also goes back to Hiuan-tsang. It is known as the Kiu-she (Kośa) school. The name is derived from the name of the famous philosophical treatise of Vasubandhu, the *Abhidharma-kośa* which contains an exposition of the philosophy of the Sarvāsti-vāda school. Vasubandhu was an adherent of this School before formulating his new philosophy of Vijñāna-vāda. The *Abhidharma-kośa* is based on the seven metaphysical works of the Sarvāsti-vāda School. Hiuan-tsang translated all these works into Chinese. He was anxious to popularize the doctrines of this School in China as they were useful for a proper understanding of the Vijñānavāda. In fact Vasubandhu himself meant his *Abhidharma-kosa* to be a stepping-stone to his Vijñāna-vāda. The philosophy of the Kośa school is a kind of materialism. True to the original teachings of the Buddha, it holds that Ātman (self) is not real; it is an ephemeral combination of the five aggregates of existence *(skandha)*. These aggregates are, however, real. They are composed of infinitely small atoms *(paramānu)* which alone are real. Their combinations are unreal and illusory. After Hiuan-tsang some of his followers continued to preach the doctrines of his School. It was then taken to Japan where it is known under the name of *Kusha*.

Another School, founded by Tao-siuan, a disciple of Hiuan-tsang, was called the Lü (Vinaya) school. In Japan it is known as Riotsu. We do not know how far its founder was influenced by his teacher Hiuan-tsang in formulating the doctrines of this School. His attitude was not inconsistent with that of other Buddhists of the period. Chi-k'ai had already taught that no branch of the sacred literature was without utility. In the same strain, Tao-siuan taught that Buddhist monastic discipline was not to be neglected. Unless one passes through the life of strict discipline, he cannot form his character and arrive at an advanced stage to practice meditation with an amount of success. For the preparation of the early career, Tao siuan recommended the *Vinaya* of the Dharmaguptaka School as the most suitable compendium of monastic discipline.

Still another School of Buddhism was introduced in China in the eighth century by Vajrabodhi and developed by his disciple Amoghavajra. It was *Tāntrika* Buddhism, already prevalent in India, especially in Nālandā and also in South India. Both Vajrabodhi and Amoghavajra carried a large number of texts to China and translated them into Chinese. The School is known in China as Chen-yen (true-word) and in Japan as Shingon. According to the teachings of this School, the primordial principle is *Mahā-vairocana.* He is identical with *bhūta-tathatā* (ultimate reality) of the philosophical Schools. The teachings of this school are concerned with three mysteries – the body, speech and the mind. They are found in all beings, either animate or inanimate. All aspects of nature are expressions of these three mysteries. These three mysteries in the human beings are the same as those in the Buddha. It is therefore possible to lead all beings to Buddhahood. This march towards Buddhahood involves a system of mental evolution through the acquisition of merits.

The philosophy was not quite new and did not attract the Chinese Buddhists very much although in Japan it had great influence. It was the magical side of this mystic Buddhism that attracted the Chinese very much. Taoism of this period had a good deal of it and when new spells, charms and magical formulae were introduced the mass of the Chinese people accepted them with great eagerness. Buddhism seems to have exhausted itself and had nothing new to bring to China.

The next few centuries form a period of decadence both in India and China. Communication between the two countries did not cease; large numbers of Chinese monks continued to visit India, the "holy land" of the Buddhists and there were also Indian monks in China who translated Buddhist texts of not much significance into Chinese.

A new period of activity starts only in the eleventh century with a new philosophical movement which though not Buddhist was greatly inspired by Buddhism and embodied certain fundamental elements of Buddhist philosophy which may be considered as lasting contributions of Buddhism to the development of Chinese thought. This new movement is the Neo-Confucianist Philosophy.

*

The new movement was started with a view to revitalizing the ancient Chinese philosophy and also with a bias against Buddhism. All previous wars against Buddhism had failed. But Buddhism was now decadent as a religion both in Indian and China. So far as the Buddhist philosophy was concerned, its scholastic systems were unintelligible to the uninitiated. Those elements of the Buddhist metaphysics which had a universal appeal had become accessible to the Chinese through the interpretations of Seng-chao, Chi-k'ai and the masters of the Dhyāna School. Buddhism, however, still enjoyed a high prestige on account of its former glory – and hence the attempt to fight it once again.

Although the new movement was directed towards a revitalization of the old philosophy, the new philosophy that was created contained less of the old and more of Buddhism which it wanted to destroy. Certain notions of positive sciences such as mathematics, astronomy, biology as applied to philosophy had been introduced by Buddhism. The Sāmkhya with its principles of *purusa* and *prakrti*, the atomism of Vaiśesika, the materialism of Sarvāsti-vāda with their theories of evolution were known to the Chinese through translations of original texts as well as through interpretations of Chinese Buddhist scholars.

The principal leaders of this new movement were Chou-tseu (1017–1073), Shao-tseu (1011–1077), Ch'eng-hao (1032–1085), Cheng-yi (1033–1107) and Chu-hi (1130–1200). The system evolved by them was perfected by Chu-hi. Contrary to the views of the ancient philosophers, Chu-hi maintained that there is no God, no sovereign power, no judge and no providence. The whole universe is composed of two co-eternal principles which are *Li* and *K'i*, the norm and the matter. Although they have distinctive characters, they are inseparable from each other. The norm is also called *T'ai-ki* because it is directing the force and *Wu-ki* because it is imperceptible and subtle. It is further described as one, infinite, eternal, immutable, unalterable, homogenous unconscious and unintelligent. It is under the impulsion of this norm that matter evolves alternately as *Yang* (progression) and *Yin* (regression). The *T'ai-ki* has no material form and thus no power to create. But in spite of its transcendental character, it has a real subsistence. Here Chu-hi distinguishes his *T'ai-ki* from the Buddhist conception of reality. He says:

> "The *T'ai-ki* consists of the *Li* of the Five Sources and the *Yin* and the *Yang*. All these are not unreal. If they were unreal they would correspond to the Buddhists idea of the nature of things".

He further says:

> "The Buddhists' idea of the unreal is not wholly wrong; but behind the unreal there must be the *Li*. If we only say that we are unreal and we do not know there are the real *Li*, that surely is inconclusive".

This seems to be a misrepresentation of the Buddhist view of life. The world is unreal but that does not mean that it is wholly unreal. From the relative point of view it is as real as anything. The highest reality is transcendental as well as immanent. It is indescribable but that does not mean that it is unattainable.

In regard to the relation between the norm and the matter and the process of evolution, Chu-hi says that the norm is not outside the matter. It puts the matter into action. It does not and cannot exist separately. While the norm itself remains immobile, it produces the manifestations which are the beings of the world. These manifestations are not successive but simultaneous. They are translations of the force into action, passage from non-perceptible to the perceptible. The norm in the individuals is only like a shoot of the universal norm and not really separate. The relation of the universal norm to the individual is best expressed by the analogy of the moon reflecting in thousands of water-pots but remaining unchanged all the time.

Chu-hi does not believe in rebirth. Everything gets dissolved with death. When a man is born his elements are derived anew from the two great reservoirs, the norm and the matter. Existence, however, is continued through descendants. Something of the ancestors is continued through them. The descendants are like waves of the sea. Each wave is complete in itself. The first is not the second, the second is not the third. But they are all modalities of the water. Likewise an individual is a modality of the universal norm and of the matter of earth and heaven. Then ancestor also is a modality of the same elements and so a man is one with his ancestor only by the community of the constituents, the norm and the matter.

The fundamental basis of this philosophy is not quite different from that of the T'ien-t'ai philosophy. Chi-k'ai, we have seen, accepted the Buddhist doctrine of Universal and eternal causality. This causality is independent of space and time. The chain is infinite, one effect becoming the cause of the other effects, and so on. The essence of the universe is eternal and the beings are only momentary small waves in this ocean of permanent reality. The waves of the ocean neither add to nor take away from its water. The same is true of the transitory phenomena. There are two causes: material and efficient. From one unique material cause, innumerable efficient causes create innumerable beings who are distinct in appearance, Chu-hi's theory of evolution in the progressive and regressive orders under the impulsion of the norm (*T'ai-ki*) which is infinite, eternal and immutable, is a translation of the same philosophy in another language.

In regard to the relation between the norm and the world, the noumenon and the phenomenon (the Buddhist *nirvāna* and *samsāra*) the Neo-Confucianist philosophers also accept the Buddhist position. Thus Ch'eng Hao says:

> "With regard to what I speak of as spiritual composure, in activity there is this composure; in stillness also. There is no anticipating and no retrospecting, no distinction of internal and external. If you take external things to be external and regard yourself as implicated in following them, then you are taking your nature to be divided into two parts, external and internal. Further, if you regard your nature as able to follow after things

> outside, then whilst it is engaged outside what is there inside you? You may have a purpose to eliminate the enticements of the external, but you are then ignoring the fact that in one's nature there is no distinction of external and internal....As to regarding the external as wrong, and the internal as right, this is not so good as forgetting that there is any external and internal. If you forget this distinction, then you are in a limpid state with nothing to disturb you. In that state you have spiritual composure. Having spiritual composure, then you are clear-minded; being clear-minded what is there which can catch you in its toils when you respond to things"?

Everything according to the Dhyāna view of life is Buddha-nature. From this point of view there is no inside and no outside, both being in the same reality. There is no difference between *nirvāna* and *samsāra*; they are also in the same reality. Ch'eng-hao also was translating the same view of life.

The Neo-Confucianists, in their attempt of synthesis of the old and the new, created a new philosophy which has been exercising a tremendous influence on the Chinese mind till now. Decadence of Buddhism in China during the subsequent centuries has led people to forget the part played by Buddhism in this new movement. There is no denying the fact that the Dhyāna and T'ien-t'ai Schools prepared the way for it. The absorption of the fundamental principles of Buddhist philosophy gave the new philosophy a universal character and made Buddhist thought almost superfluous to the Chinese intelligentsia as a separate system.

*

India had a large share in the development of the Chinese civilization. Beside certain forms of theistic religious beliefs, Buddhism introduced in China the doctrine of rebirth, the idea of causality, the belief in reward and retribution, etc. Although the Confucian ethics inculcated a certain pragmatic outlook of life, these doctrines took such a deep root in this Chinese mind that they could not be destroyed. The Buddhist philosophy, especially its conception of reality which permeates everything in nature and the notion of universal impermanence, had an abiding influence on the poets and artists and influenced the Chinese esthetic outlook. The poets of the T'ang period work under these influences. They have a deep feeling for nature and consider themselves inseparably bound up with it. They also have a consciousness about the fleeting nature of everything and feel melancholic for it. The artists discover the signs of the highest reality in nature, in the greenness of leaves, in the music of birds, and so forth. Buddhism also brought to the Chinese a deep religious feeling, a profound faith, which inspired the great works of art in China such as we find in Yun-kang, Lung-men Tun-huang and other places.

Bibliography

BAGCHI, P. C.: *India and China.*

ELIOT, SIR CHARLES: *Hinduism and Buddhism III.*

YU-LAN, Dr. FUNG: *The Spirit of Chinese Philosophy*, trans. By E. R. Hughes.

SHIH, Dr. HU: "Development of Zen Buddhism in China" (Chinese *Social and Political Science Review*, Vol. XV, 1931).

PELLIOT, P.: *Meou-Tseu on les doutes levés* (*T'oung Pao*, XIX).

WIEGER, PERE L.: *Histoire des Croyances religieuses et des opinions philosophiques en China.*

FUJISHIMA: *La Bouddhisme Japonais.*

LIBENTHAL, W: *Sacred Books of Chao.*

Note

1 The French system of transcribing Chinese words has been followed in this paper. For connecting the spellings of this paper with those of the preceding ones treat tseu as tzu, ki (k'i) as chi (ch'i), Kiu as Chiu, King as ching, Lieu ngan as Liu-an, Hiuan-tsang as Yuan Chwang, Chu Hi as Chu Hsi.

Chapter 4

A NOTE ON THE AVADĀNAŚATAKA AND ITS CHINESE TRANSLATION*

While comparing the Avādanas with the Jātaka Stories Dr. Speyer says: "The avadāna type is nearly related to the Jātaka. Both concern edifying tales told with the purpose of inculcating moral precepts as taught by the Saddharma revealed by the Buddhas".[1] The stories of the *Avadānaśataka* have also the same character. Some of the stories may be labelled as Jātaka proper. A Jātaka, judged by the Pāli collection of Jātaka stories, contains a story of the past "within the outer frame-work, constituted by the introductory episode and the concluding identification". A large number of stories of the *Avadānaśataka* contains a past story, within the frame-work of a present one with the identification. This identification is in some cases with the Buddha himself,[2] and in other cases less important persons.[3] Thus the presence of such different types of stories in the *Avadānaśataka* shows the importance of the collection in the development of the Jātaka stories.

The Chinese translation of the *Avadānaśataka* is very ancient. The title of the translation in Chinese is called *Chuan tsi pai yuan king*.[4] The translation is attributed to Upasāka Che-kien of the Yue-che country. Che-kien was an Indo-Scythian Upasāka and is mentioned as such in all the Chinese Buddhist sources. It is said that he was at first at Lo-yang but on account of the political upheaval towards the end of the reign of Han Hien-ti (190–220 A.D.) was compelled to leave the north and to go to the south. He worked at Kien-ye (Nanking) till the K'ien-hing period (252–253 A.D.) and translated a large number of texts into Chinese. The period of his activity therefore extended from about 220 to 252 A.D. and the translation of the *Avadānaśataka* also belongs to that period.[5]

As the Chinese translation of the *Avadānaśataka* belongs to the middle of the third century A.D. it is just possible that the date of the original must be placed about a hundred years earlier in the middle of the second century A.D. or a little earlier. Speyer suggests 100 A.D. as a good date for it. But this cannot

---

* *Visva-Bharati Annals* 1 (1945): 56–61.

be the date of the Sanskrit collection in its present form. A comparison of the text with the Chinese translation clearly shows that the original text was a much shorter text consisting only of the bare stories. The present text contains a large number of interpolations and amplifications.

This is clearly brought out by the absence in the Chinese translation of the stereotyped passages which have been repeated on many occasions and which Speyer would call *clichés*. Speyer is of opinion that these *clichés* "belong to the ancient Holy Writ of the oldest Buddhism". Whether they belong to the oldest Buddhism or not, it is certain that they are interpolations in the present *Avadānaśataka*. Let us examine some of these *clichés*:

(1) The description of Buddha and his followers at the commencement of the Avadānas: *buddho bhagavān satkṛto gurukṛto mānitaṛ pūjito...saśrāvakasaṅgho rājāgṛhamupaniśritya viharati veṇuvane* ... ... This long passage invariably occurs at the commencement of all the Avadānas but it is not found in the corresponding Chinese translations in which we have simply, in the manner of the old Sūtras: *"buddho viharati rājagṛhe kālandakaveṇuvane"*.

(2) The long description of the smile of Buddha which occurs in a number of Avadānas is not found in the Chinese translation. The description starts with *yasmin samaye buddhā bhagavantaḥ smitaṃ prāviṣkurvanti tasmin samaye nīlapītalohitāvadātā arciṣo mukhān niścārya... ...atha tā arciṣo bhagavantaṃ triḥpradakṣiṇīkṛtya bhagavata uṣṇīṣe'ntarhitāḥ/athāyuṣmānānandaḥ kṛtakarapuṭo bhagavantaṃ papraccha*... ... (then follows a number of gāthās).[6] The passage constitutes more than half of the Avadāna in which it occurs. Instead of the long passage we have in Chinese – "When Buddha smiled rays of five colours went out of his mouth, they illuminated the three worlds and produced different kinds of colours. They went round the Buddha three times and then entered the top of his head. Then Ānanda came to Buddha and said: It is not in vain that the Tathāgata has smiled, what is the reason". (There is nothing corresponding to the gāthās in Chinese). Speyer has drawn attention to the fact that the same description of the smile of Buddha occurs in many places of the *Dīvyāvadāna*.[7] But in the *Divyāvadāna* too it must have been a later interpolation. This becomes evident if we compare the original of some of the Avadānas of the collection with their earliest Chinese translation. The Avadānas of the Aśokan cycle were translated about 300 A.D. by Ngan Fa-k'in under the title *A yu wang chuan*.[8] The long description of the smile that occurs in the *Pāṃśupradāna-avadāna*[9] is not found in the Chinese translation;[10] we have instead the simple statement – "At this moment the Lord smiled. Ānanda bowed, joined his palms and said to Buddha – O, Lord, it is not without reason that Buddha smiles. For what reason have you smiled"? So

the occurrence of the passage in the Divyāvadāna and its absence in the corresponding Chinese translation of the 3rd century A.D., shows clearly that the passage was developed and interpolated in the Avadānas of the *Avadānaśataka* and the *Divyāvadāna* after 300 A.D.

(3) The rationalistic commonplace on the actual causes of begetting children without the direct influence of some deity cf. *Avadānaśataka*[11] – *śreṣṭī prativasati āḍhyo mahādhano mahābhogo vistīrṇaviśālaparigraho… … sāṣṭānāṃ vā navānaṃ masānāmatyayāt prasūtā / dārako jātaḥ … …*; cf. *Divyāvadāna.*[12] This passage does not occur in the Chinese translation of the *Avadānaśataka* cf. for example the translation of the third Avadāna – "There was a śreṣṭhī, exceedingly rich and famous. He had a son named Nanda".

The same thing may be said about other stereotyped passages or *clichés* of the *Avadānaśataka.* The passages do not form integral parts of the stories but are embellishments. They are interpolations concerning the qualities of the Buddha, the Arhats etc. and point out to a period when there had been a considerable development of the conception of the Buddhahood and the Buddhist doctrines. The embellishment also, must have belonged to that period.

The hundredth Avadana of the Sanskrit text is called *Saṅgīti* "Council". It has a second part which contains the story of Sundara, a story which belongs to the Aśokan cycle of legends. The story runs as follows: Aśoka, king of Pāṭalīputra, had a very beautiful son named Kuṇāla. The king was so much taken by his son's beauty that he often used to say "There is nobody so beautiful as my son in this world". Now some merchants of Gandhāra came to Pāṭalīputra. Aśoka enquired of them whether there was anybody more beautiful than his son. The merchants replied that there was in their country a youngman named Sundara who was the most beautiful among all men and that many miracles happened when he was born. Aśoka was astonished and made him come to Pāṭalīputra. When he saw him he admitted that he was the most beautiful of all men. Aśoka then asked venerable Upagupta what was the cause of this beauty. Upagupta said that in a previous birth, at the time of the first Council, Sundara had acquired merits by making offering to Kāśyapa and others of the Buddhist Saṅgha.

Mr. Przyluski made a special study of this text and after comparing it with other similar texts declared that the first portion of the story, the account of the council, closely agrees with the account in the Mūlasarvāstivādavinaya and in other texts of the same school.[13] This agreement and the association of the second part of the story with the Aśokan cycle of stories found only in the *Divyāvadāna*, which is again a work of the Mūlasarvāstivāda school shows, according to Przyluski, that the Avadānaśataka belonged to the same school.

The Chinese translation which represents the text as it was in the beginning of the 3rd century A.D. and which such a careful scholar as Przyluski, did not think of consulting, gives a different picture altogether. The story in Chinese is called the "Story of Sundara". It will appear from the English translation of the Chinese version that the first portion relating to the council (Saṅgīti) is not there. The main story, the story of Sundara is almost in the same words as those of the Sanskrit text but with important differences. The king is not Aśoka but Prasenajit. The merchants do not come from Gandhāra but from a village. Sundara in his previous life honoured not Kāśyapa, the disciple of Buddha, but Kāśyapa, the former Buddha. This is in perfect agreement with other stories of the *Avadānaśataka* in which the former Buddha Kāśyapa is honoured by the hero of the story. The time again is not the time of the first Council but some indefinite period in the Bhadrakalpa. All these go against the theory of Przyluski that the *Avadānaśataka* belonged to the Mūlasarvāstivāda. They rather show that Mūlasarvāstivādins re-edited the text sometime after the 3rd century when they introduced the story of the council in the text and rewrote the story of Sundara so that it might fit in with their scheme of the Aśokan cycle of legends. It was probably then that the long stereotyped passages or *clichés* were introduced from the *Divyāvadāna* or the Vinaya of their school in places where there were originally simple passages. It was at this stage that the name of Prasenajit was changed into Aśoka, the name of Gandhāra was introduced in the place of an unknown village and the name of Upagupta was introduced in the place of the name of Buddha, as it was not possible to pretend that Asoka could have an interlocution with Buddha himself. The substitution of the name of Kāśyapa or Mahākāśyapa for Kāśyapa the former Buddha was again another deliberate act, as Mahākāśyapa was the first patriarch according to the Mūlasarvāstivāda tradition.[14]

The idea of this rehandling probably was actuated by the name of the son of Prasenajit. In the Chinese version it is said: "The prince possessed a beauty which nobody in the world could surpass. His two eyes were clear and bright like those of a Kuṇāla bird. The king therefore named him Kuṇāla".[15] The name of Kuṇāla need not make us think at once of the son of Aśoka. The name of Aśoka's son was Dharmavivardhana. He came to be known as Kuṇāla later. On finding that the eyes of the prince were of rare beauty Aśoka one day said: "I have heard from reports that in the Himalaya, there is a bird called Kuṇāla of which the eyes are very beautiful". He then ordered a Yakṣa to find the bird for him. The Yakṣa brought it to him immediately. When he saw the bird he said: "Its small eyes are very beautiful and do not at all differ from the eyes of the child. So let him be called Kuṇāla". So the prince came to be known as Kuṇāla.[16] So it is a matter of renaming in the case of Aśoka's son while it is the original name in the case of Prasenajit's son. It is just possible that Kuṇāla was a common pet name of children in ancient times on account of the fabulous beauty of the eyes of the bird.

Notes

1 *Avadānaśataka*, Preface, p. iv.
2 Cf. nos. 31–38 – *kiṃ manyadhve bhikṣavo yo'sau tena kālena tena samayena ... ... .nāma rājā babhūvāhaṃ saḥ.*
3 Cf. no. 88 — *kiṃ manyadhve bhikṣavo yo'sau sārthavāha eṣa evāsau kapphiṇoṃ rājā tena kālena tena samayena.*
4 Nanjio 1324 and Taisho 200.
5 *Le Canon Bouddhique en Chine*, I, pp. 284–285.
6 See Sanskrit text – pp. 4–6; pp. 10–12; pp. 19–21; pp 25–27; pp. 32–34; pp. 37–40; pp. 43–45; pp. 51–53; pp. 59–61; pp 97–99; pp. 113–116; pp. 125–128; pp. 131–133; pp. 140–142; pp. 145–147;pp. 150–152; pp. 154–156; pp. 159–161; pp. 164–166.
7 Cowell and Neils' edition, pp. 67.16–69.27; 138.1–140.7; 265.15–267.7; 366.24–368.17; 568.7–570.2.
8 For the French translation of the work cf. Przyluski, *La Legende de Empereur Aśoka*, pp. 225 ff.
9 *Divy.*, pp. 366.24–368.17.
10 Cf. Przyluski, *ibid.*, p. 227.
11 p.13.6–15.7.
12 1.5–2.24, 98.18–99.17, 440.4–441.6.
13 *Le parinirvāṇa et les Funérailles du Buddha*, J.AS., 1918–20, pp. 485–526.
14 Przyluski, *La Légende de Empereur Aśoka*, p. 47.
15 Skt. *dārako jāto abhirūpo darśanīyaḥ prāsādikaḥ kuṇālasadṛśābhābhyāṃ netrābhyāṃ/... yasmādasya jātamātrasya kuṇālasadṛśe netre tasmād bhavatu dārakasya kuṇāla iti nāmeti. A.Ś.* [Pt.2], p. 201.
16 Przyluski, *La Légende* ... p. 282.

Chapter 5

BODHISATTVA-ŚĪLA OF ŚUBHĀKARASIṀHA*

Introduction

Throughout the extent of the entire Buddhist literature in Chinese it is difficult to find information on the personal activities of the Indian teachers who had worked in China. Besides translating Indian texts into Chinese, the most important of the teachers must have been engaged in teaching the fundamental doctrines of Buddhism but there is almost no information on this aspect of their activities. The text studied here, the *Wu wei san tsang ch'an yao*無畏三藏禪要 however forms a solitary exception. It is a collection of the teachings of an eminent Indian teacher, Śubhākarasiṁha, who had been to China in the beginning of the 8th century. The text is found in the standard collections of the Chinese Tripiṭaka.[1] As it was not included in the Ming Tripiṭaka there is no mention of it in the Catalogue of Nanjio.

In the preface of the Chinese text, Śubhākara is simply described as a "teacher of Tripiṭaka of the Veṇuvanavihāra of Nālandā in the city of Rājagṛha of the country of Magadha in Central India". He belonged to a noble family of the Kṣatriya race. More complete accounts of Śubhākara's life are found in the ancient catalogues of the Chinese Tripiṭaka and in the *Song kao seng chuan.* These accounts have been summarised in my *Le Canon Bouddhique en Chine II.*[2] In all these accounts the name of Śubhākarasiṁha is transcribed either as *Shu-p'o-kia-lo-seng-ho*戍婆揭羅僧訶 or as *Shu-p'o-kia-lo*輸波迦羅. The name is translated into Chinese either as *Tsing she-tseu*净師子, "pure lion" or as *Shan wu wei*善無畏, "good fearless". This last form of the name is often abridged as *Wu-wei san tsang* 無畏三藏 and this is the name that occurs in the text under consideration.

Śubhākarasiṁha was, according to all accounts, a descendant of Amṛtodana, the uncle of Śākyamuni Buddha. After ordination he first settled in the Nālandā monastery where he made a profound study of the Buddhist texts.

---

* *Sino-Indian Studies* 1.3 (1946): 132–160.

He then decided to go to foreign lands in order to preach the law of Buddha abroad. After leaving India he first travelled in the country of the Eastern Barbarians東夏. When he reached the frontier of China an official invitation was sent to him requesting him to proceed to the capital. He reached Ch'ang-ngan (Si-ngan-fu) in 716 a.d. He had with him a collection of manuscripts of Buddhist texts.He first resided in the monastery of Hing-fu sse興福寺 and then removed to the Si-ming sse 西明寺 at the imperial order. It was here that he translated some of the texts into Chinese in 717 a.d. The Śramaṇa Sita (Siddha?) who was evidently of Indian origin acted as interpreter. Śubhākara followed the Emperor to Lo-yang in 724 a.d., and settled in the monastery of Ta-fu-sien sse大福先寺. Here also he translated a few more works into Chinese. He died at Lo-yang in 735 a.d. at the age of 99 and was subsequently buried at Long-men. Śubhākara was therefore born in 636 a.d., during the reign of Emperor Harṣavardhana. It is not impossible that he had seen in his boyhood the famous Chinese pilgrim, Hiuan-tsang, either while he was residing in Nālandā or passing through Magadha. At least he had heard of him by reputation during his own residence at Nālandā.

Most of the texts translated by Śubhākara into Chinese belong to the mystic school of Mahāyāna that is generally known as Vajrayāna. These are either dhāraṇis or texts on mystic maṇdalas and mudrās employed for the worship of Mahāvairocana and other Buddhas. In fact Śubhākara was the first to introduce the teachings of this school in China in a systematic manner. He along with Vajra-bodhi and Amoghavajra are considered to be "the three great teachers of Tantrik Buddhism in China" of the K'ai-yuan period (713–741). They founded the first school of Tantrik Buddhism in that country.[3]

The title of the present text *Wu wei san tsang ch'an yao* means "The essentials of dhyāna (as taught) by the teacher of Tripiṭaka, Śubhākara". In the preface of the text it is said to be an abridgement of the essential doctrines of the Mahāyāna as taught by Śubhākara. It was compiled by a dhyāna teacher of Hui-shan sse of Song-shan named King-hien敬賢. The latter had a discussion with Śubhākara and evidently took notes which were published later on. The colophon of the text however says that it was the dhyāna teacher Hui-king慧警 of Si-ming sse西明寺 in the capital (i.e. Ch'ang-ngan) who first collected it.

About King-hien of Song-shan I have not been able to collect any information. There is however mention of one Hui-king in the *Song kao seng chuan* (k.24). It is said there that Hui-king was a monk of the Ch'ong-fu see崇福寺 in T'ai-yuan fu太原府. He translated the *Ta yun king*大雲經 – *Mahāmegha-sūtra.* There is mention of an Empress in the Sūtra. When the Empress T'ien-hou天后 came to know about it she was much moved and paid great tribute to the translator. Hui-king learnt to recite holy texts at the age of three. When the Emperor saw it, he patted him on the back and gave him a *kāṣāya.* Later on Hui-king became a monk and established himself in his own monastery. He was widely respected and feared by the Buddhist monks for his severity in regard to those who were guilty of the breach of Buddhist monastic discipline. In his later life Hui-king gave himself to the practice of the law of dhyāna and attained much success in that line. He died when he was more than 80 years old.

The above account gives us an idea of the time when Hui-king lived. He was a contemporary of the Empress T'ien-hou (684–706 ad.). He had received the *kāṣāya* in his infancy from the Emperor who was evidently Emperor Kao-tsong (650–683 a.d.). Even if we suppose that he was 20 years old when the Emperor died, he must have lived up to 743 a.d. and was thus able to establish personal contact with Śubhākara during the latter's residence in the Si-ming sse at Ch'ang-ngan. Śubhākara was at Ch'ang-ngan between 716 and 724 a.d. when he shifted to Lo-yang. Hui-king was therefore about 60 years old when he met Śubhākara and it was probably under the latter's influence that he took to the practice of dhyāna. The biographical notice on him clearly says that he took to this practice in the latter part of his life.

It is thus possible to believe that Hui-king who was originally a monk of Ch'ong-fu sse of T'ai-yuan fu had been attracted to the Si-ming sse by the reputation of Śubhākara a few years after the latter's arrival there and had found the notes taken a few years earlier by King-hien of the oral teaching of Śubhākara. These notes were edited by Hui-king and they constitute the present text. We have therefore reason to believe that these were authentic notes of the oral teachings of the famous Indian teacher.

As the preface would have us believe the text contains the essentials of the teachings on Mahāyāna. But it is Mahāyāna in the most comprehensive sense. A study of the text will show that it contains teachings of the Mahāyāna not only in the general sense of the term but also in its special sense. I have therefore divided the text into three broad divisions:

I. *Bodhisattva-śīla.*
II. *Anāsrava-dharma-śīla*; the practice of *dhyāna, dhāraṇī* and *mudrā.*
III. Breathing exercises as an expedient for the attainment of Samādhi.

I. Bodhisattva-śīla

The first part of the text deals with Bodhisattva-śīla. These contain the rules essential for initiation to the Mahāyāna. A text entitled *Bodhisattva-Prātimokṣa-sūtra* containing such rules was published by Dr. N. Dutt in the *Indian Historical Quarterly.*[4] The first part of the text, as noticed by Dr. Dutt, is a sort of manual of ordination and contains an enumeration of seven different rites: (i) *Yācanā*, entreating a *Bodhisattva* for initiation, (ii) *Pāpadeśanā*, enquiry whether sins have been committed or not, (iii) *Śaraṇagamana*, taking refuge in Buddha, Dharma and Saṅgha, (iv) *Pariṇāmanā* – offering one's own merits to all beings for the sake of Bodhi, (v) *Bodhicittotpāda* – awakening of the bodhi mind, (vi) *Ācāryābhiṣeka* – selection of an Ācarya and (vii) *Vijñapati* – announcement. The same fundamental rules are found in the *Bodhicaryāvatāra* of Śāntideva and have been enumerated by Dr. Dutt – (i) *Vandanā* and *Pūjanā*, (ii) *Saraṇagamana*, (iii) *Anumodanā* – expressions of approval of others' merits, (iv) *Yācanā* or *Adhyeṣaṇā* – entreating Buddha to be the guide of all beings, (v) *Pariṇānamanā* and (vi) *Bodhicittotpāda*.[5] The differences between the two lists are minor.

Among the late compendiums Dr. Dutt has also referred to the *Kriyāsaṁrgraha-pañjikā* of Kuladatta of which there is a detailed notice by Dr. H.P. Shastri in his *Catalogue of the Buddhist Manuscripts of the Government Collection in R.A.S.B.*[6] I have quoted the principal rules at the end of this study from the said notice of Dr. H.P. Shastri. The principal rules occur there as: (i) *Śaraṇagamana*, (ii) *Pañca Śikṣāpada*, (iii) *Yācanā* or *Adhyeṣaṇā*, (iv) *Daśa Śikṣapadā*, (v) Rules regarding robe, bowl etc., (vi) Observance of rules regarding *śīla*, *samādhi*, *prajñā*, *vimukti* and *vimukti-jñāna-darśana*. These rules as has been pointed out by Dr. Dutt have been borrowed from the Hīnayānic rules of ordination and have nothing specially Mahāyānic in character.

In fact they are enumerated as such in another Mahāyāna compendium which is entitled *Kriyāsamuccaya* which is as much used in Nepal as the *Pañjikā* of Kuladatta. The *Kriyāsamuccaya* may be later than the work of Kuladatta by about one hundred years. It contains a section called *Poṣadhavidhi*[7] which corresponds word for word with the first part of the *Bodhisattva-Prātimokṣasūtra* published by Dr. Dutt. I have reproduced the text at the end for facilitating a comparison with the text published by Dr. Dutt. The author of the *Kriyāsamuccaya* thus frankly admits that it is a *Poṣadhavidhi*, as current among the Hīnayāna schools and have no Mahāyāna character. The rules enumerated in it are almost the same as those of the *Kriyāsaṁgraha*.

The followers of Mahāyāna always admitted the necessity of primary initiation according to the rules prescribed for the Hīnayāna or Śrāvakayāna. Such initiation once received, the question arose whether one should go higher up the ladder. Rules of this higher spiritual discipline constitute the real *Bodhisattva-śīla* or *Bodhisattva-Prātimokṣa*. In this respect the text under consideration is a more comprehensive manual than the other works noticed above.

In the first section are narrated the ordinary rules that are found in the *Poṣadhavidhi* and the *Bodhisattva-Prātimokṣa* mentioned above. This section has much in common with the Hīnayāna rules of ordination. For the facility of comparison I have quoted the corresponding Sanskrit texts *in extenso* from the *Kriyāsaṁgraha* and the *Kriyāsamuccaya* at the end. This section contains the following eleven items:

I. *Cittānuśīlana* or the cultivation of the mind. It amounts to mental preparation of the candidate for initiation. The candidate first entreats all Buddhas, Bodhisattvas and other great personages for help in the matter. This corresponds to *Yācanā* of other texts.

II. *Pūjā* – the candidate then worships the Buddhas, Bodhisattvas and great personages for help in the matter of initiation. This is not separately mentioned in other sources and seems to have been a part of *Yācanā*.

III. *Anuśocanā* – the candidate is then required to repent for the various kinds of sins committed by him and seek the protection of Buddhas and Bodhisattvas against further commission of such sins. This is not mentioned in other sources.

IV. *Śaraṇagamana* – The candidate then takes refuge in the three jewels – Buddha, Dharma and Saṅgha. Here there is a departure from the Hīnayāna conception of three jewels as the candidate takes refuge in: (i) *tri-kāya* of the Tathāgata, (ii) *vaipulya-Mahāyāna -dharma* and (iii) *avaivartika- saṅgha*. In the other texts mentioned above there is provision for *Saraṇagamana* but in the Hīnayāna sense of the term.

V. *Bodhicittānuśīlana* – cultivation of the Bodhicitta. This occurs in all the sources as it is the most important of all Bodhisattvaśīlas. The candidate is required to take the vow that he will go on cultivating the Bodhicitta so long as he does not attain the Bodhi knowledge.

VI. *Pāpadeśanā* – is the same as found in the other texts. The candidate has to be first questioned by the teacher whether he has committed the seven offences viz. killing a Buddha, killing the Arhats, killing the Upādhyāyas and Ācāryas and destroying the unity of the Saṅgha. If the teacher is satisfied that the candidate is immune from such offences then he may give him ordination.

VII. *Ācāryābhiṣeka* – it is not the selection of Ācāryas in the Hīnayāna sense. The candidate invites Buddha Śākyamuni to be his Upādhyāya, Mañjuśrī to be the Karmācārya, and all Bodhisattvas and Mahāsattvas to be his fellow students.

VIII. *Karma* – it does not occur in the other texts as a separate item. In the present text it consists of the observance of three kinds of śīla – *saṁvara-śīla*, *kuśala-śīla* and *sattvārtha-kriya-śīla*. These three kinds of śīlas are mentioned in the other texts and specially discussed in the *Bodhisattva-bhūmi*. Dr. Dutt (*ibid*) has explained these terms with the help of the last mentioned work. *Saṁvara-śīla* are the disciplinary rules for the Bodhisattvas and are to be practised by all candidates for Bodhisattvahood. *Kuśala-śīla*, also called *Kuśaladharma-*

saṅgrāhaka- śīla consists of study, contemplation, meditation, insight (*śamathā*, *cittaikāgralā*, *samādhi*, *vipaśyā*) etc. which a candidate practises after being established in śīla. *Sattvānugrahaśīla* are eleven kinds of śīlas to be practised for the benefit of others such as helping all beings in their various useful works, helping them in their sufferings from disease etc., warning persons through religious discourses and so forth.

IX. *Sīmābandha* – this does not occur in other sources. It is not quite clear what it really means. It is explained in the text as simply a warning from the teacher to keep the three śīlas of the Buddhas and Bodhisattvas so long as one does not attain the highest Bodhi.

X *The practice of the four adhiṣṭhnās* – the four *adhiṣṭhnā-dharmas* as enumerated in the text are: *priyavāditā*, *dānaṁ*, *artha-caryā* and *samārthatā*. These are the same as found in the *Mahā-vyutpatti.* They are not mentioned in the other sources.

XI. *The ten important śīlas* seem to be more or less the same as the *Mūlāpattis* and *Sthūlāpattis* described in later literatures. The number of the *Mūlāpattis* is given as fourteen and that of the *Sthūlāpattis* as eight in the *Advayavajrasaṁgraha.*[8] They are also mentioned in the *Kriyāsamuccaya*[9] sometimes under more correct forms. The ten injunctions of Śubhākara may be compared with the *Āpattis:*

1. Not to turn down the Bodhicitta, cf. Mūlāpatti no. 5 – *bodhi-citta-parityāga.*
2. Not to abandon the three jewels, cf. Mūla. no. 2 – *sugatā-jñāvilaṁghana.*
3. Not to speak ill of the three jewels, cf. Mūla. no. 6 – *yāna-tritaya-nindana.*
4. Not to have doubts as to the meaning of the *Mahāyāna-sūtras*, cf. Mūla. no. 9 – *śudhātma- dhdrma-sandeha* (*Kriyā-samuccaya*: *svabhāva-śuddhadharmeṣu vicikitsā*).

5–6. Not to speak such laws as may drive others to the two yānas, i.e. Śrāvaka and Pratyeka-Buddha-yānas, cf. Sthūlāpatti no. 5 – *yaḥ śrāddheṣu sattveṣu guhyadharmarateṣu ca viparītam samākhyātam*, nos. 6 and 8 of the Sthūlapattis are also similar – there are prohibitions of not to live with the Śrāvakas even for a week and not to divulge the true law to those who are attached to other laws.

7. Not to speak of the highest and excellent Mahāyāna before those who follow the Hīnayāna, cf. Sthūlapattis no. 4 – *guhya-dharmaṁ yadā duṣṭa na gopayati naṣṭadhīḥ* (?), Mūlāpatti no. 7 – *guhyākhyāne jane pakṣe* (Kriyā, *aparivārita-sattveṣu guhyākhyna*).
8. Not to cultivate wrong views, cf. Mūlāpattis no. 8 and 11 – *jinātmaskhandha-dūṣaṇe*, *dharmeṣvanadvayārope.*

9. Not to speak before the Tīrthikas that you keep the excellent śīla for the highest bodhi, cf. Mūlāpatti no. 7 – referred to above.
10. Not to do anything injurious to living beings, cf, Mūlāpatti no. 4 – *mahāhumaitrī-vivarjana*.

The agreement between the injunctions of Śubhākara and the *āpattis* is very close in many cases. But it is probable that the *āpattis* had not been formulated in the time of Śubhākara in the form we get them in the later compendiums. The fourteen *Mūlāpattis* and the eight *Sthūlāpattis* in their present forms were conceived later than the eighth century.

With the enumeration of the ten injunctions the section of Bodhisattva-śīla proper comes to an end. Śubhākara then deals with other practices of Mahāyāna that properly belong to the domain of Vajrayāna or Tantrayāna.

II. Anāsrava-dharma-śila

In the next section Śubhākara teaches the mystic upāya by which one may quickly attain Bodhi knowledge. He calls it *anāsrava-dharma-śila*. It is also called the śīla of the true law (*satya-dharma-śila*). It consists of the practice of *dhyāna*, *dhārna* and *mudrā*. The dhāranīs are to be recited after entering the *dhyāna* at different stages. The dhāranīs prescribed by Śubhākara are five in number of which the intermediate three are the most important as by practising them one may realise the Bodhicitta, attain the Bodhi knowledge and enter the mystic maṇḍala respectively. The dhāranīs are to be recited three times each. If they are recited for a greater number of times the result comes more quickly.

The practise of dhyāna and mudrā is essential for the attainment of samādhi. These are to be practised in a solitary place where the mind is not disturbed by the external things. The mudrā to be employed is explained by Śubhākara by symbolical terms. The words for the *pāramitās* stand for the various fingers. This is a practice commonly current in the Tantrik schools. The right hand is called puṇya福 and the left jñāna智. The fingers of the right hand beginning with the thumb are respectively called – *dhyāna*禪, *vīrya*進, *kṣānti*忍, *śīla*戒 and *dāna*施, and those of the left hand in the same order are *jñāna*智, *bala*力, *praṇidhāna*願, *upāya*方, and *prajñā*慧. These are also enumerated in the same way in the ordinary Chinese Buddhist compilations. Śubhākara recommends that the mudrā is to be made in seven different places in the upper part of the body. After making the mudrā one should repeat the dhāraṇīs on the rosary as many times as possible in one sitting. If one can tell them up to one hundred thousand times then various kinds of spiritual powers may be quickly attained. As regards the sitting posture Śubhākara is in agreement with the earlier Yoga-śāstras. He does not believe in sitting in postures that are painful. One should sit, according to him, in any easy pose, the best way being to sit with legs half-crossed. It is reasonable to believe, on Śubhākara's evidence, that the various complicated methods of sitting (āsana) had not yet come into use. Śubhākara also gives other details of the practice of dhyāna. The eyes, he says, should not be either fully closed or kept fully open as both the practices are bad for attaining concentration of mind. The eyes should be kept, according to him, half shut. That this was the common practice among the yogis is also corroborated by other texts as well as old sculptural representations of Buddha and other famous religious teachers. The object of dhyāna, according to Śubhākara, is Buddha. But it is not the historical Buddha but all Buddhas in ten directions in the Dharmadhātu. The dharmadhātu is no longer an empty region but a world which is filled with innumerable Buddhas, Bodhisattvas etc. One has to approach all these Buddhas in dhyāna and offer them worship in order to acquire their help and blessing in his upward march. This practice leads to the complete purification of the mind and the ultimate attainment of samādhi.

III. Breathing Exercises and Other Practices

In the last part of the text, Śubhākara gives instruction on the breathing exercises and other expedients, for the attainment of samādhi. That the breathing exercises were current among the Buddhists from the very earliest times can be seen from the various teachings on *āmapāna*. The Chinese translations of some of these *Ānapāna-sūtras* go back to the second century and are attributed to Ngan She-kao. We will deal with one of these ancient texts in a future article. Śubhākara's method of breathing exercise is very simple. He says: "First think of breathing in and breathing out. It must go inside our body through all the joints and muscles. Afterwards it goes out slowly through the mouth... One should follow the distance it goes. It again slowly comes in through the nose. It goes to the joints and muscles all over the body. It is then allowed to go out and come in three times". This is heeded, according to Śubhākara, for keeping the body fit. If one takes this exercise the body is not affected either by cold, heat or wind. Such a condition of the body is needed for the attainment of samādhi. In course of the breathing exercise the breath stops at a certain moment and different kinds of thoughts both *kuśala* and *akuśala*, arise in the mind. The *akuśala* thoughts are to be avoided as they are the cause of fear to the yogin. The *kuśala* thoughts should be retained as they help in attaining *samyak smṛti* and purity of mind.

Śubhākara describes another peculiar practice which I have not been able to find elsewhere. It is a means of attaining concentration of mind and samādhi.

Śubhākara describes it in the following words: "At a quiet place make the ground level and clean. Its surface should have a length of 25 cubits. Erect two posts at the two ends. Pass a rope through them and attach it to the two ends. It is hung high up to the chest. Hold the rope by means of a bamboo tube which is big enough to be held in the hands. Turn the bamboo tube with the sun on the right. Go and come in a balanced way. The mind, quite composed, sees in the front up to 6 feet".

Although the Chinese text seems to be clear enough I have not been able to understand in what this peculiar practice consisted. It looks like dancing on the rope for which one must hold a bamboo in the hands in order to keep the balance.

Śubhākara also prescribes another means for attaining samādhi. It is a mental exercise, which is described in the following words: "Imagine a bright disc like the clear moon at a distance of four feet from the body, direct in front neither high nor low. It measures one cubit and is completely circular. Its colour is bright, it is shining both inside and outside and is without a like. At first you will not be able to get a long view of it but if you try attentively you will get it. After searching you can have a large view of it. Then you will find its expansion increasing up to four feet, or double that size or becoming as big as to fill up the *tri-sāhasra-mahāsāhasra* worlds".

Śubhākara also gives an explanation why this practice is helpful in the attainment of samādhi. The moon is composed of four elements and is bright. So it is compared with the intellect which has the same characteristics. Śubhākara probably means to say that concentration of the mind on the brightness of the moon outside leads to the attainment of an identity between the two, the mind and the moon and an ultimate projection of the mental faculties. The result is: "Then you see only brightness and nothing else, not even the body and the mind. All dharmas are lost in emptiness". Śubhākara says that this emptiness should not be taken in the ordinary sense. It means "absence of thought" or *āyatana-śūnyatā* and not vacuity. These are some of the peculiar practices which Śubhākara teaches. According to him *samādhi* is *nirvikalpa-dharma.* The Buddhas as well as the lowest creatures are all the same. It is only the bad thoughts which cover them with *avidyā* and *viśaya.* This is the reason of their floating in the world of transmigration and becoming subject to birth and death. The state of *samādhi* is free from this *avidyā*. In this regard Śubhākara repeats the fundamental teachings of Buddhism. He also mentions several kinds of *samādhis* and *bhūmis* or stages of spiritual progress. He states in this regard that a practised mind has five different aspects: (i) *kṣaṇa-citta*, (ii) *srotāpanna-citta*, (iii) *madhura-citta*, (iv) *vidhvaṁhsana-vikṣipta-citta*, (v) *ādarśa-citta.* These indicate different capacities of the mind for realisation of the truth.

On the whole the teachings of Śubhākara as embodied in the present text offer a complete practical code of the Mahāyānists of the 7th and 8th centuries a.d. They indicate the peculiar mystic bent of the faith that was developing in that period. As such the text supplies us with an important landmark in the development of the Mahāyāna Buddhism.

Translation – Wu wei san tsang ch'an yao

[I]

Śubhākara was a Śramaṇa, the teacher of Tripiṭaka of the Veṇu-vanavihāra 竹林寺 at Nālandā in the city of Rājagṛha of the country of Magadha in Central India. His name is translated in the T'ang language (i.e. Chinese) as Shan wu wei善無畏 "good fearless". He belonged to a rich and noble family of the Kṣatriya race. He discussed the law of Buddha with the Venerable Dhyāna teacher of the monastery of Hui shan sse會善寺 of Song-shan嵩山, the Ho-shang King-hien敬賢. He abridged the essential doctrines旨要of Mahāyāna which quickly open the mind so that all beings quickly realise the law. He received the Karmavidhi of the Bodhisattvaśīla which is as follows:

He who wants to enter the Mahāyāna must first of all cultivate the excellent bodhicitta, observe the Bodhisattvaśīla and keep the body-vessel (*deha-bhāṇḍa* 身器) pure. Then he can receive the law. Briefly speaking it is of eleven kinds:

i. *Cittānuśilana*, the cultivation of the mind 發心.
ii. *Pūjā,* worship供養.
iii. *Anuśocanā*, repentance懺悔.
iv. *Śaraṇagamana*, taking refuge歸依.
v. *Bodhicitlānuśīlana,* cultivation of Bodhicitta發菩提心.
vi. *Pāpadeśanā* – Enquiry whether sins have been committed or not問遮難.
vii. *Ācāryābhiṣeka* – choosing the *Ācārya*請師.
viii. *Karmavācā*羯摩.
ix. *Śīmābandha*結界.
x. The practice of four *adhiṣṭhāna dharmas*修四攝.
xi. The ten important śīlas十重戒 (Mūlāpattis?).

I. *Cittānuśilana* – I disciple so and so take refuge in all Buddhas, great Bodhisattvas and great Bodhi minds in ten directions. We make them our guide. May they save us from falling in the evil existence and show the men and gods the great road to nirvāṇa. So we worship them to-day with great attention.

II. *Pūjā* – We disciples so and so worship all the Buddhas, great Bodhisattvas and the great Bodhi minds with all that is best in the world in the ten directions and with fragrant incense, flowers, banners and different kinds of good things. We now cultivate the mind for all times to come and worship with full attention.[10]

III. *Anuśocanā* – I disciple so and so (realise) that from the past without beginning till to-day all beings have been suffering from misery (*kleśa*煩惱), such as greed, anger, ignorance, hatred, etc. The miseries much disturb the body and mind and make us commit all kinds of sins. The deeds of the body which are not good (akuśala) are killing, robbing and committing sexual offence. The deeds of the speech which are not good are telling lies, using bad words and practising duplicity. The deeds of the mind that are not good are greediness, anger and holding wrong view. All these miseries which are without beginning and end (i.e. numberless) continually fetter the mind and the body. They let the body, mouth and the mind commit sins without limit. Some kill their parents, some kill the Athats, some cause the blood flow from the body of a Buddha, some destroy the united Saṅgha, some calumniate the three jewels, some cause violence to living beings, some spoil the fast and the rules of conduct (śīla), some drink wine, some eat meat and some commit similar other offences, endless and unthinkable. To-day with a sincere mind we practise repentance. Once we repent we destroy the continuity (of sins) for ever and we will not venture to commit them again. We place ourselves under the protection of the Buddhas and the great Bodhisattvas in ten directions. Let our sins be destroyed. (So we worship them) with complete attention.

IV. *Śaraṇagamana* – I disciple so and so take refuge in the excellent tri-kāya of the Tathāgata from the beginning of the present body up to the sitting on the Bodhimaṇḍa. I place myself under the protection of the *Vaipulya-mahāyāna-piṭaka*方廣大乘法藏. I take refuge in the community of the *avaivartika*不退 Bodhisattvas. Let the Buddhas and the great Bodhisattvas in ten directions recognise us. We worship them with complete attention.

V. *Bodhicitlānuśīlana* – I disciple so and so take the vow to cultivate the highest Bodhicitta beginning with the present body up to sitting on the Bodhimaṇḍa.

Living beings without limit take the vow of crossing,
Merit and knowledge without limit (they) wish to collect,
Means without limit they wish to learn,
Tathāgatas without limit they wish to serve,
The path of anuttara Buddha they wish to attain.

We now cultivate the mind and remove from it the two characteristics (*lakṣaṇa*) of *ātmadharma*我法. It clearly reveals the original knowledge本

覺, i.e. *bodhi* which is the truth. By considering all things equal we attain the right knowledge. The mind is then fully attained and becomes all-good (samantabhadra). Let the Buddhas and the great Bodhisattvas in ten directions recognise us. We repent with complete attention (i.e. sincerely).

VI. *Pāpadeśanā* – First enquire if the seven sins have been committed. (If they are committed) the teacher should not give ordination. He should advise the disciple to repent. He must repent sincerely either for one week, two weeks, seven weeks or one year and become one of good character. If he does not become so, no ordination can be given.[11]

You children of Buddha, have you killed father since the time of your birth? Have you killed mother? Have you caused the blood of the Buddha's body flow? Have you killed the Arhats, Upādhyāyas and Ācāryas? Have you destroyed the unity of the Saṅgha? If you have committed any of the above sins you must confess it in the midst of all and practice repentance. Do not hide it. If you do so you will fall to the avīci hell and have unlimited suffering. If you follow the teachings of Buddha, make the confession. Great sin will be destroyed and you will have a pure body. You will enter Buddha's knowledge and get enlightened by the highest and right bodhi knowledge. If you have not committed it (sin) you should answer "no". You children of the Buddha, from to-day up to your sitting on the Bodhimaṇḍa, can you energetically keep the highest śīlas of all the Buddhas and the great Bodhisattvas and the best *saṃvaraśīla*律儀戒? So it has been called the *tri-śaraṇa-śīla*. Keep the *saṃvaraśīla*. Keep the *kuśāla-śīla* 善法戒. Keep the *sattvārtha-kriyā-śīla*饒益有情戒. You should follow it in this body up to your attainment of Bodhi.

Can you keep this vow without lapses during all this time?

[Yes.]

Can you do that during all this time without giving up the tri-śaraṇa and the four vows?

[Yes.]

Then cultivate the Bodhicitta and receive the Bodhisattva-śīla. Let the Buddhas and the great Bodhisattvas in ten directions recognise and protect us. Let us not go back. Let us worship with complete attention.

VII. *Ācāryābhiṣeka* – We disciples so and so invite all the Buddhas and Bodhisattvas in ten directions, the Bodhisattva Avalokiteśvara, the Bodhisattva Maitreya, Ākāśagarbha Bodhisattva, Samantabhadra Bodhisattva, Vajradhara Bodhisattva, Mañjuśrī Bodhisattva, Vajragarbha Bodhisattva, Sarvanivāraṇa Bodhisattva, and the assembly of all great Bodhisattvas who according to their previous vow came to the Bodhimaṇḍa to recognise us. We worship them with full attention.

I disciple so and so invite the Buddha Śākyamuni to be our Upādhyāya. We respectfully invite the Buddhas in ten directions to be our teacher for recognising the śīla. We respectfully invite all Bodhisattvas and Mahāsattvas to be our fellow-students of law. May all the Buddhas and the great Bodhisattvas have compassion for us and kindly accept our invitation. We worship them with complete attention.

VIII. *Karma* – Listen, you all children of Buddha. Now for you is given the *karma-dāna-śīla.* It is time to receive the *śīla.* Listen attentively to what has been written on *kie-mo* (karma).

All the Buddhas and Bodhisattvas of the three worlds in ten directions may remember their merciful intentions. You all children of Buddha, beginning from today till you sit on the Bodhimanda, learn the pure śīla of all the Buddhas and Bodhisattvas of the past, present and future ... It means keeping the *saṃvara-śīla,* keeping the *kuśala-śīla* and *sattvārtha-kriyā-śīla.* These three pure śīlas have been completely received.[12] We worship with full attention.

IX. *Sīmābandha* – You all children of Buddha, beginning from today till you attain the highest Bodhi, should fully keep the three pure śīlas of all the Buddhas and Bodhisattvas. Now you have received the pure śīla. Keep it thus.[13] We worship with full attention.

X. *The practice of the four adhiṣṭhāna dharmas*: You all children of Buddha, you have cultivated the Bodhicitta and practised the Bodhisattvaśīla as mentioned above. You should then practise the four *adhiṣṭhāna dharmas* and the ten important śīlas. You must not violate them. The four dharmas are: to make charity, *dānam*布施; to use agreeable words, *priyavāditā*愛語; to do beneficial acts, *artha-caryā*利行 and to work in unity, *samānarthatā*同事. If you wish to curb your endless desire and to do good to other living beings practise charity. If you wish to control anger, vanity and other troubles of the mind and to do good to others use agreeable words. If you wish to do good to others and fulfill your original vow, do acts beneficial to others. If you wish to be acquainted with learned men and not to let good minds be destroyed, work in unity (with them).[14]

XI. *The ten important-śīlas*: You all children of Buddha receive the Bodhisattva-śīla. I shall now speak on the ten important-śīlas. You should carefully listen:

1. You should not turn down the Bodhicitta. It is harmful for those who want to become Buddha.
2. You should not abandon the three jewels and take refuge in the religion of the Tīrthikas which is harmful to the law.
3. You should not speak ill of the three jewels and the teachings of the three Yānas. It goes against the Buddha-sattva.
4. If you cannot understand the deep meaning of the Mahāyāna sūtras, do not have any doubts. A common man (pṛthag-jana) cannot understand it.

5. Even to men who have not cultivated the Bodhicitta you should not speak such laws as may drive them to the practice, of the two Yānas. Otherwise you will violate the original vow.
6. When some people have already cultivated the Bodhicitta do not speak to them such laws as may destroy the Bodhicitta and lead them to the two Yānas. You will otherwise destroy the seed of the three jewels.
7. To those who follow these Yānas and have wrong views you should not speak at once of the highest and excellent Mahāyāna. For there is fear of abuse and great mischief.
8. You should not cultivate the wrong views. It will lead to the destruction of the good foundation.
9. You should not yourself speak before the Tīrthikas that you keep the excellent śīla for the highest bodhi. This makes them jealous and seek for such śīlas. When they cannot keep them they abandon Bodhisattvaśīla. Both are harmful.
10. You should not do anything injurious or not beneficial to the living beings. You should not ask others to do that or feel happy when you see others doing that. It is contrary to the law of doing good to others and to the nature of a compassionate mind.

Such is the Bodhisattvaśīla that I have now given you. You should observe these pure śīlas and let no mistakes be committed. Then the pure śīlas concerning the three refuges are received.

[II]

You should also gradually receive the *vipaśyanā jñāna*觀智, its methods, the law of *dhāyna* and other excellent things of the Mahāyāna. You should have a desire to receive this law. It is very deep and profound and you should not reveal it to others as a believer is rarely found. Give the secret religion according to capacity. First of all speak on the different upāyas and then communicate the teachings of the Āryas. Let firm belief grow so that the net of doubts may be destroyed. Then one's mind is fully illuminated.

The master of the Tripiṭaka, Śubhākara, then said: The force of the *Kuśalamūla*根機 of all beings is not the same. The teachings of the Āryas have not been given in the same way. You should not hold one law against others. Even you cannot obtain birth amongst the gods and men, not to speak of attaining the highest law. One may become Buddha by doing charity *(dāna)*. One may also become a Buddha by observing the *śīla*. One may also become Buddha by patience (*kṣānti*), energy (*vīrya*), meditation (*dhyāna*), *prajñā* etc, or by following any of the eighty-four thousand ways of the law. Today, according to the *Vajrauṣṇīṣa-sūtra*金剛頂經, I am going to give you an *upāya* by practising which you may become a Buddha. If you listen to what I say, purify your mind and practise meditation peacefully.

The master of the Tripiṭaka then remained seated in his place in the midst of the assembly not moving from his seat, quiet as if entering the dhyāna. After a long time he woke up from his meditation and looked on four kinds of people (around him). All of them bowed to him with folded hands and showed respects to him again and again.

The master of the Tripiṭaka after a while said: Formerly you received the pure Bodhisattva-śīla. New you should receive the śīla of the pure undefiled law (*anāsrava-dharma-sīla*無漏清法戒) which is the very essence of all Buddhas. You can then enter the dhyāna.

On entering the dhyāna you should recite the dhāraṇī. The dhāraṇī is ultimately the same as the law of Buddha. This leads to an ocean of all knowledge. It is the śīla of the true law (*satya-dharma-śīla*).

Nobody should be allowed to hear the secret of this law at once. If one wants to hear it he should first receive the following dhāraṇī:

oṃ samaya strāṃ (?)

This dhāraṇī should be recited three times. Then let him hear the śīla and other secret laws so that he may have all the rules of the pure Vinaya of the Bodhisattvas. Its merits are innumerable. Then for cultivating the mind the following dhāraṇī is given:

oṃ bodhicittam utpādayāmi

This dhāraṇī should be recited three times. Then the Bodhicitta should be cultivated with firmness and without any lapse up to the attainment of Buddhahood. Then for realisation the following dhāraṇī is given:

oṃ cittapratibodhaṃ karomi

This dhāraṇī should be recited three times. Thereby one may get the treasures of the deep simultaneously. Then for entering the domain of the Boddhisattva-caryā the following dhāraṇī is given:

oṃ vajramaṇḍalaṃ praveśāmi

If this dhāraṇī is recited three times it leads to all kinds of nitiation (abhiṣeka) and establishment in the maṇḍala. One can then hear all the secret laws without hindrance. After getting the Bodhisattvābhiṣeka (initiation to Bodhisattvahood) one gets the dhyāna. This is the śīla of the undefiled secret law (anāsrava). Then for the protection of the initiated the following dhāraṇī is given:

oṃ śudhā śudhā

By repeating it one hundred times you can remove all obstacles. The three karmas are purified. The sins are removed. The evil one (māra) can no longer disturb you. The practice is like the pure white silk which may be easily coloured. When the sins and obstacles are all destroyed you realise the samādhi quickly. Then for the Caryā the following dhāraṇī is given:

oṃ sarvavide svāhā

The method of recitation is to repeat either of the two dhāraṇīs (at a time) but not in pairs. Otherwise there is fear of taxing the mind too much and losing full attention. Those who want to enter Samādhi should keep away from all worldly affairs at the time of first learning. Alone, in a solitary place he should sit cross-legged. First make the mudrā for your protection. Combine the *dāna* (the little finger of the right hand) with the *prajñā* (the little finger of the left), raise *śīla* (ring finger of the right hand), *kṣānti* (middle finger of the right hand), *upāya* (ring finger of the left hand) and *praṇidhāna* (middle finger of the left). The two hands are in an interlacing position. Then *vīrya* (fore-finger of the right hand) and *bala* (fore-finger of the left) are joined and raised. Then open the heart開心 (?) a little, and join the *dhyāna* (thumb of the right hand) and the *jñāna* (thumb of the left) and raise them. This makes the mudrā (complete). The first mudrā is made on the top of the head, the second on the forehead, the third oil the right shoulder, the fourth on the left shoulder, the fifth on the heart, the sixth on the right knee and seventh on the left knee. While making the mudrās, repeat each of the dhāraṇīs mentioned above, seven times in all the seven places, the last mudrā being made on the top of the head. Then repeat the dhāraṇīs on the rosary. If you can repeat it from 200 or 300 times to 3000 or 5000 times at each sitting then repeat them fully for a lo-ch'a (*lakṣā*) times. By doing so you can attain various siddhis. It increases the strength and sustaining power of the body. The body is to be kept erect as before with legs half-crossed, the right leg on the left. They need not be fully crossed. When legs are fully crossed it becomes painful.

The mind is then distracted by pain. It is then difficult to attain concentration of mind. If from the beginning one can sit fully cross-legged then that is the best thing. The head is kept straight looking in a level, the eyes are neither fully opened nor completely closed. If they are fully opened the mind is distracted. If they are fully closed then also the mind is distracted. Don't be attracted by outside object. After sitting peacefully one should direct the mind to worship and repentance. First let the mind see Buddhas in ten directions in the assembly of men and gods, teaching the law to the four assemblies. Then you should see your own self doing the three acts of respecting, worshipping and praising all the Buddhas one by one. The man who gets this vision should clearly distinguish himself and see it as if it were before his own eyes. After this he should take his mind to the world of all gods and men in ten directions and worship with flowers, scents, banners, drink and food and various kinds of precious things. The emptiness of all the Dharmadhātu is then filled up. Worship all the Buddhas, the great Bodhisattvas, the Dharmakāya, the Sambhogakāya, and the Nirmāṇa-kāya, the Caryāphala and the great assembly. The man who worships them can direct his mind to the presence of each of the Buddhas and the great Bodhisattvas and can acquire the highest sincerity. This leads to repentance: We, from time immemorial till now, have been floating in birth and death with mind afflicted by troubles. We have been doing acts of body, speech and mind in numberless ways. Today we are only full of repentance. By once repenting we destroy the continuity of karma. We will not do any more karma. We only wish that all the Buddhas and Bodhisattvas by the power of their great mercy may protect us and accept our repentance. Let our sins be immediately destroyed.[15]

You should then take the following vow: I have been long floating in the past, then practised the Bodhisattvacaryā, obtained benefit for the numberless living beings. By practising the dhyāna and by steadfastly practising the Vīrya we have protected the three karmas業. By doing this we have acquired merits as numerous as the sands of the Ganges. So also we have acquired the Buddhaphala. We now wish that all the Buddhas and Bodhisattvas through their merciful power may protect us and let us win these merits, and quickly allow us to attain *Samādhimukha-yoga* and *Dhāraṇī -yoga*. May they allow us to acquire all the purity of nature (*svabhānvaśuddhatā*). If you fully take this vow you will immediately attain spiritual success (*siddhi*) without hindrance.

[III]

After this you should learn breathing. Breathing is as follows: First think of breathing in and breathing out. It must go inside our body through all the joints and muscles. Afterwards it goes out slowly through the mouth. You should think that the breath is as white as snow and as liquid as milk. One should follow the distance it goes. It again slowly comes in through nose. It goes to the joints and muscles all over the body. It is then allowed to go out and come in three times. If you do this breathing the body will no longer suffer from cold, heat, wind etc., and all will be pacified. After this learn Samādhi.

The master of the Tripiṭaka, Śubhākara then said: The first learners may get frightened at the thoughts that arise when the breath stops. So some try to get rid of thoughts completely. It is not possible to succeed in that. The thoughts are of two kinds – *kuśala* and *akuśala.* The akuśala thoughts should be avoided from the beginning. Don't let the kuśala thoughts be destroyed. The man who follows the true and correct practice should first of all follow right memory *(samyaksmṛti)* in an increasing manner. Afterwards this leads to complete purity. As a man who learns to shoot becomes a good marksman by long practice so also (by long practice) one can attain the *niścitta-samjñm*無心想 and remain firm in samādhi. Then there is no more fear of the rising of thoughts. There is fear of it only at the time of the first practice.

Next you should practice samādhi. What is meant by samādhi is nothing but *nirvikalpa-dharma*無別法. So it is called the knowledge of the great and full mirror大圓鏡智. Beginning with all Buddhas above down to the senseless creatures all are of the same class, no more and no less. But impure and bad thoughts cover them with avidyā and viṣaya. This is why they float in the world of transmigration, are subject to birth and death and cannot attain Buddhahood. So those who practise should remain firm and peaceful. They should not be attracted by objects. Imagine a bright disc like the clear moon at a distance of four feet from the body, direct in the front neither high nor low. It measures one cubit and is completely circular. Its colour is bright, it is shining both inside and outside and is without a like. At first you will not be able to get a long view of it but if you try attentively you will get it. After searching you can have a large view of it. Then you will find its expansion increasing up to four feet, or double that size or becoming as big as to fill up the *tri-sahasra-mahāsahasra* worlds. You can clearly distinguish it. It appears clearly to you although it is beyond (the ordinary) sight. Then slowly return to the original nature. When you first saw it, it looked like a moon. But when you will have gone round, it no longer looks square or circular. This sort of seeing enables you to remove all hindrances and attain samādhi. This samādhi is known as *ti ts'ien san hien*地前三賢. With its help you can advance slowly through the dharmadhātu. It has been spoken of in the Sūtras as the first bhūmi – so it is known as the *prathamā-bhūmi.* This method was not known before but now you can get it for the first time. As you get great joy from it the first bhūmi is called *kuan-hi*歡喜– *muditā.* No distinction is made (in this bhūmi). Furthermore, as in the case of the moon, the purity of nature has three aspects: firstly it is purity of nature *(svabhāva-śuddhatā)* free from greed, desire and impurities secondly, it is perfectly cool being free from anger and passions; thirdly, it is bright being free from ignorance and foolishness (lit darkness).

The moon is composed of the four elements (*mahābhūtas*), which are ultimately destroyed. So is the moon seen by all people. They take it for comparison with the intellect. Practice means seeing it for a long time and attaining success (*siddhi*). One should not go either too slow or too fast. Then you see only brightness and nothing else, not even the body and the mind. Ah dharmas are lost in emptiness. But this should not be taken as emptiness. It is absence of thought無念 and hence it is *āyatana-śūnyatā* and not vacuity. It may be realised after a long practice. Then you are in a state of yoga without obstacle無所罣礙 whether walking, sitting, staying or lying down or thinking at all times and in all places. You are then no longer moved by wrong thought, greediness, anger, foolishness or any other trouble (kleśa). Once destroyed they will not arise again. Nature is always pure. Go on practising in this way till you attain Buddha-hood. This is the only method and there is no other method. This is the way of the inner light of the Buddhas and Bodhisattvas. It is not within the access of the two yānas and the Tīrthikas. The merits of the law of all Buddhas are as numerous as the sands of the Ganges. They cannot be attained by any other method. You can realise them with this (method) alone. If you can unfold one letter you can speak on numberless laws. In one moment (*kṣaṇa*) you awaken all Dharmas. This is the state of Īśvara自在 in which there is no obstacle. There is then no going, no coming, no rise and no destruction. All attain samatā平等. By advancing slowly you can at last attain self-illumination. It is not possible to speak more fully about it.

The master of the Tripiṭaka, Śubhākara, then said: After practice and attainment of success you will be in that state of mind which has five aspects: the first is *kṣaṇa-citta*. This citta sees the way by one *smṛti-yoga*念相應. It is quickly lost and forgotten. It is like the lightning at night which quickly appears and disappears. So it is called kṣaṇa. The second is the *srotāpanna-citta*流注心– when one has already seen the way and thinks of it more and more without stopping. It is like the current falling. So it is called srotāpannacitta. The third is the *madkura-citta*甜美心– when through the accumulation of endless efforts śūnyatā is attained and the body and mind become light (i.e. to attain praśrabdhi) and a taste of the way is obtained. So it is called madhura. The fourth is the *vidhvaṁsana-vikṣipta-citt*a催散心 by this either you energetically rise at once or give up the practice. Both are against the way and so it is called the *vidhvaṁsana-vikṣipta-citta*. The fifth is the *ādarśa-citta*明鏡心– one goes away from the scattered and troubled state of mind and sees the round bright light. Then nothing else remains. So it is called ādarśa-*citta*.

If these five cittas are understood and realised by oneself then the three yānas, the common people (pṛthag-jana) and the sages (āryas) will be distinguished. All of you who are practising, first practise meditation定. You should practise the secret methods (guhyopāya秘密方便) of all the past Buddhas and hold and practise the law of meditation. First of all get the yoga of all the dhāraṇīs. So you should practise the four dhāraṇīs that follow:

oṃ sūkṣma vajra

This dhāraṇī can make you attain the *vipaśyanā-siddhx*.

oṃ tiṣṭha vajra

This dhāraṇī can make your *vipaśyanā* undecaying.

oṃ supra vajra

This dhāraṇī can make your *vipaśyanā* gradually attain vastness.

oṃ samhāra vajra

This dhāraṇī can make your *vipaśyanā* vast and then make again gradually contracted.

These are the four dhāraṇīs. This is the Bhagavan. It is the secret upāya of the self-illumined law which opens the mind of the students and quickly enlighten them. If you wish to attain samādhi in the four iryāpathas威儀 then always repeat these dhāraṇīs. Always cultivate it in your mind and do not give it up for a moment. It will never fail you. You ail who practise samādhi should know the rule of walking經行.

At a quiet place make the ground level and clean. Its surface should have a length of 25 cubits. Erect (two) posts at the two ends. Pass a rope through them and attach it to the two ends. It is hung high up to the chest. Hold the rope by means of a bamboo tube which is big enough to be held in the hands. Turn the bamboo tube with the sun on the right. Go and come in a balanced way. The mind, quite composed, sees in the front up to 6 feet. In this way practise samādhi and control the mind in its original state. Clearly realise the truth and don't let it be lost. Put one foot down and repeat a dhāraṇī . In this way repeat the four dhāraṇīs from the beginning to the end. Repeat them without stop. If you feel tired then sit quietly.

The man who practices it thus, realises the upāya, if he goes deep and proceeds energetically. The mind then becomes as strong as the vajra, unshakable, unchangeable and armed with a very strong armour. The mind becomes strong and sharp. Take vow to practise it till the end. Do not go back and get moved to the last. Do not learn many things that raise doubt in the mind. It is passing time in vain. The law has no two characters. Both the mind and speech are lost in it. Without the means (upāya) you cannot enter it orherwise.

Sanskrit梵 and Chinese漢 are different languages. One cannot understand the one without translating it into the other. I have instructed what I remember to be written down so that those who are ignorant about it may be instructed to do this. The dhyāna teacher Hui-king慧警 of the Si-ming sse西明寺 in the capital first collected it. It has now been found out again and put in order. With our heads bent let us say fully:

Obeissance to the Buddhas in ten directions.
Truth is like the nectar in the bottom of the sea.
To the three sages, the ten Āryas, the Arhats and the Bhikṣhusaṅgha,
We pray so that they may increase the power of our memory
(*smṛti-balo'*) by their wonderful power.
Rare are the dharanls and the essentials of the dhyāna.
Cultivate the full, bright, vast, great mind.
We accordingly praise it now
And get benefit for all beings of the dharmadhātu.

Kriyāsamuccaya
[pp. 137^b–139^b]

[I] tatoguruṇā'dhyāśayapravṛttaṃśiṣyamālokyayathāśaktiprayacchāmīti svīkārapuraḥ saraṃ evaṃ dātavyaṃ || vadatvāyuṣman[16] samanvāharantu māṃ daśadig lokadhātu saṃnipatitā buddhā bhaga- vanto mahābodhisatvāś cal samanvāharantu ācāryyo'ham evaṃnāmā yatkiñcit kāyavāṅmanobhir buddha-bodhisatvān mātapitarau tadanyān vā satvān samāgamya ihajanmani anyeṣu vā janmāntareṣu mayā pāpakaṃ karma kṛtaṃ kāritaṃ vā anumoditaṃ vā tatsarvam ekadhyam abhisaṃkṣipya piṇḍayitvā tulayitvā sarvabuddbabodhisatvāḥ nāma

ācāryasya vā antike agrayā pravarayā deśanayā pratideśayāmi | jānan smaraṇ praticchādayāmi || trirevam ||

[II] so'ham evaṃnāmā evaṃ deśitātyaya imaṃ divasam upādāya yāvadābodhimaṇḍaniṣadanāt buddhaṃ bhagavantaṃ mahākāruṇikaṃ sarvajñaṃ sarvadarśinaṃ sarvavairabhayātītaṃ mahāpuruṣaṃ abhedyakāyaṃ anuttarakāyaṃ dharmakāyaṃ śaraṇaṃ gacchāmi dvipadānām agram l so'ham evaṃnāmā evaṃ deśitātyayaḥ | imaṃ divasam upādāya yāvadābodhimaṇḍaniṣadanāt dharmaśaraṇaṃ gacchāmi anuttaraṃ mahāyānaṃ dharmānāṃ pravalaṃ | so'ham evaṃ deśitātyayaḥ | imaṃ divasam upādāya yāvadābodhimaṇḍaṇiṣadanāt avaivarttikabodhisatvasaṃghaśaraṇaṃ gacchāmi dāntaṃ ganānāṃ srestham | | trirevam | |

[III] so'ham evaṃnāmā evam deśitātyayaḥ | imam divasam upādāya triśaraṇagato'anantasatvadhātuntāranāyabhyuddharaṇāya ca saṃsāraduḥkhāt paritrāṇāya sarvajñāne pratiṣṭhāpanāya | yathātītānāgatapratyutpannābuddhā bhagatanto mahābodhisatvāś ca bodhi- cittam utpādya buddhatvam adhigatavanto'dhigacchanti adhigami-
syanti ca | yathā te sarvasaṃbuddhā anāvaraṇena buddhajñānena buddhacakṣuṣā jāananti paśyanti yathādharmānāṃ dharmatāṃ jñātvādutyanujānanti | tena vidhinā aham evaṃnāmna ācāryas ya antikāt sambuddhabodhisatvānāṃ ca purato'nuttarāyāṃ samyaksambaudhau cittam utpādayāṃi | | trirevam | | trirevaṃ ādyāgreṇabodhisatvāṃ māṃ sarvabuddhabodhisatvā ācāryaś ca dhārayanta | | iti ratnatrayaśaraṇagamanaṃ bodhicittotpādapūtvakam | |

[IV] pañcaśikṣāpadagrahaṇam upāsakasamvara savādhyeṣitavate śiṣyāyaṃ evaṃ datavyaṃ II vadatvamāyuṣman samanvāhara ācāryya yathā te ācāryā arhanto yāvajjīvaṃ prāṇātipātaṃ grahāya prāṇātipātāt prativiratāḥ | evamevāhamukanāmā imaṃ divasaṃ upādāya yāvajjīvaṃ prāṇātipātaṃ prahāya prāṇātipātāt prativiramāmi | anenāhaṃ prathamenāṅgena teṣām āryāṇam arhatāṃ śikṣāyām anuśikṣe anuvidhīye anukaromi | punaraparaṃ samanvāhara ācārya yathā te ācārya arhanto yāvajjīvam adattādanaṃ kāmamithyācārarṃ mṛṣāvādaṃ surāmaireyamadyapramādasthānaṃ ca prahāya adattādānāt kāmamithyācārāt mṛṣārsavādāt surāmaireyamadya pramādasthānāt ca prativiratāḥ | tathāhamukanāmā imaṃ divasam upādāya yāvajjīivaṃ adattādanaṃ kāmamithyācāraṃ mṛṣārvādaṃ surāmaireyamadyapramādasthānaṃ ca prahāya adattādānāt kāmamithyācārāt mṛṣāvādāt surāmaireyamadyapramādasthānāt ca prativiramāmi | anenāhaṃ pañcamenāṅgena teṣām āryyānaṃ arhatāṃ śikṣāyām anuśikṣe anuvidhīye anukaromi upāsakaṃ ca māṃ ācāryā dhārayatu | evaṃ dvirapi trirapi | |

[V] āryyāṣṭāṅgikapoṣadhaṃ karttum icchati tadā pūrvavadadhyeṣitavate trīṇiśaraṇagamanāni datvā'ṣṭauśikṣāpadāny eva dātavyāni | vadatvāmāyuṣman samanvāhara ācāryā ahaṃ amukanāmā imāṃ velām upādāya yāvacca rātrigāminī yāvataś ca suryyodayo'trāntarāḥ sarvaprāṇivadhāt parasvaharaṇād abrahmacaryyāt tathā vāgbhedād anṛtāt madīyajananānyātādvikālāsanānmānaṃ varṇakaṃnṛtyagītalalitāt śayyāsanād ucchritād adyāhaṃ virataḥ karomy arhatāṃ vṛtraṃ guṇair aṣṭabhiḥ | | trirevaṃ | |

[VI] idaṃ me poṣadhaṃ śīlasamvarasamādānaṃ cittālaṅkārāpacittapariṣkārāya sarvasatvāmantarajñanaphalāvāptay a iti | atra gurunā vaktavyaṃ aupayikaṃ | śiṣyeṇasādhviti | puṣṇāti yasmāt kuśalasamagraṃ kṛtaṃ ca saṃśodhayatīha pāyatat poṣaṇāc cittaviśodhanāc ca tathāgataḥ poṣadhamittuvāca | poṣadhavidhi | |

KRIYĀSAṀGRAHAPAÑJIKĀ
(H.P. Shastri, Catalogue …, pp. 123–126)

(I) aham itthaṃnāmā yāvajjīvaṃ buddhaśaraṇaṃ gacchāmi dvipadānām agryam I dharmaṃ śaraṇaṃ gacchāmi virāgāṇām agryam | saṅghaṃ śaraṇaṃ gacchāmi gaṇānām agryam |
(dvirapi)

(II) aham itthaṃnāmā yāvajjīvaṃ prāṇātipātāt prativiramāmi |
aham itthaṃnāmā yāvajjīvaṃ adattādānāt prativiramāmi |
aham itthaṃnāmā yāvajjīvaṃ kāmāmithyācārāt prativiramāmi |
aham itthaṃnāmā yāvajjīvaṃ mṛṣāvādāt prativiramāmi |
aham itthaṃ yāvajjīvaṃ mūrāmaireyamadyapramāda-sthānāt prativiramāmi | (trirapi)

(III) aham itthaṃnāmā ācāryyaṃ yāce I ācāryyeṇāhaṃ pravrajiṣye | |
(dvirapi)
aham itthaṃnāmā upādhyāyena pravrajiṣye | (trirapi)
aham itthaṃnāmā yāvajjīvaṃ gṛhaliṅgaṃ parityājāmi pravrajyāliṅgaṃ samādade I (trirapi)
aham itthaṃnāmā yāvajjīvaṃ buddhaṃ śaraṇaṃ gacchāmi dvipadānāgryam |
aham itthaṃnāmā yāvajjīvaṃ dharmaṃ śaraṇaṃ gacchāmi virāgānāmagryam |
aham itthaṃnāmā yāvajjīvaṃ saṃghaṃ śaraṇaṃ gacchāmi gaṇānāmagryam | (trirapi)

(IV) aham itthaṃnāmā yāvajjīvaṃ prāṇātipātavairamaṇā śrāmaṇeraśikṣaḥ samādade I evam evāham prathamenāṅhgena teṣām āryyāṇām arhatā śikṣāyām anuśikṣe anuvidhīye anukaromi yathā te āryyā arhanto yāvajjīvaṃ adattādānamabrahmacaryyamṛṣārvāda-surāmaireyamadyapramādasthānāt nṛtyagīitāvaditramālāgandha- vile panvarṇakadhāraṇamuccaśayanamahāśayānakālabhojanajāta-rūparajatapratigrahāt prativiratāḥ |
aham itthaṃnāmā yāvajjīvaṃ adattādānavairamaṇa śrāmaṇera śikṣāpadaṃ samāpādayāmi |
aham itthaṃnāmā yāvajjīvaṃ abrahmacaryyavairamaṇa-śikṣāpadaṃ samādade |

aham itthaṃnāmā yāvajjīvaṃ mṛṣāvādavairamaṇaśikṣāpadaṃsamāda yāmi |
aham itthaṃnāmā yāvajjīvaṃ suramaireyamadyapramada-sthānavairamaṇaśikṣāpadam samādayāmi |
aham itthaṃnāmā yāvajjīvaṃ uccaśayānamahāśayānaśikṣāpadaṃ samādayāmi |
aham itthaṃnāmā yāvajjīvaṃ nṛtyagītavādyavairamaṇaṃ śikṣāpadaṃ samādayāmi |
aham itthaṃnāmā yāvajjīvaṃ mālāgandhavilepanavairamaṇaṃ śikṣāpadaṃ samādayāmi |
aham itthaṃnāmā yāvajjīvaṃ jātarūparajatapratigrahaṇavaira-maṇaṃ śikṣāpadaṃ samādayāmi | (trirapi)

(V) aham itthaṃnāmā ācāryya adhyeṣayāmi idaṃ *Cīvaraṃ* saṃghasya viśvāse saṃghaparibhogāyādhiṣṭhatu |
aham itthaṃnāmā ācāryya adhyeṣayāmi idaṃ cīvaraṃ rājākula-gamanāyādhitiṣṭhatu |
aham itthaṃnāmā ācāryya adhyeṣayāmi idaṃ cīvaraṃ grāma-nagarajinārāmapallīpattanagamanāyādhitiṣṭhatu |
aham itthaṃnāmā ācāryya adhyeṣayāmi idaṃ *Pātraṃ* ṛṣibhāja-naṃ śikṣābhājanabhojanaparibhogikam adhitiṣṭhatu |
aham itthaṃnāmā ācāryya adhyeṣayāmi imāṃ *śikṣābhājana-kuṇḍikāṃ* adhitiṣṭhatu |
aham itthaṃnāmā ācāryya śradhyeṣayāmi imāṃ *khikṣirikāṃ* adhitiṣṭhatu | [trirapi]
upādhyāya ... [trirapi]
ācāryyasaṃgha ... [trirapi]
aham itthaṃnāmā idaṃ cīvaraṃ saṃghasya viśvāsaparibhogāya dhārayāmi ...
rājakulagamanāya dhārayāmi ... grāmanagaranigama-pallīpattanagamanāya dhārayāmi
pātraṃ ṛṣibhājanaṃ śikṣābhājanaṃ bhojanopabhogāya dhārayāmi ... ... śikṣāmājanakuṇḍikaṃ dhārayāmi ... ... khikṣirikāṃ-dhārayāmi
aham itthaṃnāmā āryyākhyāsamvaram āsaṃpatsye |

(VI) aham itthaṃnāmā yadā saṃghasya sāmagrīṃ lapsye tadā anena saṃghena sārddhaṃ poṣadhaṃ kariṣye |
...Śīlaikandha ... Samādhiskandha ... Prajñāskandha ... Vimukti-jñānadarśana... ... (*trirapi*)

Notes

1 Tokyo XXV, 1; Shanghai XXV, 1; Taisho 917.
2 pp. 561 ff.
3 *Sino-Indian Studies*, I, 2, p. 86.
4 Vol. VII, 2.
5 *Aspects of Mahāyāna Buddhism*, pp. 302–5.
6 pp. 123–6.
7 pp. 138–193, of the manuscript in my possession.
8 ed. by H.P. Shastri, p. 13.
9 fol. 163 of my ms.
10 A Chinese note says: You should teach the disciple to let his mind act. Let him think of all Buddhas in ten directions and present himself before the Buddhas and Bodhisattvas, numberless like the sands of the Ganges, in the limitless dhātus and lands and seas as many as the atoms. Let him worship, praise and make offerings to each of the Buddhas.
11 Chinese note – If the sin committed is light you should confess the guilt. You must not hide it. Otherwise great retribution will be in store for you. If other sins are not committed you should answer "no".
12 Chinese note – to be said three times.
13 Chinese note – to be said three times.
14 Chinese note – these four laws relate to conduct.
15 Chinese note – it is called adhyātma-guhya-anuśocanā which is the highest and the best.
16 From here up to the end of the 3rd paragraph the text agrees closely with the text of Bodhisattva-Pratimokṣa-sūtra published by Dr. N. Dutt (loc. cit.).

Chapter 6

A FRAGMENT OF THE KĀŚYAPA SAṀHITĀ IN CHINESE*

A short medical treatise entitled *Kia-ye sien jen shuo yi niu jen king* 迦葉仙人說醫女人經 *(= Kāśyapa-ṛṣi-prokta-strīcikitsā- sūtra)* has been preserved in Chinese translation and is included in the Tripitaka.[1] The translation is due to an Indian scholar who is known in Chinese either as Fa-t'ien (Dharmadeva) or as Fa-hien (Dharmabhadra). Dharmabhadra was a Buddhist monk of the Nālandā monastery. He went to China in 973 A.D. and was much honoured by the Song Emperor. He lived till 1001 A.D. He was very active during his long sojourn in China and translated 118 works into Chinese. Another medical treatise translated by him is the *Kumāra-tantra* of Rāvaṇa which has been studied and translated by me in another article.[2] The **Strīcikītsā (Sūtra)* of Kāśyapa was translated by Fa-t'ien sometime between 982 and 1001 A.D.

In my article on the *Kumāra-tantra* of Rāvaṇa I pointed out its affinity with a newly published medical text entitled *Kāśyapa-saṁhitā*. The **Strīcikitśā-sūtra* translated by Fa-hien also bears the name of sage Kāśyapa and seems to have been connected with the school to which the Kāśyapa-samhitā belonged. The **Strī-cikitsā* is in the form of an interlocution between the sage Ji-p'o-kia (= Jīvaka) and the sage Kia-ye (= Kāśyapa). Jīvaka felt great pity for those women who suffer from various kinds of troubles during the period of pregnancy and went to Kāśyapa "a great teacher possessed of vast knowledge" to ascertain the method of their treatment. At his request Kāśyapa narrated the method of treating the diseases of pregnant women according to the various stages of their pregnancy. The *Kāśyapa-saṁhitā* is also in the form of an interlocution between Jīvaka and Kāśyapa. Although the text is mutilated and incomplete there are many indications which clearly

---

* *Indian Culture* 9.1 (1942/43): 53–64.

bring out this form of the presentation; cf. for example the beginning of the *Lehādhyāya* (Sūtrasthāna) Jīvaka asks:–

> ... ...
> ... ...
> Kiṁvā lehayitavyaṁ ca kiṁvā lehitalakṣaṇam/
> Atilehitadoṣāḥ ke ke ca doṣā alehite//
> Mandalīḍhasya kiṁ rūpaṁ gunadoṣāśca tatra ke/
> Ke lehanodbhavā rogāḥ kaśca teṣamupakramaḥ//
> Etanme bhagavan sarvaṁ vaktumarhasi tattvataḥ/
> Sukhaṁ duḥkhaṁ hi bālānāṁ dṛśyate lehanāśrayam//
> Iti pṛṣto mahābhāgaḥ kaśyapo lokapūjitaḥ/
> Praśnaṁ provāca nikhilaṁ prajānāṁ hitakāmyayā//

[Jīvaka asks Kāśyapa]....

> "What is fit for licking? What are the things to be licked? What are the evil effects of overlicking? What is bad in not licking? What are the things difficult to lick, and what are their bad and good effects? What are the diseases that arise from licking? How do they arise? Bhagavan, you should tell me all about it. It seems that the health and the disease of children depend on licking. The great sage Kāśyapa venerated by all, being thus requested replied to the question thus for the good of all beings".

A comparison of this form of the narration of the *Kāśyapa-saṁhitā* with the commencement of the **Strīciktsā-sūtra* of Kāśyapa of which I have given a translation below will clearly show that the two texts are very closely connected. I believe that the **Stricikitsā* is only an extract from the *Kāśyapa-saṁhitā*. That there is room for such supposition will be clear from a further examination of the *Kāśyapa-saṁhitā*.

About the authorship of the *Kāśyapa-saṁhitā* the text itself records the following tradition.[3] "Kāśyapa, being appointed by Brahmā, compiled this Tantra for the good of mankind. Jīvaka, the son of Ṛcika, received this great Tantra and summarised it. Jīvaka later on came to be known as Vṛddha-Jīvaka. The Tantra was then preserved by Anāyāsa Yakṣa who narrated it later to Vātsya, a descendent of Vṛddha-Jīvaka. Vātsya revised and edited the work". Hence the work is known under both the names: Kāśyapa-saṁhitā and *Vṛddha-jīvakīyaṁ Tantram.*

The Rājaguru Hemrāj Śarmā in his learned introduction to the *Kāśyapa-saṁhitā* has compared the work with other medical treatises and come to the conclusion that the treatment of subjects in the present work is similar to that in the *Caraka-saṁhitā* and the *Bheḍa-tantra.* The Śuśruta differs from all other works in this respect.

	Kāśyapa	Caraka	Bheḍa
Sūtrasthāna, Chaps.	30	30	30
Nidāna⁰ ,,	8	8	8
Vimāna⁰ ,,	8	8	8
Śārīra⁰ ,,	8	8	8
Indriya⁰ ,,	12	12	12
Cikitsā⁰ ,,	30	30	30
Siddhi⁰ ,,	12	12	9 (?)
Kalpa⁰ ,,	12	12	8 (?)

The *Kāśyapa-saṁhitā* has besides a supplement *(Khila)* which is its 9th section. This is evidently a later addition and contains many repetitions of subjects treated in the main body of the work.

The complete text of the *Kāśyapa-saṁhitā* has not yet been discovered. The unique manuscript from which the text has been edited was fragmentary and hence long portions of the text are missing. A considerable portion of the *Cikitsādhyāya* is missing. In the chapter on *Garbhiṇi cikitsādhyāya* the treatment of certain diseases of pregnant women have been described, such as *pravāhikā, kāmalā, śūla, urdhvanīla, ikkāśvāsa* etc. Something must have been said on the treatment of miscarriage in this connection, but that portion is missing.

The **Strīcikitsā* of Kāśyapa however is more concerned with prenatal care than with regular medical treatment. This text shows considerable agreement with the 31st chapter of the 8th section of the *Śārīrasthāna* of Caraka. In fact the whole of the 8th section of *Śārīrasthāna* deals with pre-natal and post-natal care *(Jātisūtrīyam śārīram),* – conception, the diet of a pregnant woman, the causes of miscarriage, preventive measures prescribed month by month. As a general method of treatment Caraka prescribes for the preservation of the foetus the decoction of the following drugs with milk or ghee – *aindrī, brāhmī, śatavīrya, sahasravīrya, amogha, avyathā, śivā, balāariṣṭa, vātyapuṣpī, viśvakasenā* and *kāntā*. It is also recommended that the expectant mother should rub her body daily with an ointment of these drugs and bathe in the water in which these drugs have been boiled.[4]

Caraka then gives the following prescription to be followed by pregnant women month by month.[5]

"In the *first* month the diet should mainly consist of medicated milk which has been properly boiled and cooled and given in proper measure. Her principal meals should consist of such items as may be easily assimilated. In the *second* month her diet principally should consist of milk boiled with the group of drugs called sweets (*Kākolī* etc.). In the *third* month the milk is to be mixed with ghee and honey. In the *fourth* month two *tolus* of cheese should be given. In the *fifth* month the quantity of ghee should be increased. In the *sixth* and *seventh* months ghee should be boiled with the drugs, called sweets (*Kākolī* etc). In the *seventh* month is to be performed the *dohada* ceremony. The general food should be given in small measures, should consist of such items as are regarded sweet and alleviative of wind and should contain oil and salts as little as possible. In the *eighth* month she should be given daily, at proper intervals, a drink prepared of milk, barley gruel *(yavāgu)* and ghee boiled together. In the ninth month she should have as an additional measure an enema of oil in which the drugs called sweets (*Kākolī* etc) are boiled".

Caraka also gives the method of treatment in case the chest is affected which is usual in the seventh month of pregnancy. He prescribes first of all a decoction of *badara* mixed with cheese and boiled with the drugs called sweets (*Kākolī* etc.). For application on the affected parts he recommends a paste of *candana* and *mṛṇāla*, or of *śirīṣa, dhātakī*, *sarṣapa* and liquorice, or of *kuṭaja, arjjaka* seeds, *musta* and turmeric or of *nimba, kola, surasā* and *mañjiṣṭhā* or an oil medicated with the leaves of *karavīra*. For washing he recommends an infusion of *triphala* mixed with the blood of small deer (pṛṣat) and of a hare and also water boiled with *mālatī* and liquorice.

There is also a similar chapter in the *Śārīrasthāna* of the *Kāśyapa-saṁhitā* which is equally called *Jātisutriya*. This is also, as in Caraka, the last and the 8th chapter of the *Śārīrasthāna*. The first portion of the chapter shows a general agreement with the corresponding chapter of Caraka, but its middle portion where we should have expected the more specific prescriptions for the pregnant woman according to the various stages of pregnancy is lost. One complete palm-leaf (the 85th folio) is missing. This seems to have contained the matter now found in the **Strīcikitsā* of Kāśyapa. The introductory portion of the **Strīcikitsā* dealing with the meeting of Jīvaka and Kāśyapa might not have been there, but the remaining portion of the text giving prescription, month by month, seems to have been taken from this chapter of the *Kāśyapa-saṁhitā*.

In the supplement *(Khilasthāna)* of the *Kāśyapa-saṁhitā* there is a chapter called *Antarvatnīcikitsā* (chap. x) which contains similar information on the treatment of pregnant women. As the supplement is a sort of later elaboration of the matter given in the main text it gives an idea of the missing portion of the chapter of *Jātisūtrīya* of the *Kāśyapasaṁhitā*. The 10th chapter of the supplement says that regular treatment of pregnant women should be undertaken from the fourth month of pregnancy (*māsāccaturthāt prabhṛti bhisagbhesajamācaret.* śl.11). This method of treatment is given in slokas 147 ff.

Caturthe māsi nārīṇāmidaṁ kuryāccikitsitam //147//
Sarpirbhirannapānairvā kṣīreṇekṣurasena vā /
Vāsayet phalayuktena yathāvaditi kaśyapaḥ //148//
Caturangulasiddhena rasena payasā pi vā /
Virecayettu matimān ya icchet sukhamātmanaḥ //149//
Pūtikapatrairbhṛṣṭairvā puṣpairvāṭyālakasya vā /
Amlāṁ yavāgūṁprapivennātivegā yathā bhavet //150//
Eraṇḍapatraṁ kṣīreṇa vātarogānvitā pivet /
Vātamūtravirodhe tu śūle vā'pi samutthite //151//
Pancame māsi garbhiṇyā vyaktamlavaṇaṁ tataḥ /
Āsthāpanaṁ hitaṁ nāryā madhuraṁ cāmuvāsanam //152//
Granthīnāṁ pīḍakānāṁ ca śothe caiva viśāmpate /
Rohiṇyāṁ vidradhau vā'pi ṣaṣthamāse viśeṣataḥ /
Yathāmlaṁ bheṣajaṁ kuryāddāruṇaṁ śāstrapāragaḥ //153//
Pīnamāmsopasamanam kṣārakarmāgnikarma ca /
Bhagnāsthiśleṣanam caiva śastrakarma tathaiva ca //154//
Saptame māsi nārīnām sarvametat prayojayet /

The *Bheḍa-saṁhitā*, which, we have seen, follows the same tradition as that of Caraka, has also in its extant South Indian version a chapter called *Jātisūtrīyam* (which is the chapter viii of its *Śārī-rasthāna*). It is an abridged version, but still it agrees with the corresponding passages of the *Carakasaṁhitā* and the *Kāśyapa-saṁhitā* (specially the supplement). It may be quoted here for a comparison with other texts: –

> Caturthe khalu māse prativihite kṣīre navanītam prāsnīyāt/ Pancame kṣīrayavaguh/ṣaṣthe kṣīssarpih, saptaṃe tu khalu māse garbhaprapīḍitā pittasmāno prāpya vidahyamānā kandum janayanti/tena cikkisāni jāyante/strīnām triphalacurṇam sasarudhiraṇa piṣṭstvā tenāsyāh stanānyavalepayet/aṣṭame tu khalu māse prativihite sati sutikāgāram samyak prāgdvāramudagdvāram vā kārayet tindukapalāśāśvatthaih// (Bheḍasamhitā, p. 95).

Thus a comparison of the mutilated *Jātisūtrīyam* section of the *Kāśyapa-saṁhitā* with the corresponding chapters of the Caraka-saṁhitā, the Bheḍasaṁhitā and the Khilasthānam of the Kāśyapa-saṁhitā itself shows that the short treatise in Chinese translation, the **Strīcikitsā* of Kāśyapa formed a part of *the Jātisūtrīyam* of the Kāśyapa-saṁhitā. It must have been based on that portion of the *Jātisūtrīyam* which is now lost.

The two medical treatises translated by Fa-t'ien (Dharmadeva) a monk of Nālandā – the Kumāra-tantra of Rāvaṇa and the **Strīcikitsā* of Kāśyapa bear a Buddhist stamp. The *Kumāra-tantra*, as we have said in another article[6] is of Buddhist inspiration. Rāvaṇa is a Yakṣa and it is only in Buddhism that the Yakṣa have been considered as beneficent beings. The *Kāśyapa-saṁhitā* of which **Strīcikitsā* is a part, is also said to have been handed down by another Yakṣa – Yakṣa Anāyāsa, who is invoked in the Mahāmāyūrī.[7] Rāvaṇa is the Yakṣa protector of the country of Ramaṭha in North-Western India, while Anāyāsa is the Yakṣa protector of the city of Kauśāmbī. The *Kāśyapa-saṁhitā* like the **Strīcikitsā* has another Buddhist association. Its author was Jīvaka. The sage Kāśyapa communicated it to Jīvaka who recorded it and gave publicity to it for the good of humanity. Jīvaka is well-known in the Buddhist texts as a great authority on medicine. He was a contemporary of Buddha and was educated in medical science at Takṣaśilā under Ātreya.[8]

The contents of the **Strīcikitsā* of Kāśyapa may now be discussed and compared with prescriptions in other sources. It will be seen that the prescription given in the **Strīcikitsā* is much more detailed than that in other sources. This is probably because the *Kāśyapa-saṁhitā* with which the **Strīcikitsā* is directly connected is specially a *Kaumārabhṛtyam* and as such is more concerned with the diseases of expectant mothers and children.

First month (of pregnancy) – The medicine prescribed is a powder of *candana* scent and *utpala* flower mixed with milk and milk-sugar. *Ju-t'ang* 乳糖 literally means 'milk-sugar' but I do not know what kind of sugar it really is. Caraka prescribes only milk properly boiled and cooled.

Second month – The medicine prescribed is the powder of blue utpala flower, root of *ku-mu-na* (kumuda), *ling-kio* and *kie-si-iu-kia*, mixed with milk. *Ling-kio* 陵角 is supposed to be *Gokṣuraka* - tribulus lanuginosus in Mahāvyutpatti (Sakaki–5782 (ii). But it is really *śṛṅgāṭka* – trapa bicornis or a kind of water caltrops. *Kie-si-lu-kia* 羯細嚕迦 is kaśeruka. It is a kind of root which when taken helps the regular secretion of biles and cools the system *(raktapitta-praśmanatvaṁ, śītatvaṁ, dāhaśramāpahatvañca* – cf. Śabdakalpa-druma). Caraka prescribes for the second month – 'milk boiled with drugs called sweets *(madhura)*'. The group of these drugs, according to the commentary, begins with *kākolī*. *Kākolī* however is prescribed here from the third month.

Third month – The medicine prescribed in equal portions of *kia-kiu-lei, ch'e-lo-kia-kiu-lei* and the root of *pi-ma* rubbed and mixed with milk, milk sugar and honey. *Kia kiu lei* 迦俱隸 and *ch'e-lo-kia-kiu-lei* 叱囉迦俱隸 are *kākolī* and *kṣīra-kākolī*. *Kākolī* is described as a medical plant with aromatic berries – Luvunga Scandens. Kṣīra-kākolī is described as a "root from the Himalayas yielding a milky juice" – Trittiliria Stacheyi.[9] *Pi-ma* 蓖 麻 is castor oil plant, Sanskrit *eraṇḍa* – Ricinus Communis. Caraka prescribes for the 3rd month only 'milk mixed with ghee and honey'.

Fourth month – The medicine prescribed is the equal proportion of the root of *tsi-li* 蒺藜, its branch and leaf, utpala flower and its stalk, rubbed and mixed with milk. *Tsi-li* is Tribulus terrestris. In the *Fan yu tsa ming*[10] *Tsi-li* is *kokṣura (gokṣura)*. Caraka and Bheḍa prescribe for the fourth month only cheese and milk. But the supplementary section of the Kāśyapa-saṁhitā already referred to gives a more detailed prescription for the fourth month according to the nature of the troubles, – *ghee*, milk, juice of sugarcane, leaf of castor oil plant boiled in milk etc.

Fifth month – The medicine prescribed is the powder of equal proportion of the root of gourd plant (*hu tseu* 瓠子), and utpala flower mixed with grape-juice (*p' u-t'ao che* 葡萄子), milk and milk-sugar. Caraka prescribes simply 'milk and ghee', while Bheḍa only barley-gruel (yavāgū) and milk. *Hu tseu* is literally 'gourd plant' but it is not clear what sort of gourd it is, *P' u-t'ao* literally means 'grape juice' – *drākṣā pāṇaka.*[11] *Pu't'ao* has been proved by Laufer[12] to be a borrowed Iranian word; p'u-t'ao *(*bu-daw)* has been restored by him in its old Iranian form **budāwa* or **budawa* formed with a suffix *wa* or *awa*, from a stem *buda* which may be connected with new persian *bāda* "wine" – probably a dialectal form of Avestan *madav*, "wine from berries". In the present case however *P'ut'ao che* means "fresh grape juice" and not a variety of grape wine.

Sixth month – The medicine prescribed is equal proportions of *pi-o-lo, mo-ti-kia-lo-jo* and *sa-ki-t'o-fu* herbs rubbed and boiled in milk mixed with milk-sugar and honey. *Pi-o-lo* 閉阿羅 is *Piyāla, mo-ti-kia-lo-jo* 摩地迦羅惹 is probably a wrong transcription for mātuluṅga which is a kind of citron plant, and *sa-ki(hi)-lo-fu is sahetava.* The properties of *piyāla* are given as – *madhuratvam, snigdhatvam, vātapittanāśitvam* etc, and the properties of *mātuluṅga* are – *hṛdyatvam, amlatvam, laghutvam, agnidīpatvam* etc.[13] Caraka prescribes for the sixth month the drugs called sweet – *Kākolī* etc. boiled in ghee, whereas Bheḍa prescribes ghee and milk only.

Seventh month – The medicine prescribed is pills made with the powder of *tsi-li* – tribulus terrestris-branch and leaf mixed with milk-sugar and honey, to be taken with meat soup. Caraka prescribes for general treatment the same medicine as for the previous month. Bheḍa follows him. For the skin infection which is usual in the 7th month Caraka makes an elaborate prescription; our text however does not refer to it.

Eighth month – The medicine prescribed is equal portions of *san-hanngo* lotus flower, blue utpala flower and tribulus terrestris, rubbed and mixed with milk, milk-sugar and honey. I have not been able to find out what plant *san-han-ngo* is. For the eighth month Caraka prescribes a drink made of ghee, barley gruel and milk mixed together.

Ninth month – The medicine prescribed is equal portions of the roots of pi-ma – castor oil plant, *kia-ku-lei-kākolī, she-lo-po-han-ni– Śārapāhanī* (?), *mei-li-han-ti* (Bṛhatī?) rubbed and boiled in milk. I have not been able to find out what *she-lo-po-han-ni* is. The last mei-li-han-ti 沒哩賀底 seems to be *Bṛhatī* which is according to some sources the same as *kaṇṭakari*. Its properties are given as – *tiktatvam, uṣṇatvam, vāta-jvarārocakāśvāhṛdroganāśitvam.*[14] Caraka prescribes only for outer use 'oil in which kakoli has been boiled'.

Tenth month – The medicine prescribed is equal portions of *liu-teu* 菉豆 beans, and utpala flower, rubbed and boiled in milk mixed with milk-sugar and honey. Caraka and other sources do not give any prescription for the 10th, 11th and 12th months, as these stages of pregnancy are uncommon. Bheḍa stops with the eighth month and recommends that the labour room should be made ready in the 8th month. I have not been able to find out what kind of beans was *liu-teu*.

Eleventh month – The medicine prescribed is equal portions of blue utpala flower, *sha-lu-kang* 娑路剛 *(Śāluka)* plant, lotus flower and lotus stalk, rubbed in cold water and boiled in milk mixed with milk-sugar. *Sha-lu-kang* is *Śāluka* – a plant like the lotus which grows in water. There is no prescription for the eleventh month in other sources.

Twelfth month – The medicine prescribed is equal portions of *kia-kiu-lei (kākolī), ch'e-lo-kia-kiu-lei (kṣīra-kākolī)* liquorice (*kan ts'ao* 甘草) and utpala flower ground and boiled in milk. *Kan-ts'ao* is liquorice – Skt. *Yaṣṭimadhu.*

(Kāśyaparṣiprokta-strīcikitā-sūtra) "The sutra on curing women spoken by the sage Kāśyapa". –

Once upon a time the sage Jīvaka was worried by this thought: In the world all beings get their body from women. The women at first get pregnant for full ten months and some even longer for twelve months and then they give birth (to the child). In this period they suffer from sickness which afflicts them with pain. I shall now ask the teachers about the means of getting the medicine for curing their diseases. On thinking thus he went to see the teacher, the sage Kāśyapa. He prostrated himself before the teacher and after saluting him said – The great teacher Kāśyapa is possessed of vast knowledge. I want to ask him a question and pray him to listen to me and reply. The sage Kāśyapa replied: What do you want to ask me? Then the sage Jīvaka said: The woman remains pregnant for ten months or twelve months. When the days are completed she gives birth to the child. Why do they suffer from diseases in this period for which the foetus gets shaky and uneasy. Some get spoilt whereas others suffer from unlimited pain. My teacher is all-knowing. I request him to speak on the treatment of these diseases and on the medicine to cure them. When he had finished he waited quietly to listen (to the reply).

Then the sage Kāśyapa said to the sage Jīvaka: The women, when pregnant, do not know how to protect themselves. So the foetus gets unsteady. I shall now briefly speak, month by month on the medicine for protecting it.

If the foetus gets unsteady in the first month of pregnancy the woman should take the *chen-tan (candana)* scent, the lotus flower, the *yu-po-lo* (utpala) flower, put them in water and grind them. She should then mix it with milk and the milk-sugar boiled together. This medicine if taken when tepid, can save the foetus from all harm and pain and make it steady in the first month of pregnancy.

He then told Jīvaka: If in the second month of pregnancy the foetus get unsteady then take the blue Utpala flower, the root of the *kiu-mu-na (kumuda)*, water-caltrops *(ling kio)*, *kie-si-lu-kia (kaśeruka* ?). Grind equal portions of these herbs into powder, mix the powder with milk and boil it. It should be taken when cool. This medicine can keep the foetus in its place, remove the pain and keep the pregnant woman in good condition.

If in the third month of pregnancy the foetus gets unsteady then take equal portions of *kia-kiu-lei (kākolī)*, *ch'e-lo kia-kiu-lei* (kṣīra-kākolī) and the root of *pi-ma*; rub them in water and make them exceedingly fine, put them in milk and boil it well. Put some milk-sugar and honey in it, mix up and take it when cool. This medicine can keep the foatus in its place, remove pain and fear and keep the pregnant woman in good condition.

If in the fourth month of pregnancy the foetus gets unsteady then take the root of the *tribulus terrestris (tsi-li)* take also its branch and leaf, utpala flower and its stalk, take equal portion of each, rub them in water and make them exceedingly fine, put them in milk and boil. Give it when cool. This medicine can keep the foetus in its place, remove pain and fear and keep the pregnant woman in good condition.

If in the fifth month of pregnancy the foetus gets unsteady take the root of the gourd plant *(hu-tseu)*, the utpala flower, equal portion of each, grind them and make them fine, mix them with grape juice *(p'u-t'ao)*, milk and milk-sugar, boil them and give it when cool. This medicine can keep the foetus in its place, remove pain and fear and keep the pregnant woman in good condition.

If in the sixth month of pregnancy the foetus gets unsteady then take *pi-po-lo (piyāla)*, *mo-ti-kia-lo-jo (mātulaṅga?)*, *sa-hi-to-fu (Sahetava?)* herbs, equal portion of each, rub them in water and make them extremely fine, boil them in milk, and then put some milk-sugar and honey in it. Give it when cool. This medicine can keep the foetus in its place, remove pain and fear and keep the pregnant woman in good condition.

If in the seventh month of pregnancy the foetus gets unsteady then take the *tribulus terrestris*, its branch, leaf and root, grind them into powder, put some milk-sugar and honey and make pills. Give each pill with meat soups. It may be taken also as food with the meat soup or with the soup of green beans. Whether taken as medicine or food it can keep the foetus in its place, remove pain and fear and keep the pregnant woman in good condition.

If in the eighth month of pregnancy the foetus gets unsteady then take *san-han-ngo* (medicine), lotus flower, blue utpala flower and *tribulus terrestris*, equal portion of each, rub them in cold water and make them extremely fine, mix them with milk, sugar and honey, boil them and give it when cool. This medicine can keep the foetus in its place, remove pain and fear and keep the pregnant woman in good condition.

If in the ninth month of pregnancy the foetus gets unsteady then the root of *pi-ma* (castor oil plant), *kia-kiu-lei (kākolī)*, *she-lo-po-han-ni (Śārapā?)* herb and *mei-li-han-ti (bṛhatī)* herb, equal portion of each rub them in cold water and make exceedingly fine, put them in milk and boil. Give when cool. This medicine can keep the foetus in its place, remove pain and fear and keep the pregnant woman in good condition.

If in the tenth month of pregnancy the foetus gets unsteady then take green beans *(liu-teu)* and utpala flower, equal portion of each mix them with water, rub them extremely fine, put some milk-sugar and honey in them and boil them in milk. Give it when cool. This medicine can keep the foetus in its place, remove pain and fear and keep the pregnant woman in good condition.

In the eleventh month of pregnancy the foetus gets unsteady then take blue utpala flower, *sha-lu-hang (Śāluka)* herb, lotus flower and stalk, equal portion of each, rub them in cold water and make them extremely fine, mix them with milk, put some milk-sugar in it and boil. Give one dose of it when cool. This medicine can keep the foetus in its place, remove pain and fear and keep the pregnant woman in good condition.

If in the twelfth month of pregnancy the foetus gets unsteady, then take *kia-kiu-lei (kākolī)*, *ch'e-lo kia-kiu-lei (kṣīra-kākolī)*, herbs liquorice *(kan-t'sao, yaṣṭimadhu)*, and utpala flower, equal portion of each, grind them and make them fine, rub them in water and boil in milk. Give one dose of it when cool. This medicine can keep the pregnant woman in good condition.

When Jīvaka Ṛsi had heard the master on this method of treating pregnant women he became exceedingly happy, bowed unto him and went away. Cf. *Carakhasaṁhitā*, *Śārīra*⁰ VIII-31.

Paramato nirvikāramāpyāyamānasya garbhasya ṁāse mase karmo-padekṣyāmaḥ prathame māse śanket ced-garbhamāpannā, kṣīramanu-paskṛtaṃ mātrāvacchītam kāle kāle pibedantarvatnī, sātmyameva ca punarbhojanaṃ sāyaṃ prātanca bhunjīta/dvitīye māse kṣīrameva ca madhurauṣadhasiddham, tṛtīye māse kṣīram madhusarpirbhyāmupasamsṛjyay caturthe māse kṣīranavanītamakṣa mātramasnīyāta, pañcame māse kṣīrasarpiḥ, ṣaṣṭhe māse kṣīrasarpiḥ madhurauṣadhasiddham, tadeva saptame māsi, tartra garbhasya keśā jāyamānā māturvidāham janayantīti striyo bhāṣante; tanneti bhagavānātreyaḥ, kintu garbhotpīḍanāddhi vātapittaśleṣmāṇa uraḥ prāpya vidahanti/tataḥ kandūrupajāyate; kandūmūlā kikkisāvāptiḥ; tatra kolodakena navanītasya madhurauṣadhasiddhasya pānitalamātram kāle kāle'sya dadyāt, candanamṛṇālakalkaiṣcāsyāḥ stanodaraṃ vimṛdnīyāt/śirīṣadhātakīsarṣappamadhūkacūrnaiḥ kuta jājakabijamustaharidrākalkairvā nimbakolakasurasamanjiṣṭākalkairvā pṛṣataharinaśaśarudhirayu-tayā triphalayā vā, karavīpatrakasiddhena vā tailenābhyaṅgaḥ, pariṣekaḥ punarmālatīmadhukasiddhenāmbhasā, jātakandūśca kandūyanaṃ varjayet tvagbhedavairūpyaparihārārtham, asahyā-yāntu kandvāmunnmardanodgharṣaṇābhyāṃ parihārah syāt, madhuramāhārjātaṃ vātaharamalpamasnehalavanamalpoda kā-nupānaṃ bhuñjīta. aṣṭame tu māse kṣīrayavāgūṃ sarpiṣmatīṃ kāle kāle pibet; neti bhadrakāpyah paingālyabādho hi āsyā garbham āgacchedītī; astūtvapainglyābādha ityāha bhagavān Punarvasurātreyaḥ. Na tvevaitanna kāryam, evaṃ kurvatī hyarogāroga-balavarṇa-svrasaṃ-hananasampadupetaṃ jñātīnāṃ śreṣṭhama-patyam janayati, Navame tu khalvenām māse madhurauṣadha-siddhena tailenāmevāsayet. Ataścavāsyastailapicuṃ yono pranayet garbhasthānamārgasnehanārtham, yadidaṃ karma prathamaṃ māsaṃ samupādāyopadiṣṭamānavamamāsāt, tena garbheṇyā garbhaṣamaye garbhadhāraṇe kukṣikaṭipārśva prīṣṭaṃ mrīdu bhavati, vātaścānulomah sampadyate, mūtra purīṣe ca prakṛtibhūte sukhen mārgāvāpadyete carmanakhānī ca mārdavamupyānti, balavanou copacīyete putraṃ ceṣtaṃ sampadupetaṃ sukhinaṃ sukhenaisā kāle prajāyate. iti.

Notes

1 *Nanjio*, 883; *Hobogirin* 1385; Bagchi–*Le Canon Bouddhique II*, p. 589.
2 *Indian Culture*, VII, pp. 269 ff.
3 *Kalpasthāna*, p. 191.
4 *Sārira* VIII, 21.
5 *ibid* VIII 31.
6 *Indian culture*, VII, pp.269ff.
7 S. Lévi *Le catalogue Géogarphique des Yakṣa*, J. As. 1915.
8 For a detailed study on Jīvaka, his role as a medical authority, his association with Buddha etc., see the *History of Indian Medicine* by G. N. Mukherji Vol. III, pp. 681ff.
9 Woolner J.R.A.S. 1925, p.631.
10 Bagchi, *Deux Lexiques*, 1003.
11 *Mahāvyutpatti* 5717–36.
12 *Sino-Iranica*, p.225.
13 Śabdakalpadruma.
14 Śabdakalpadruma.

Chapter 7

THE CHINESE MYSTICISM*

The Chinese mind, generally speaking, has no mystic bent. The Confucian positivism is its best expression and the greater bulk of the people have been ardent followers of the Confucian ethics. The abolition of imperialism, round which this Confucianism centered in ancient times, has made no difference in the country and the Confucian attitude of mind has not been disturbed in the least. The Confucian ethics is mainly based on conservative social dogmas. There is no place of divine revelation in it, and it insists on the reciprocal duties of the Emperor and his subjects, father and children, and the fellow-citizens. The respect of the subjects for the Emperor, and the respect of the children for their ancestors, constitute the real foundation of the Government and family. This is why it has been given the place of a national religion in Confucian ethics. In Confucian philosophy there is no place for a Creator God, and in fact Confucius himself refused more than once to be dragged into the speculation on the existence of a Godhead. He explains the mystery of the Universe by the formulation of two principles which he calls *Yin* and *Yang*. *Yin* is the female principle which is passive and *Yang* is the male principle which is active. These two in conjunction create the beings which populate the earth.

Such a simple positivist creed could not have given rise to mysticism, but still China witnessed very early the birth and growth of a very intricate mysticism. This mysticism known as Taoism was, if we are to rely on tradition, first introduced by Lao-tse in the 6th century B.C. Lao-tse was an elder contemporary of Confucius and lived between 570 and 490 B.C. Lao-tse which means the "Old Philosopher" was only the nickname of the teacher and the real name still remains in obscurity. In fact, the personal history of the "Old Philosopher" is not much known. It is admitted by all sources that he was the librarian in the court of the Cheou princes and while engaged in the study of the old documents he discovered his new mystic philosophy. About his last days there are two different stories: according to one, he left his office and went away to the West (West of China) and was never heard of

* *The Calcutta Review* (1933): 66–69.

afterwards; according to the other he lived in China till his death. His mystic philosophy is contained in a canonical work which is called the *Tao-te-king* and attributed to him. About this treatise there are two stories: according to one, Lao-tse composed it during his journey in the West for his friend Yin hi who was the guard of the Western pass; according to the other, admitted to be more authentic, he discovered it or at least records containing the exposition of analogous doctrines in the ministerial archives. If we are to rely on the second, we have to admit that the history of Taoism did not commence with Lao-tse, it had its pre-history, or, in other words, Lao-tse had his precursors. But this pre-history is lost in oblivion and for all practical purposes the *Tao-te king* is our oldest authority on the subject.

About Lao-tse, what the famous Chinese historians Sse-ma-ts'ien of the 2nd century B.C. has said still remains true: "of the Old Teacher some say this, while others say that, and it can be only affirmed that this man deliberately effaced all the traces of his life because he loved obscurity above all". It is not known if he had any following during his life time but in later times some of the well-known Chinese writers and philosophers professed his mystic doctrines and amongst them were counted Lie-tse, Chuang-tse and Yang-chu who lived in the 4th century B.C, wrote comments on the famous work and contributed to the spread and development of Taoist philosophy. The Taoist literature which consists of about two thousand treatises forms an important section of Chinese literature.

Tao literally means the way and is generally rendered as the *principle.* This *Tao* is conceived as the unique principle which existed before everything else. It is both transcendent and immanent and has no form, sound or colour. It can not be expressed or defined in language and "if a name has been given to it, it is as a symbol, if not of its unfathomable essence, but of the way in which it manifests itself on earth". Says the *Tao-te-king*:

> "The principle which may be enunciated is not that which always existed. The being that may be named is not that which always existed. Before all times, there was an ineffable and unnameable being. When he was still unnameable he conceived the heaven and the earth. He then became nameable and gave birth to all beings. Man's knowledge of the universal principle depends on the state of his mind. The mind which is habitually free from passion knows its mysterious essence. The mind which is habitually full of passion knows only its effects".

The commentators, discussing this passage of the *Tao-te-king*, say: Before times and before all times there was a being who was self-existent, eternal, infinite, complete and omnipresent. It is impossible to name him or speak of him because human words apply to perceptible beings. But the primordial being was at the beginning, and is even now, essentially imperceptible to the senses. Before the origin of the world there was nothing beyond him. His essence alone existed at the beginning. This essence possessed two immanent properties – the *yin*, concentration and the *yang*, expansion, which were once exteriorised under the two perceptible forms of heaven and earth. This was the commencement of times and since then the principle came to be named. The state of *yin, i.e.* the state of concentration and repose which the principle had before time is his real state. The state of *yang, i.e.* the state of expansion and action, the state of manifestation in perceptible beings, is his condition in time – a condition which is illusory. To these two conditions of the principle correspond in the mental faculty of man repose and activity or in other words void and fullness. When the mind is productive of ideas it is full of images, it is moved by passions and at that time it is able only to recognise the effects of the principle. But when the cogitation of the mind is absolutely stopped it becomes completely void and calm, it is then like a pure and unstained mirror in which is reflected the ineffable and unnameable essence of the principle itself.

This principle is further defined in the *Tao-te-king* as the *true nature*. The superior kind of wisdom consists in knowing this true nature of self. It can be attained by imposing one's own will on himself and in mastering his passions. It can be realised by renouncing all forms of conventional knowledge and worldly activities. In the words of Lao-tse a true sage "acts without acting, is busy without being busy, tastes without tasting, sees with the same eye the great and small, much and little". These words of Lao-tse are capable of only one interpretation. Man ought to realise the universal principle or the true nature of his self. This principle or true nature cannot be defined by words, it can be only felt or realised. This realisation is possible only when the passions have been mastered, the worldly ideas and images have been removed from the mind and a perfect calm has been attained. The mind goes back to its real nature or gets the image of its real self when it is completely clean and void. This cannot be attained through conventional knowledge. When the mind attains this true nature its attitude undergoes a complete change. The man then moves in the world but not as other do. As he has then no desire and passions he acts but he is not moved by any of his actions, he looks at others but sees in them only one universal principle and does not distinguish between this man or that man.

There is however a practical side of this mysticism. The method by which the transcendental state can be reached is indicated by Lao-tse in the following words:

> "Close your mouth and nostrils and you will run to the end of your days without any decadence. To talk too much and indulge in too many

> anxieties is to waste yourself away and shorten your life. To concentrate the rays of intelligence on the intelligence and not to allow the mental functions to disturb your body is to cover (or protect) the body so that it may endure long".

Chuang-tse states this method more clearly: One should retire to river banks or solitary places and abstain from doing anything just as those who really love nature and like to enjoy leisure, do. To take in breath in a measured way, to evacuate the air contained in the lungs and to replace it by fresh air lengthens one's life. However simple this method might have been at the beginning, it gave rise later on to a very complicated system of breath control.

The pantheistic conception of the universal principle and breath control and concentration prescribed for realising that principle within the self have no doubt close similarity with the Upanishadic conception of Brahma and certain Yogic methods adopted for its realisation within the self. The agreement is so close that one feels tempted to say that Lao-tse derived his ideas from the Indian source and his traditional journey to the West may supply its confirmatory evidence. In fact some Sinologists have expressed such an opinion. But there is a very great difficulty in accepting such a view because the ancient Chinese annals do not officially admit of any relation of China with India before the close of the 1st century A.D.

But whether of Indian extraction or of independent growth there is no doubt that the mystic philosophy of the "Old Philosopher" attain "a rare elevation although its very sublimity renders it sometimes obscure".

Chapter 8

SOME EARLY BUDDHIST MISSIONARIES OF PERSIA IN CHINA*

China came in contact with the Iranian world for the first time towards the end of the 2nd century before Christ when Chang Kien, the famous Chinese explorer came back to China (126 B.C.) after a long absence of twelve years. Chang Kien was sent to negotiate with the western powers, especially with the Scythians, established at that time in the valley of the Oxus, in view of forming an alliance against the Huns who were a formidable menace to empire. Though the political mission of Chang Kien did not immediately succeed he brought definite information about the kingdoms which were flourishing at that time in the western region – especially *Ta-yuan* (Ferganah), *K'ang Kiu* (Sogdiana), *Ngan-si* (Parthia), etc.

Subsequently when the first official embassy of China was sent to Parthia under the reign of Emperor Wu-ti (140–86 B.C.), the King of the country ordered twenty thousand cavalry to meet them on the eastern frontier and entertained them well. All the Chinese annals trace their relation with Parthia from this date. Parthia came to be known to the Chinese as *Ngan-si* through the name of the dynasty ruling over Parthia in that period namely the Arsacidan. Ngan-si (An-si) in ancient Chinese pronunciation would give as Ar-śak (Arsak). The description of the country, as given by the Chinese historians of that period answer very well to the empire of the Arsacides. "The king of the country of Ngan-si (Parthia) rules at the city of *P'an-tou* (Parthian? παρθοι of Herodotus). It bounds north *K'ang Kiu* (Sogdiana), east on *Wu-yi-shan-li* (Alexandra, i.e., Herat), west on *T' iao-che* (Chaldea). Several hundred small and large cities are subject to it and the country is several thousand *li* in extent that is very large country. It lies on the banks of the *Kuei-shwei* (the Oxus). The carts and ships of their merchants go to the neighbouring countries".[1]

Parthia was, in this period, playing an important role in the eastern commerce. The Chinese commodities passed to the Roman world through Parthia. The Chinese soon came to know about this western power, the territory of which was

* *The Calcutta Review* (July 1927): 60–64.

bounded on Parthia on the east and felt the necessity of coming in direct touch with the Roman orient (called *Ta-ts'in*, by the Chinese). In 97 A.D. the famous general Pan-ch'ao during his Central-Asian campaigns sent a certain Kan-ying as ambassador to the Roman orient (*Ta-ts'in*). He arrived in *Tiao-che* (Chaldea) on the coast of the great sea. When about to take his passage across the sea, the sailors of the western frontier of Ngan-si (Parthia) told Kan-ying that the voyage was a long and a terrible one. Kan-ying therefore returned home without fulfilling his mission. Direct relation with the Roman orient was established as late as 156 A.D. when an embassy of Marcus Aurelius Antonius reached Tonkin (then a Chinese province), with presents. The motive of this embassy was very probably to ruin the monopoly of eastern trade which Parthia was exercising by the land route. The Roman world wanted to have direct commercial relation with China. The official relation was established but we do not know how far the project of direct commerce was realised.

Whatever it might have been there was an active commercial relation between China and the Parthian world in the beginning of the Christian era. It is very probable that the Parthian merchants had formed a community by themselves in the capital of China (*Si-ngan-fu*) already in this period. The existence of such communities of different nationalities, Indian, Persian, Indo-Chinese, etc., are attested in a later age. Whatever might have been the position of the foreigners in the capital of China during the first centuries of the Christian era, it is certain that the commercial exchange of the merchants of different countries facilitated also an intellectual cooperation and China gradually began to get interested in foreign religion, art and literature.[2]

It was in this period in 148 A.D. that a Parthian Buddhist missionary reached the capital of China with the intention of propagating the new religion. He is known as Ngan She-kao or She-kao the Parthian.[3] If Shekao be a Buddhist church name it may be reconstructed as *Lokottama*. He was prince of real royal descent of Parthia and most probably of the Arsacidan dynasty. From his childhood he had a religious bent of mind; so he abdicated the throne in favour of his uncle, embraced Buddhism and became a monk. He devoted himself to the study of the Buddhist scripture and determined to travel in different centres of Buddhist learning, evidently for a better knowledge of the scriptures. Though it is not known if he ever visited India, he certainly was acquainted with some Indian language (probably, Sanskrit) as is evident from the vast number of translations of Buddhist texts he made into Chinese. He travelled extensively and reached China in 148 A.D. He worked there till 168 A.D. and is said to have translated 176 Buddhist texts. Fifty-five of his translations still exist in the present collection of the Chinese Tripiṭaka published from Japan. We have no sure information about the end of She-kao, but all traditions agree in relating that after 168 A.D. She-kao travelled in

South China for preaching Buddhism till the end of the century when he met with some mishap which caused his death.

The fifty-five works which still exist amply show that She-kao was very well-read in the Buddhist scriptures. Many of them are judicious selections from the mass of Buddhist texts and the translations, though not literal are good adaptations of the original texts, many of which are missing. She-kao was not satisfied only with the work, he did himself but founded a school of translators which did such an admirable work that it came to be known as "*unrivalled*". In this school, there were Sogdian, Scythian and Indian monks working side by side for the propagation of Buddhism, and Buddhist scripture.

Buddhism was introduced in China in the year 2 B.C. and the first missionaries, Dharmaratna and Kāśyapa Mātaṅga are said to have come to China in 65 A.D. They translated four or five texts, one of which still exists. But the informations on these two first preachers are all very hazy and do not seem to be very reliable. Real history of the Buddhist literature in China begins with the works of She-kao and his collaborators, though it is certain that some of the works attributed to him are either later additions or apocryphal. The very style proves it. But many of them are, without doubt, authentic. We will not enter here into a detailed discussion of his works. Almost all of them are texts from the Āgamas (corresponding to the Pāli *nikāyas* but greatly differing from the latter). Though some Mahāyāna texts are attributed to him, they seem to be spurious. An important question, about the original language of the texts translated by She-kao, has not been replied to. It is certain that it was not Pāli. A study of the transcription of proper names do not allow us to, say that the original language of these texts was Sanskrit either. We have two alternatives to suppose, either an Indian Prakrit, or an Iranian language which She-kao learnt easily. An analysis of the Chinese Āgamas might prove one day, that some of these Āgama texts, specially those translated by Parthian or Sogdian monks are of Iranian *provenance* and point to an incomplete Iranian version of the comparatively more ancient part of the Buddhist scripture.

From Ngan She-kao, we pass to two other Parthian names Ngan Hiuan and Ngan Fa-K'in. Ngan Hiuan came to Si-ngan-fu in 181 A.D. as a merchant. On account of some distinguished services, which he rendered to the public, he received an official favour and was made "the chief officer of cavalry". But his temperament was religious and he therefore joined the Buddhist community founded by She-kao and devoted himself to study. He translated two Buddhist texts into Chinese and both of them exist in the present collection of the Tripiṭaka. Ngan Fa-K'in came to Si-ngan-fu in 281 A.D. and translated Buddhist texts till 306 A.D. Five works are ascribed to him, and two of these still exist.

These few names of the early period have been preserved along with the names of other translators. But they are sufficient to point a past history which now remains forgotten. They break the silence of this voiceless past and present new problems to us, which remains to be answered. We do not know as yet anything about the propagation of Buddhism in Persia as early as the beginning of the Christian era. The conversion of Ngan She-kao presupposes the presence of Buddhists in the capital of the Arsacides and their history is still to be traced out. The Parthian monks who went to China are not isolated figures and are only landmarks in the history of Indo-Parthian relation.

Notes

1 F. Hirth, *China and the Roman Orient*, pp. 139–140.

2 For the commercial relation between China and Persia, and for the names of Persian commodities preserved in Chinese and the Chinese commodities preserved in Persia, see the work of Berthold Laufer – *Sino-Iranian.*

3 The Chinese had the habit of adding a prefix to the name of a foreigner to indicate his nationality. An element of the name of the country was generally prefixed to the name of the person e.g. She-Kao of Parthia (Ngan-si) – Ngan She-Kao; Seng hoeui of Sogdiana (K'ang-Kiu) – K'ang Seng houei; Nandi of India (T'ien chu) –*Chu* Nan-ti, etc. In the Buddhist Church of China, the pious disciple of a foreign teacher sometimes used to attribute to himself the same nationality as his teacher, e.g. Fa-hu (Dharmarakṣa) born of Scythian parents in Kan-su used to call himself *Chu* Fa-hu as his teacher was an Indian. There are many other similar cases.

Chapter 9

SOME LETTERS OF HIUAN-TSANG AND HIS INDIAN FRIENDS*

The great Chinese pilgrim Hiuan-tsang was in India for about sixteen years from 630 to 645 A.D. He passed a considerable time at Nālandā in the study of the Buddhist philosophy with the then abbot of the monastery – Śīlabhadra. King Harṣa invited him thrice to the capital and he turned down his request every time. Later on when Harṣa met the pilgrim he asked the latter about the cause of his refusal. Thereupon Hiuan-tsang replied that he had come from far in search of the law of Buddha and for the sake of learning the Buddhist philosophy and that he did not go to meet the king then as he had not finished his studies.[1] This testifies to his great attachment to his studies at Nālandā. His attachment to his Guru Śīlabhadra and to his fellow-students especially to Jñāna-prabha, the chief disciple of Śīlabhadra, was also great.

His Indian friends also reciprocated the same sentiments towards him. This is best shown by the incident which happened at the time of his departure from Nālandā. On hearing that he had decided to go back to China all the monks of the Nālandā monastery came to him in a body and begged him not to go back. They pointed out to him that India was the land of Buddha and that China was not a holy land. They also said that Buddha could never be born in China and that hence the people there could not be meritorious. But Hiuan-tsang replied that the law of Buddha was designed for universal diffusion and that China could not be deprived of Buddha's favour. When all arguments were of no avail they carried the sad news to Śīlabhadra. Śīlabhadra then called for Hiuan-tsang and said: "Why, Sir, have you come to this resolution?" Hiuan-tsang replied: "This country is the place of Buddha's birth: it is impossible not to regard it with affection; only Hiuan-tsang's intention in coming hither was to inquire after the great law for the benefit of his fellow creatures... My visit here has been of the utmost profit. I desire now to go back and translate and explain to others what I have heard, so as to cause others also to be equally grateful to you". Śīlabhadra joyfully replied: "These are thought worthy of a great Bodhisattva;

---

* *Journal of the U. P. History Society* 18.1–2 (N.D.): 74–81.

my heart anticipates your own wishes". He then arranged for the departure of the pilgrim.[2] The separation must have been very painful to both the parties.

The personal contact of the pilgrim with his Indian friends continued even after his return to China. Three letters which have been preserved in Hui-li's Life of Hiuan-tsang[3] are supposed to be letters which were originally written by the pilgrim and his Indian friends in Sanskrit. Two of them, partially preserved in the Chinese Buddhist Encyclopaedia – *Fo-tsu li tai t'ong tsai* were translated by Chavannes in French.[4] Full translations of the three letters are given here as they throw considerable light on the personal ties that existed between Indian and foreign scholars in such an early period.

Hiuan-tsang had two Sanskrit names. The Mahayanists used to call him *Mahāyāna-deva* while the Hinayanists called him *Mokṣadeva* or *Mokṣācārya*. It is under this latter name that he is addressed in the following letter.

I. Letter of Prajñādeva and Jñānaprabha to Hiuan-tsang[5]

In the summer, 5th month of the year 652 A.D., the Venerable monks Che-kuang (Jñānaprabha), Hui-t'ien (Prajñādeva)[6] and others of the Mahābodhi-vihāra in Middle India sent a letter to the Master of the Law (i.e. Hiuan-tsang). Jñānaprabha was a great scholar of both the Hīnayāna and Mahāyāna literature, and of the literature of other religions such as the four Vedas, the five vidyās, etc. He was at the top of all disciples of the great teacher of law, Śīlabhadra. He was honoured by all learners of the Five Indies. Prajñādeva was well acquainted and exercised in the literature of the eighteen schools of Hīnayāna. His knowledge and great virtue had won for him universal esteem. While in India Hiuan-tsang had occasion to defend the teachings of Mahāyāna against the attacks of the partisans of Hīnayāna but the courteous polemics had not at all diminished the esteem and sympathy which they had for him. So Prajñādeva sent with the Bhikṣu Dharma-vardhana (? Fa-chang)[7] of the same Vihāra a letter to Hiuan-tsang with the copy of a Stotra which he had composed and a pair of white cloths. The letter was the following:

> "The Sthavira Prajñādeva who associates with men of great wisdom in the temple of Mahābodhi near the Vajrāsana of Lord Buddha sends this letter to Mokṣācarya of Mahācīna who knows well and has penetrated well into the Sūtras, Vinayas and the innumerable Śāstras. He humbly wishes that the latter may ever be free from illness and suffering.
>
> I, Bhikṣu, Prajñādeva, have now composed an eulogy on the great divine transformations of Buddha (Trikāyastotra ?) and also a "Comparative estimate of the Sūtras, Śāstras, etc". I hand them over to Bhikṣu Fa-chang who will carry them to you. Among us the Ācārya, the

Venerable Bhadanta Jñānaprabha, possessed of numerous and limitless knowledge, joins me in enquiring about you. The Upāsakas, here, always offer their salutations to you. We all are sending you a pair of white cloths to show that we are not forgetful. The road is long. So do not mind the smallness of the present. We wish you may accept it. As regards the Sūtras and Śāstras which you may require, please send us a list. We will copy them and send them to you. This is Mokṣācarya, all that we want to inform you. This is for conveying to you from a distance our loving thoughts".

II. Letter of Hiuan-tsang to Jñānaprabha

Fa-chang (Dharmavardhana ?) returned in the 2nd month, spring, of the 5th year yong-hoei (654). The following letter was written by Hiuan-tsang to Jñānaprabha, the same year and sent through Fa-chang.

"The Bhikṣu Hiuan-tsang of the country of the Great T'ang rulers humbly writes to the Master of Law, the teacher of Tripiṭaka, Bhadanta Jñānaprabha of Magadha in Middle India. I returned more than 10 years ago. The frontiers of the countries are far away from each other. I had no news from you. My anxiety went on increasing. By enquiring from Bhikṣu Fa-chang I learn that you are all well. My eyes become bright and it seems I see your face. Pen cannot describe the joy I feel at the news. The climate now is becoming hot and I cannot say how it will be afterwards.[8]

I learnt from an ambassador who recently came back from India that the great teacher Śīlabhadra is no more in this world. On getting this news I was overwhelmed with sorrow that knew no bounds. Alas! the boat of this sea of suffering has foundered: the eye of men and gods has closed. How to express the sorrow that his disappearance causes us? In the past when the Great Buddha withdrew his light Kāśyapa continued his work and extended it; while Śāṇavāsa left this world. Upagupta continued to give exposition of his beautiful law. Now that a general of the Law has returned to his true place let the masters of law in their turn perform their duties. I only wish that the pure explanations and the subtle discussions (of the law) may spread in vast waves like the waves of the four seas and that the holy knowledge may be eternal like the five mountains.

Among the Sūtras and Śāstras that I, Hiuan-tsang, had brought with me, I have already translated the *Yogācāra-bhūmi-śāstra* and other works in all 30 volumes. The *Kośa* and the *Nyāyānusāra-śāstra*[9] are not yet fully translated. They will certainly be completed this year.

At present the Devaputra (i.e. the Emperor) of the great T'ang dynasty through his personal holiness and by his numerous felicities guides the country and brings peace to the people. With the affection of a Cakravartī king and like a Dharmarāja, he helps the propagation of the law to far away places. In regard to the Sūtras and Śāstras translated we have obtained the favour of a preface from his divine pen. In regard to them the officers have received the order for circulating the texts in all the kingdoms. Even the neighbouring countries will receive all of them when the order is executed. Although we are near the end of the *kalpa* the shining glory of the law is still very sweet and perfect. It is not at all different from its manifestation in the Jetavana at Śrāvasti.

I should humbly like to let you know that while crossing the Indus I had lost a load of sacred texts. I now send you a list of those texts annexed to this letter. I request you to send them to me if you get the chance. I am sending some small articles as present. Please accept them. The road is long and it is not possible to send much. Do not disdain it.

With the salutations of Hiuan-tsang".

III. Letter of Hiuan-tsang to Prajñādeva

"The Bhikṣu Hiuan-tsang of the great T'ang country respectfully writes to the Master of Law, the teacher of Tripiṭaka, Prajñādeva of the Mahābodhi-vihāra: A long time has elapsed. There was no news from you and so I was greatly anxious. There was no means of calming the anxiety. When Bhikṣu Dharmavardhana (Fa-chang?) came with your letter, I came to learn that you are all well. This gave me great joy. I have received the pair of fine white cloths and the bundle of Stotras (sent by you). It is a great honour to me which I did not merit. I feel much ashamed. The weather is gradually becoming hot. I do not know what it will be afterwards and how you will keep.

You have reduced to nothingness the Śāstras of hundred schools and maintained the integrity of the Sūtras with its nine divisions *(navāṅga-budhaśāsana)*. You have raised the banner of the Right Law and led every one to the goal. You have beaten the drum of victory and defeated the opponents. Supreme in knowledge you have challenged all the kings. You must therefore feel very happy.

I, Hiuan-tsang, am a fool. I am also growing old and failing in strength. I remember your merits and respect you for your kindness. These thoughts tire me more. When I was in India I met you in the Assembly at Kānyakubja and discussed the Śāstras together before the kings, and their numerous followers in order to settle the doctrinal issues. One party defended the Mahāyāna and the other defended the incomplete religion (lit. half religion, i.e., the Hīnayāna). During the debate the atmosphere sometimes grew very tense and sometimes very low. My only intention was to follow the logic and not to show any partiality. It is due to this that we were opposed to each other. When the meeting ended our mutual opposition also ended. Now the messenger has brought your letter and your apology.[10] Why do you keep it in mind? You are deeply learned, your style is lucid, your determination is strong, and your character is high. Even the waves of the Anavatapta lake cannot be compared to yours. The clearness of a *maṇi* cannot equal yours. You are a bright example to your disciples. I wish you had followed the good law (i.e., Mahāyāna) in your elucidation of the religion. When the logic is perfect speech reaches its limit. Nothing can surpass the Mahāyāna. I am sorry that you have not yet imbibed a deep faith in it. You prefer goat and deer to the white cow, and crystal to a *maṇi*. You possess brightness and great virtue. Why do you ignore it? Your body is brittle and short-lived like an earthen pot. You should decide to have faith in Alaṁkāra (? *Mahāyāna-sūtrālaṁkāra*) so that you may not have to regret before your death.

The messenger is now going back. I send you this advice which is an expression of my love for you. I am sending you a small thing as an expression of my gratefulness for your present. This cannot represent my deep respect for you. I hope you understand me. During my return while crossing the Indus I lost a load of the holy texts, I am sending you a list of them with this letter. I request you to send them to me.

With respects of Bhikṣu Hiuan-tsang".

Notes

1 Beal - *Life of Hiuan-Tsang* pp. 173–174.
2 Beal - *ibid.,* p. 169.
3 Chinese text, chap. vii.
4 *Les Inscriptions Chinoises de Bodhgayā*, Revue de l'Histoire des Religions 1896.
5 Life of Hiuan-tsang, Nanking edition, III, chap. vii, pp. 15a–15b.
6 The restoration of the name of Prajñādeva is not very certain. Literally it means: "Mind-God" – *Matideva,* but the Chinese word Hui (in Hui-t'ien) is sometimes confused with another Hui which means – "Prajñā".
7 Chinese Fa-chang literally means "Dharma – long". This may be restored as Dharma – vardhana.
8 This is evidently a reference to the terribly hot summer of Northern India which must have been very trying for the pilgrim during his stay in India.
9 *Kośa* here refers to *Abhidharmakoṣa-vyākhyā* of Vasubandhu in 30 chapters (Nanjio 1267). The translation was commenced on 10th of the 5th month of 651 and completed on the 27th of the 7th month of 654. The other work is the *Nyāyānu-sāra-śāstra* of

Saṅghabhadra (Nanjio 1265). Its translation was commenced on the 1st day of the first month of 653 and completed on the 10th day of the 7th month of 654. The date of the letter is the 5th month of 654.

10 The apology referred to by Hiuan-tsang must have been contained in the 'Comparative estimate of the Sūtras and Śāstras' mentioned in Prajñādeva's letter. It was evidently composed to answer some of the points raised by Hiuan-tsang.

Chapter 10

NEW LIGHTS ON THE CHINESE INSCRIPTIONS OF BODHGAYĀ*

With Chou Ta-fu

Chavannes was the first to publish an authoritative reading of the five Chinese inscriptions found at Bodhgayā with translation and notes (*Les Inscriptions Chinoises de Bodhgayā*, Revue de l'Histoire des Religions, T. XXXIV, Paris, 1896). His readings were based on estampages and photographs sent by Prof. A. Foucher who was then in India on a scientific mission. A faulty reading and a summary of two of these inscriptions had been previously published by Beal (J.R.A.S. 1881, vol. XIII, pp. 552–572, Indian Antiquary X, p. 193). The same note was reproduced without any revision in Cunningham's *Mahahodhi.* The original of the first four of the five inscriptions studied by Chavannes are now in the Indian Museum at Calcutta.

A re-examination of the original of Inscription no. 1 has now made it possible to suggest some improvements on its reading as given by Chavannes. The stone not being in a good condition the estampages was not evidently clear enough and Chavannes was obliged to leave a few lacunae in his reading of the inscription. These lacunae have now been filled up by an examination of the original inscription. The correct reading and a revised translation are given below.

Translation

The monk Che-yi of the great Han country had first taken the vow to exhort three hundred thousand men to practise the conduct which assures a higher birth, to make a charity of three hundred thousand copies (lit. fasciculi) of the *Shang sheng king* (Sūtra on the higher birth), and

* *Sino-Indian Studies* 1.2 (1944): 111–114.

himself to recite (it) three hundred thousand times (lit. fasciculi). Such a merit, as mentioned above conduces to birth in the inner Tusita (heaven). Now on arriving in Magadha, he has admired (?) the Diamond-throne (Vajrāsana) and has humbly met the abbot of Vijñanamātra (School) Kui-pao and a group of venerable monks and together taken the vow to go to be born in the Tusita. Among three hundred thousand persons Kui-pao the first, Che-yi the second, Kuang-fong the third and others mentioned in order are Hui-yen, Ch'ong-ta, Ts'iuan-tsun, Yuan-chen, Yi-sien, Hui-siu, Che-yong, Fong-sheng, Ts'ing-yun etc. have together desired to pay homage to Maitreya, the compassionate and the honoured one and have now engraved the (images of) seven Buddhas which they place on record.

大漢國僧志義先發願勸三十萬人修上生行，施三十萬卷上生經，自誦三十萬卷：如上功德，向回同生內陀。今至摩竭國，金剛座，伏遇唯識座主歸寶與諸大德等同發願往生內陀。三十萬人中，歸寶為第一人，志義第二，廣峰第三，下依？次第：惠嚴，重達，全遵，緣真，義暹，惠秀，智永，奉升，清蘊等，並願親奉彌勒慈尊。今結良緣，成此七佛已，為記之。

The precise date of the inscription is not given. From an examination of the style of the sculpture Cunningham suggested that the inscription could not be older than 1000 A.D. Che-yi calls himself "a monk of the great Han country". This Han dynasty could not be the great Han dynasty which ruled from 206 B.C. to 220 A.D. There was a dynasty of later Hans which ruled in a small part of China for five years only from 947 to 951 A.D. Chavannes suggested that Che-yi possibly refers to that short-lived dynasty and that Che-yi most probably came to India during the reign of these later Hans. The inscription therefore should be placed according to Chavannes between 947 and 951 A.D.

But it seems that we have now more precise indication of the date. The beginning of the third line of the inscription contains the names of monks who accompanied Kui-pao which Chavannes could not correctly read from the estampage. He read only one name Hui-shen (which is a mistake for Hui-yen) and failed to recognise the other names. These names have now been read as Hui-yen, Ch'ong-ta, Ta'iuan-tsun, Yuan-chen, Hui-siu, Che-yong, Fon-sheng, Ts'ing-yun etc. One of these names, Ch'ong-ta (重達) is otherwise known. While dealing with the notices on Chinese monks who came to China in the Sung period, Chavannes in the same article (p. 51) refers to a monk named Ch'ong-ta. It is said in the *Fo-tsu-tong-ki* from which Chavannes collected the informations (Chap-XLIII, second year *toan-hong* 989 A.D. which Chavannes would correct as the third year *toan-hong* 990 A.D.) that Chong-ta, a Sramana of T'ai Yuan, came back from India in that year (990 A.D.) after ten years of absence. Chong-ta therefore had started in 980-981 A.D. and must have reached India within a year. If this Ch'ong-ta is identified with Chong-ta who was in India with Che-yi then we should place the Bodhgayā inscription sometime between 981 and 990 A.D. This brings us much nearer to the date suggested by Cunningham. The great Hans referred to by Che-yi would be the earlier Hans,who were really great and of whom China had always been proud and not the petty Hans of the middle of the 10th century who had gained an insignificant political power only for five years.

The expression *sheng nei t'o* (生内陀) which occurs in lines 1 and 2 may be interpreted in the way we have done; *t'o* is an abbreviation for *Tou shuai t'o* (兜率陀) i.e. Tusita, the heaven of Maitreya Buddha. The Sūtra of which 300,000 copies were made by Che-yi and his associates, Shang sheng king, is also a text dedicated to Maitreya. This was identified by Chavannes in one of his later contributions (*T'oung Pao*, 1911, pp. 441–446). The text referred to is the *Kuan mi lei p'u sa shang sheng tou shuai t'ien king* (觀彌勒菩薩上生兜率天經) Nanjio 204, Taisho 452, which was translated by Tsu-k'iu King-sheng in 455 A.D. The text was so largely popular in the Chinese Buddhist world that 100,000 copies of its Si-hia translation were distributed in 1189 A.D. by the Si-hia king among his people. Information on this Si-hia text is given by lvanov in his article *Stranitsa iz istorii Si-hia* (Bulletin de l'Academie imp. des Sciences de St. Petersbourg, 1911, noticed by Chavannes in T'oung Pao, XII, pp. 441 ff.).

Chavannes had some difficulty in the interpretation of the first few words of line 2 as he had read 過 "to pass before" instead of 遇 "to meet accidentally" and separated 主 from 座. The words 座主 should be taken together as an attribute of Kui-pao. 座 is evidently an abbreviation of the 上座 which stands for an "elder", "sthavira". Kui-pao was therefore the chief of the elders of the Wei-she or Vijñānamātra school that was founded by Hiuan-tsang and had won a great prestige for it in China in later times.

A close examination of the inscription has permitted us to read the names of the monks that occur after the name of Kui-pao in the way we have done. It was not possible for Chavannes to read the names correctly from the estampage and so he took some of the rest not as proper names but as words which he tried to translate.

The last two words of the inscription can now be read as 記之 and so it has been translated as "they place on record".

The oldest Chinese inscription of Bodhgayā may therefore be placed in the last quarter of the 10th century sometime between 981 and 990 A.D. It was set up by the Chinese monk named Che-yi in collaboration with Kui-pao and a number of other Chinese monks whom Che-yi met in India probably at Mahābodhi.

*

The second Chinese inscription of Bodhgayā studied by Chavannes is dated 1022 A.D. and attributed to a Chinese monk named Yun-shu. It is an eulogy of the three kāyas of Buddha. An examination of the original inscription confirms the reading of Chavannes except in the case of the name.

The name of the monk occurs in three places, twice in line 1 and once in line 2. Chavannes read the two lines, so far as the name goes in the following manner:

> 僧蕴述赞佛身座记。蕴述别帝…蕴述竭馀资
>
> "Memoir on the bodies (kāya) and the thrones of Buddha by monk Yun-shu ... Yun-shu left the imperial country ... Yun-shu exhausted all his remaining resource ..." .

From the point of view of Chinese grammar the construction is not without difficulty as the three verbs (赞别竭) are without their principal compliments. But an examination of the original inscription allows the improvement that is needed.

The character Yun (蘊) in all the three places is preceded by another character K'o (可) within the same square space and this was not noticed by Chavannes. This is an old palaeographic device occasionally found in old Japanese inscriptions. The name of the monk therefore should be read not as Yun-shu but as K'o-yun (可蘊). The verbs therefore may be completed as follows – in the first case it is 述讚 "praising, eulogizing", in the second case 遠別 "left" and in the third case it is 遂竭 "to use entirely, to exhaust". In the last two cases the first characters were wrongly read by Chavannes as 述. It is now clear that the name of the monk was not Yun-shu but K'o-yun.

Chapter 11

A BUDDHIST MONK OF NĀLANDĀ AMONGST THE WESTERN TURKS*

The Western Turks separated from their brethren of the North in 582 A.D. But before their final separation they already had formed a distinct group with their "ten tribes". Their chief *She-tie-mi* (Istami) with the help of his elder brother *Tou men* had already extended their power to different parts of Central Asia. They had two great powers to combat – the *Joan-joan* and the *Hephthalite*. The power of the *Joan-joan* hordes established since 400 A.D. had developed their power to such an extent that in the middle of the 6th century (652 A.D.) they were holding their sway over almost the whole of the northern part of Central Asia. *T'ou-men* with the help of some Tunguse chiefs succeeded in destroying altogether the power of the *Joan-joan* and their vast territory fell into the hands of the Turks in 555 A.D. The next onslaught of the Turks was directed against the Hephthalites. The Hephthalites had already established their sway over the people in the valley of the Oxus in the middle of the 5th century A.D. They had attained the apogic of their power in the period 502–556 A.D. when they carried their victorious armies not only to Persia but also to Kapisa, Karasahr, Kucha, Kashgar, Bai, Khoten, etc. Their territory comprised also Tash-Kourgane, Wakhan, Zebak, the valley of Chitral and Gandhara and their capital was situated at Bamian. When Song-Yun visited Gandhara (in 520 A.D.) the country had already been conquered by the Hephthalites.

The invasion of the Turks in the middle of the 6th century changed the whole political atmosphere and the powerful empire of the Hephthalites crumbled to dust. Their power was completely destroyed between 563–567 A.D. and the territory of the Turks soon extended up to Kapisa. A few years after this in 582 A.D. the Western Turks separated and established their autonomy under their own Khagan the descendant of the line of Istami.

Though many Buddhist countries had thus come under the sway of the Western Turks their Khagan does not seem to have taken at first much interest

* *The Buddhist India* (2 March 1928): 7–9.

in Buddhism. The first introduction of Buddhism does not seem to have taken place before the beginning of the next century. Hiuan Tsang passed through the Kingdom of the Western Turks in 630 A.D. and met with the great Khagan *She-hon* (yabghu) a place called *Bin-ghyul* ("Thousand springs") near Tashkend. The Khagan had transferred his head quarters there in 619 A.D. Hiuan Tsang was warmly received and entertained by the Khagan who invited him "to improve the occasion, whereupon the pilgrim expounded the doctrines of the *ten virtues*, compassion for animal life, and the Paramitas and emancipation. The Khagan raising his hands bowed and gladly believed and accepted the teaching". Through the kindness of the Khagan Hiuan Tsang was safely conducted across the vast territory of the Western Turks up to the valley of the Indus.

If Hiuan Tsang was received well by the *She-hon* Khagan and requested to expound the Buddhist doctrine to him the way was already prepared by an Indian monk of Nālandā shortly before 626 A.D. This is our famous Prabhākaramitra who was, in all probability, the first to have taught the Buddhist doctrine to *She-hon* Khagan.

The Chinese sources have preserved an account of Prabhākaramitra and his works. His name is faithfully transcribed by all these sources as *Po-lo-p'o-kia-lo-mi-to-lo*. He was also simply known as Prabhāmitra *Po-lo-p'o-mi-to-lo*. He was born in royal family of Ksatriya descent in Central India, (Madhyadesa). He left home, at the age of 10 years and studied under an able teacher. He at first studied the *Mahāyāna-Sútras*. On receiving *upasampada* he took to the study of *Vinayapitika* and applied himself to a strict observance of disciplinary rules. But he was by temperament meditative and liked the study of Buddhist metaphysics.

At the end of his study he went out to travel in different parts of India. Having travelled in South India he returned to his country and went to the monastery of *Na-lan-to* (Nālandā) in the kingdom of Magadha. There he met Silabhadra (*Kie-hien* in Chinese) who was lecturing on the Saptadasabhūmi Sāstra *(She-tsi-ti-louen)* at that time. Prabhākara attended these lectures, studied and collected information on the *Hīnayāna-Sāstras*.

Thus being possessed of a deep knowledge of both Hīnayāna and Mahāyāna Sāstras, he was appointed a teacher of Ahhidharma at Nālandā and soon won the admiration of all his companions and disciples. He had many disciples at Nālandā and some of them, Prajñāvarman, Indravarman and others were famous for their profound erudition. Prabhākara was admired not only by the people but also by the king of the Country.

As the Buddhist disciplinary rules do not permit a Śākyaputra, who have adopted the life of a monk, to live in one place for more than six months Prabhākara thought of leaving Nālandā. He heard that nobody had as yet preached the Law of Buddha amongst the barbarians of the north. As there were many to propagate the religion at home but nobody to go to foreign countries he left for the northern countries with 10 disciples, both monks and laymen. After travelling in different countries he reached the camp of Yabghu (*She-hou*),† the Khagan of the Western Turks. He taught him the Law of Buddha.

After a period of ten days he discovered in the barbarian sovereign a spirit of confidence and submission. Every day the Khagan sent for Prabhākara and his companions necessary food; every morning and evening he sent them offerings with respect: All of them received excellent treatment from the Turkish chief and found with joy in him an ever-increasing faith for Buddha and his religion.

In 620 A.D. the king of *Kao-p'ing* came from China, to the country of the barbarian hordes as ambassador. Prabhākara met him and taking this opportunity prepared himself for going to China. But the Khagan and his subjects would not let him go away. The king of *Kao-p'ing* therefore sent a note to the Emperor (of China) and the latter soon issued an official order inviting Prabhākara to come to the Capital of China. He arrived at the Capital with the king of *Kao-p'ing* towards the end of the same year (626 A.D.). At the request of the Emperor Prabhākara, was lodged in the monastery of *Hing-Shen* at the Captial.

The Emperor was soon attracted by the great abilities and profound learning of Prabhákara and began to entertain a great respect for him. In the 3rd month of the year 629 A.D. the Emperor requested him to translate Buddhist texts into Chinese. A Committee of 19 eminent monks was appointed to help him. There were two Indian monks known as Sangha (*Seng-Kīa*) and Gupta *Kiu-to* on the Committee and one of them served as interpreter.

The work of translation continued till the year 630 A.D. These translations won him great honour from the Chinese Buddhist scholars. But the Confucian literati soon got jealous of Prabhākara's influence. They began to poison the ear of the Emperor who gradually began to show indifference towards Prabhākara. Thus a little disappointed at the end of his life Prabhākara died in the Capital of China on the 6th day of the 4th month of the year 633 A.D. at the age of 69. His disciples erected a *Stūpa* to honour his memory.

Three Sanskrit Buddhist works were translated by Prabhākara and all the three are Mahāyāna works. The first work, translated in 620 A.D., and called *Ratnatārā-dhāranī-sūtra* (Nanjio 84), is only an extract from the *Mahāvaipulya-mahā-Sannipāta-Sūtra.* The second one, translated in 632 A.D. the *Prajñāpradipa-*

† The head quarters of the Khagan must have been situated somewhere in the region of *Bin-ghyal* north of Tashkend. It had been transferred there in 619 A.D.

sāstra-kārikā (Nanjio 1185) is a work of Āryadeva. It is a commentary on *Prajñāpradipa-sāstra*, attributed to the authorship of Nāgārjuna. The third one, translated in 630 A.D. and published in 633 A.D. is the famous philosophical treatise of Asanga – the *Mahāyānālamkāra-sāstra* otherwise known as *Sūtrālamkāra-sāstra.* The Sanskrit original has now been discovered from Nepal by Professor Sylvain Lévi. It has been edited and translated into French by him.

Chapter 12

POLITICAL RELATIONS BETWEEN BENGAL AND CHINA IN THE PATHAN PERIOD*

Sources of Information

Political relations between India and China practically come to a close with the end of the Buddhist period. There is no reference in the Chinese records to any exchange of ambassadors after the T'ang period. There is neither any mention of Indian missionaries going to China after the middle of the 11th century. There was however an attempt to resume political relations between the two countries in the Ming period but it succeeded only temporarily. The Chinese official records of this period reveal a complete ignorance of the former relations between the two countries. The records sometimes show that the Chinese writers had even forgotten the geography of India and considered parts of it as countries outside India.

There are a number of records on the exchange of embassies between Bengal and China during the first half of the 15th century. These records have a special interest in so far as they throw light from an unexpected quarter on the political, social and economic condition of Bengal in the 15th century. Two of these records had been formerly translated by Rockhill in *T'oung Pao*, 1915, pp. 436–444. There are however a few more which are more complete and precise than the former in certain respects. They have now been, translated with the help of my friend and colleague in the Visva-Bharati, Mr. Hsiao-ling Wu. I have thought it fit to publish these records here along with those previously translated by Rockhill which also have been partly revised. It would not have been possible to present these records without the kind collaboration of Mr. Wu. I therefore take this opportunity of expressing my gratefulness for the help he has rendered in this work.

---

* *Visva-Bharati Annals* 1 (1945): 96–134.

The records of which the translations are being published are the following:

1. *Ying yai sheng lan* which was compiled by Ma Huan between 1425 and 1432 A.D. It is a general account of Bengal without any reference to the king or the court. It was translated by Rockhill in *T'oung Pao*, 1915, pp. 436–440.
2. *Sing ch'a sheng lan*, compiled by Fei-sin in 1436 A.D. This is also a general account of Bengal with some information on the king and the court but the name of the king does not occur in it. It is an account of Hou-hien's visit to Bengal in 1415. It was also translated by Rockhill in *T'oung Pao*, 1915, pp. 440–444.
3. *Si yang ch'ao kung tien lu* compiled by Huang Sing-ts'eng in 1520 A.D. So far as the general account of Bengal goes it agrees with the second account. It contains in addition the name of the king and a reference to the various embassies sent by him to the Chinese court till 1438 A.D. A translation of this account was published in *J.R.A.S.*, 1895, pp. 529–33 by G. Phillips, but ours is an independent translation. A preliminary note was published by Prof. Sujitkumar Mukhopādhyāya and Mr. Hsiao-ling Wu in *Modern Review*, 1945, March, pp. 121–122.
4. *Shu yu chou tseu lu* compiled in 1574 by Yen Ts'ong-kien. This is the most complete of all accounts. It must have been based not only on the previous accounts but also on other sources not known to us at present. It has also a commentary from which some extracts have been translated by us. The edition used by us is the reprint of the only Ming edition published by the Palace Museum Peiping, 1930.
5. *Ming-she*, the official compilation was completed in 1739 but the materials are old. Its chapter on *Wai kuo chuan* was compiled by You T'ung (1618–1704). You T'ung was a poet and wrote poems on the foreign countries which may now be found in his complete work *Si t'ang tsiuan tsi*. There are two poems on Bengal but there is nothing new for us in them.

There are a few other records of the commercial intercourse between China and Bengal of the Yuan and Ming periods. Chao Ju-kua in his *Chu fan che* (translation by Hirth and Rockhill, p. 97) mentions the kingdom of *P'eng-kie-lo* as a country of the west. He says: "The city walls were 120 li circuit. The people of the country used white conch shells ground into shape as money. The native products include fine swords, *tu-lo* cotton stuffs and common cotton cloth". Hirth and Rockhill had some hesitation in identifying the country with Bengal and suggested that probably 'the kingdom of Balhara' was meant.[1] This was probably due to its being mentioned as a country in the west. But this must be understood in relation to China and not as Western India. The use of white, conch shells (cowrie) as money, the mention of the native products – specially *tu-lo mien* and also common cotton stuff, also point out to Bengal. It will be evident from texts translated below that Bengal was specially noted for these things.

There is however a little difficulty about the identification of the capital of Bengal as mentioned by Chao Ju-kua. The capital of Bengal is mentioned by him as the city of *Ch'a-na-ki* 茶那咭. Hirth and Rockhill did not suggest any identification. But I believe that the complete form of the name was [Pen]-ch'a-na-ki-[lo]（奔）茶那咭（羅）which has been either wrongly copied by the copyist or abbreviated. This name stands for Puṇḍanagara. The ancient transcriptions of the name have been discussed by Pelliot in *B.E.E.E.O.*, IV, p. 380. Puṇḍanagara of the later period was not however Puṇḍranagara or Puṇḍravardhana of earlier period of which the ruins have been discovered at Mahāsthān in the district of Bogra, but Pandua further to the north.

The next work which mentions Bengal is a compilation of Yuan period. It is the *Tao yi che leo* – "A Description of the Barbarians of the Isles". It was compiled by Wang Ta-yuan most probably in the winter of 1349–50 A.D.[2] The *Tao yi che leo* is more reliable than the *Chu fan che*. The author of the latter, Chao Ju-kua did not write from personal observations. He was the Customs Officer of Fu-kien and wrote from informations supplied by the foreign sailors and merchants. But Wang Ta-yuan visited many of the localities described by him for purposes of trade. Although it is not certain if he had come up to Bengal, his short description of the country is more precise than that of Chao Ju-kua. It has also been translated by Rockhill in *T'oung Pao*.[3] Wang Ta-yuan speaks of Bengal as a country of luxuriant fields which yield three crops a year, the people being highly industrious. He found the usages and customs of the people as pure and virtuous. His estimate of the people is noteworthy:

"These people owe all their tranquility and prosperity to themselves, for its source lies in their devotion to agriculture whereby a land originally covered with jungle has been reclaimed by their unremitting toil in tilling and planting. The seasons of Heaven have scattered the Wealth of the Earth over this kingdom the riches and integrity of its people surpass, perhaps, those of Ch'iu-chiang (Palembang) and equal those of Chao-wa (Java)".

About the Government and the economic products of Bengal the author says:

> "The government tax is two-tenths. The government casts a silver coin called a *t'ang-ka* (tangka) which weigh eight can-dareens (or eight hundredths of an ounce Chinese). In their dealings they use cowrie shells, 10.520 odd being exchanged for a small coin (*i.e.*, tangka). It is an extremely convenient currency for the people. The native products

comprise cotton stuffs (like our Chinese) *pi-pu*, *kao-ni-pu* and *tu-lo-kin* and also king-fisher's feathers. The goods used in trading are southern and northern silks, coloured taffetas, satins, cloves, nut-megs, blue and white, white China ware, white (yak hair ?) tassels, and the like".

We will see later on that this account of Bengal is amply confirmed by a number of other records of the Ming period.

Political Missions to Bengal

The Chinese texts of which translations are given below refer to exchange of embassies between China and Bengal as well as to a Chinese mission to the state of Jaunpur during the first half of 15th century. Bengal was then ruled by Pathan rulers independent of the Government at Delhi. The capital of Bengal was then Pandua in the district of Maldah.

A full account of the political missions is found in the *Si yang ch'ao kung tien lu* which was compiled in 1520 and the *Shu yu chou tseu lu* compiled in 1574. According to the first text the first mission was sent from Bengal by king Ngai-ya-sse-ting (Ghiyās-ud-din) in the 6th year yong-lo (1408 A.D.). It reached T'ai-ts'ang in Kiang-su with presents for the Emperor, the next year (1409). The next mission from Bengal reached China in the 12th year yong-lo (1414) and the third in the 3rd year cheng-t'ong (1438).

The second text gives some additional information on these missions. It says that the first mission from Bengal sent by Ghiyās-ud-din reached China in the 3rd year yong-lo (1405). The second mission went in 1408, the third in 1414 but it does not mention the last mission sent in 1438. The *Ming-she* throws some more light on these events.

The *Ming-she* says that since 1409 the Emperor Yong-lo initiated a policy of opening up relations with foreign countries. This probably occurred to the Emperor after the first two visits of the ambassadors of Bengal in 1405 and 1408. The *Ming-she* further says that since then ambassadors came from Bengal every year. It is not known whether they really came every year, but the text refers to a mission that was expected to arrive in 1412. It is said that in the 10th year yong-lo (1412) officials were sent to Chen-kiang for the reception of the ambassador of Bengal. The ambassador reached China with the news of the death of the king of Bengal. The name of the king however is not mentioned. Officials were then sent to Bengal to attend the coronation of the Prince Sai-wu-ting 賽勿丁. The *Ming-she* further adds that this new king sent a mission to China in the 12th year yong-lo (1414). It was probably on this account that in the 13th year yong-lo (1415) the Emperor ordered the eunuch Hou-hien to go to Bengal with presents for the king, queen and ministers of the country.

The route followed by Hou-hien to the capital of Bengal was the usual route of those days mentioned in other records as, well. He disembarked at the port of Cha-ti-kiang (Chittagong). Thence they went in small boats up to Suo-na-eul-kiang (Sonargaon) which was apparently the emporium of trade "where all goods were collected and distributed". The distance between Chittagong and Sonargaon is given in one source as 500 li and in another as 16 stages. From Sonargaon to Pandua, the capital, the route lay overland and the distance was 20 Stages. This gives the idea that the distance from Sonargaon to Pandua was greater than that from Chittagong to Sonargaon. This seems to be incorrect. One of the sources, the *Si yang ch'ao kung tien lu* mentions the distance between Chittagong and Sonargaon as 500 li and that between Sonargaon and Pandua as 35 li. This also is incorrect. The latter distance seems to have been 200 li.

From the account discussed above it is clear that ambassadors were sent from Bengal in 1405, 1408, 1409, 1412, 1414, 1438–39. The Chinese envoys were sent to Bengal for the first time soon after the Bengal mission of 1409. The second Chinese mission was sent soon after 1412, probably in 1413, to attend the coronation of the king of Bengal. The third mission was sent in 1415 and it was then that Hou-hien led the mission. On the first two occasions it was apparently the eunuch Cheng-ho who led the missions to Bengal. These were the third and fourth sailings of Cheng-ho to the west. Ma Huan, the compiler of the first account, the *Ying yai sheng lan,* came as his interpreter.

The biography of Cheng-ho in the *Ming-she* gives a complete account of his sailings. It is said that he sailed seven times at the Imperial order between 1405 and 1433. The dates of these sailings are given as follows:

(1) Yong-lo 3rd year to 5th year (1405–1407)
(2) „ 5th year to 7th year (1407–1409)
(3) „ 7th year to 9th year (1409–1411)
(4) „ 11th year to 13th year (1413–1415)
(5) „ 15th year to 17th year (1417–1419)
(6) „ 19th year to 20th year (1421–1422)
(7) Hiuan-to 6th year to 8th year (1431–1433)

Some of the dates given by Groeneveldt in his *Notes on Malay Archipelago* on the basis of the *Ming-she* and quoted by Rockhill[4] seem to be wrong. His information is stated to have been derived from the "Biography of Cheng-ho" in the *Ming-she* but the dates as given by him are: (1) 1405–1407, (2) 1408–1411, (3) 1412–1415, (4) 1417–1419, (5) 1421–1421, (6) 1424–1425, and (7) 1430 – date of return not known. We have stated above the dates as given in the said Biography.

"The Biography of Cheng-ho" mentions 36 or 37 countries which were visited by Cheng-ho during his various sailings. These include Peng-kola i.e. Bengal and another place in Northern India called Sha-li-wan-ni 沙里一泥 which cannot be identified. It may be a scribe's error for Sha-ni-p'u-ni 沙泥普泥. Admitting this correction it may be identified with Jaunpur which was then a powerful state in Bihar and which, we shall see later on, was visited by a Chinese ambassador who was in all likelihood Cheng-ho. Cheng-ho also visited other places in the south, specially Cochin, Kulam, Quilon, Coromondel coast, Cail, Cambay, Ceylon and Maladives.

The information supplied by the Biography of Cheng-ho in the *Ming-she* is also confirmed by an inscription left by Cheng-ho. This inscription was set up by him in 1431 in the port of Liu-kia at T'ai-ts'ang when he was starting on his last voyage. It is found in the *Wu tu wen suei siu tsi* 吳都文粹續集 edited by Ts'ien-ku of the Ming dynasty, chap. 26. The inscription is, entitled: "The Record of the events of communication with the barbarians (set up) in the T'ien-fei kong at the port of Liu-kia at T'ai-tsang" 劉家港天妃宮石刻通番事蹟記. The record states that it was set up by Cheng-ho in 1431 while starting on his 7th mission in the courtyard of the temple of T'ien-fei at Liu-kia. Cheng-ho had great veneration for this goddess and believed that it was due to her grace that he had successfully completed all his voyages. T'ien-fei is simply stated to be a "goddess of the waters" in the Dictionaries.[5] She might have been a goddess of the type of Manimekhalā worshipped in the South sea Islands and Southern India.[6]

The record further says that Cheng-ho's party consisted of two ambassadors, himself and Wang King-hong and four Vice-ambassadors Chu-liang, Chou-fu, Hong-pao and Yang-chen. The following dates of his voyages are given in the inscription:

(1) Yong-lo 3rd year to 5th year, (1405–1407).
(2) „ 5th year to 7th year, (1407–1409).
(3) „ 7th year to 9th year, (1409–1411).
(4) „ 12th year to 13th year, (1414–1415).
(5) „ 15th year (1417), date of return not given.
(6) „ 19th year (1421), date of return not given.
(7) Hiuan-to 5th year, (1430).

The last date is probably not correct as the inscription is dated 1431. He might have intended to start in the previous year but the voyage was evidently postponed for a year. The date of his last voyage as given in the *Ming-she* as 1431–1433 seems to be the correct date. All other dates mentioned in the inscription agree with those of the *Ming-she* except the initial year of his 4th voyage which is given here as 1414 but in the *Ming-she* as 1413.

Political Missions to Jaunpur

But Cheng-ho's inscription does not throw any light on his missions to Bengal. There is some additional information on the events of Bengal between 1415 and 1420 in the *Ming-she* under the notice on Jaunpur. The *Sing ch'a skeng tan* of Fei-sin refers to the country of *Chao-na-fu-eui* 紹納福兒 which was to the west of Bengal, the country of the Diamond Seat (Vajrāsana) where Buddha attained spiritual enlightenment. This is without any doubt the kingdom of Jaunpur which had come to be founded in 1393. Gayā, the place of Buddha's enlightenment was included in it. The *Ming-she* contains the following notices on Jaunpur.

(1) *Ming-she* (ch. 340, lie-chuan 196 – "the Biography of Hou-hien") – "In the 7th month of the 13th year yong-lo (1415) the Emperor wishing to communicate with Bengal and other countries, asked Hou-hien to go (to those countries) with a navy". That country (i.e. Bengal) is East India. It is very far from China. Their king Sai-fo-ting 賽佛丁 sent ambassador with a tribute of K'i-lin and many native products. The Emperor was much pleased. He presented more in return. To the west of Bengal there is a kingdom called Sse-na-p'u-eul 紹納樸兒 which is situated in the middle of the Five Indies. This is the ancient country of Buddha. The king of the country had invaded Bengal. Sai-fo-ting informed the Chinese court. In the 9th month of the 38th year yong-lo (1420) the Emperor ordered Hou-hien to go and pacify them. Gold and money were then presented (to the king of Sse-na-p'u-eul) and the war was stopped".

(2) *Ming-she* (chap 326): "Sse-na-p'u-eul (Jaunpur) – It is to the west of Bengal. It is also called Middle India. In ancient times it was the place of Buddha. In the 10th year of yong-lo (1412) an ambassador was sent to that kingdom with the Imperial mandate and gold embroidered silk and decorated clothes were presented to their king Yi-pu-la 亦不剌. In the 18th year young-lo (1420), the ambassador of Bengal informed (the Chinese court) that their king had invaded Bengal several times. Hou-hien was then sent with the orders of the Emperor to tell him (i.e. the king of Jaunpur) that by being good to a neighbour he could save his own. Presents of silk and money were given to him. Hou-hien then visited the Vajrāsana and made a gift to it. That kingdom is very far from China. So it did not send any present to China".

(3) *Siu-t'ong-tien,* chap. 140. It was compiled, in 1769. The information on Jaunpur given in it is exactly the same as the previous one of the *Ming-she,* ch. 326. Some of the spellings only are differently given. Jaunpur is written Sse-na-p'u-eul 沼納樸兒 and the name of the king as Ngo-pu-lo 額布勒.

These accounts clearly say that a Chinese ambassador was first sent in 1412 to the king of Jaunpur with presents with the hope of opening up diplomatic and commercial relations with him. This ambassador seems to have been Cheng-ho. This probably refers to his 4th sailing which was undertaken either in 1413 or in the year following. It is probable that the Imperial order was passed in 1412 but it was executed a year later. In 1415 the Emperor sent Hou-hien with a navy to communicate with Bengal and other countries. It is not known if he had gone up to Jaunpur at that time. Hou-hien was sent for the second time in the 9th month of 1420 to stop the war between Jaunpur and Bengal. The war was stopped by making a payment to the king of Jaunpur. The name of the king of Jaunpur is given as *Yi-pu-la* in one source and *Ngo-pu-lo* in another. Both the forms may be restored as "Ibra-" which certainly stands for Ibrahim or Ibrahim Sharqi of Jaunpur who was on the throne from 1402 to 1436. The ambassador of Bengal who went to China in 1420 reported that his country had been invaded several times by the king of Jaunpur. In fact Bengal was invaded several times between 1409 and 1414 by Ibrahim Sharqi and his attacks were directed against the Hindu regime set up by Raja Ganesh in Bengal during this period.[7]

Chronology of the Kings of Bengal

The political situation in Bengal in this period was very complicated and the chronology of kings so far worked out by scholars is far from certain. According to the *Cambridge History of India* (vol. III) it stands thus:

1. Ghiyās-ud-din Azam Shah–(1370–1396).
2. Saif-ud-din Hamza Shah–(1396–1406). (The son of Ghiyās-ud-din who was probably defeated by Ganesh in 1404 but continued to rule till 1406).
3. Shams-ud-din—(1406–1409). (A son or an adopted son of Saif-ud-din, as a puppet in the hands of Ganesh).
4. Shihāb-ud-din Bayazid Shah–(1409–1414). (His connection with Saifud-din and Shams-ud-din not known, a puppet in the hands of Ganesh).
5. Jalal-ud-din Muhammad Shah–(1414–1431). (The son of Ganesh who embraced Islam and ascended the throne in 1414 after the death of his father).
6. Shams-ud-din Ahmad Shah–(1431–1432) (The son of Jalal-ud-din).

But the Chinese accounts under consideration state the position in a different way altogether:

> 3rd year yong-lo (1405) – the king of Bengal was Ngai-ya-see-ting (Ghiyās-ud-din).
>
> 6th year yong-lo (1408) – the same king of Bengal.
>
> 10th year yong-lo (1412) – the news of the death of the king reaches China – officials sent to attend the coronation of the new king Sai-wu-ting.
>
> 13th year yong-lo (1414) – presents to China from the new king Sai-fo-ting.[8] Hou-hien sent in 1415 with presents to Bengal.
>
> 18th year young-lo (1420) – ambassador came from king Sai-fo-ting of Bengal for help against the attacks of Ibra(him), king of Jaunpur.

This shows that Ghiyās-ud-din was alive when the mission of Bengal started in 1408. This mission reached China in 1409. Who was the king of whom the death news was carried to China by the mission of 1412? The importance attached to the news by the Emperor of China leads us to think that the king was Ghiyās-ud-din.

The problem becomes more complicated when the question of the coronation of the new king comes in. The name of the new king is given in the *Ming-she* as Sai-wu-ting and in the 'Biography of Hou-hien' which also is incorporated in the *Ming-she* as Sai-fo-ting. There is no doubt that both the forms stand for the name of Saif-ud-din. The Mahomedan historians also tell us that Ghiyās-ud-din was succeeded by his son Saif-ud-din. According to one source this letter was on the throne for three years and seven months but according to another for 10 years.[9] In the latter case he must have been on the throne till 1421. This agrees well with the information in the Chinese record about his sending an envoy to China in 1420 for help against Jaunpur.

So the chronology according to the Chinese records stands thus: Ghiyās-ud-din died in 1411 and Saif-ud-din succeeded him. His official coronation took place either in 1412 or in 1413 and it was attended by Chinese officials. Saif-ud-din was still alive in 1420 when Hou-hien, the Chinese envoy came to help him against Ibrahim Sharqi of Jaunpur. Saif-ud-din might have been on the throne till 1421 if we believe that he ruled for 10 years.

But we get the name of an enigmatic ruler named Shihāb-ud-din Bayazid Shah who issued coins in his name from Hij. 812 (1409)[10] to Hij. 817 (1414). According to some sources it was only another name of Shams-ud-din, the son of Saif-ud-din, but this is not accepted by most of the authorities. This is also impossible according to the Chinese records which clearly say that Saif-ud-din who succeeded Ghiyās-ud-din in 1412–3 was still on the throne in 1420. Shihāb-ud-din Bayarid Shah therefore was issuing coins in his name during the latter part of the reign of Ghiyasud-din and the first part of the reign of Saif-ud-din.

Moreover the Mahomedan historians tell us that Jalal-ud-din Muhammad Shah, the son of Raja Ganesh, who had embraced Islam came to the throne in 1414 when Ganesh died. Jalal-ud-din issued coins in his own name from Hij. 818 (1415). Jalal-ud-din was on the throne till 1431 when his son Shams-ud-din Ahmad Shah succeeded. The latter ruled till 1442. This shows that Jalal-ud-din was also issuing coins, in his own name when Saif-ud-din was on the throne. The Chinese records along with the evidence of coins therefore raise a problem which can be solved only by supposing the existence of a dual government in his period:

Ghiyās-ud-din (died 1411) : Shihāb-ud-din (1409–14).

↓ ⋮

Saif-ud-din (1412–1421) : Jalal-ud-din (1414–1431).

What part did then Raja Ganesh play? He was at first a minister of Ghiyās-ud-din and then assumed the sole authority. He might nave been responsible for the death of Ghiyās-ud-din, but that is not certain. The Chinese records do not speak of any violent death of the king. Saif-uddin's succession was also peaceful. Ganesh was in power till his death in 1414. A suggestion was made by some scholars that it was probably Raja Ganesh who had assumed the Mahomedan name of Shihāb-ud-din Bayazid Shah in order to please the Mahomedans. His son's acceptance of Islam was only one step further. The suggestion perfectly agrees with the order of things. Ganesh rose to power in 1409 during the latter part of the reign of Ghiyās-ud-din and died in 1414 when Saif-ud-din had been on throne only for two or three years. Ghiyās-ud-din evidently became a puppet in the hands of Ganesh in his last years, and the *de facto* ruler of the country was Raja Ganesh *alias* Shihāb-ud-din Bayazid Shah.[11] Saif-ud-din was similarly a puppet first in the hands of Raja Ganesh and subsequently in the hands of his son Jalal-ud-din. It is difficult to say if Jalal-ud-din became the sole ruler of the country in 1421 after the death of Saif-ud-din or allowed the latter's son or adopted son who is also called Shams-ud-din to rule for a few years more as a puppet. The repeated attacks of Ibrahim Sharqi were not directed so much against Ghiyās-ud-din and Saif-ud-din as against Ganesh (*alias* Shihāb-ud-din) and his son Jalal-ud-din who had become the real rulers of the land. The Mahomedan historians tell us that Ibrahim Sharqi was specially requested by Qutb-ul-'Alam, a Mahomedan saint of Bengal, to intervene in favour of the Mahomedans.

We are further told that Ganesh got out of this difficulty by allowing his son to be converted by Qutb. His assumption of a Mahomedan name might have also been to pacify the Mahomedan subjects. The Chinese money, as the *Ming-she* tells us, might have also succeeded in pacifying Ibrahim Sharqi for the time being.[12]

The Chinese envoys had no chance of knowing the real situation in Bengal. Ghiyās-ud-din and his successors were certainly presented to them as the *de jure* rulers of Bengal on such ceremonial occasions as the reception of foreign ambassadors. This practice is not unknown in some states in modern times. The Hindu predominance in the court is also suggested by the oldest Chinese account of the official banquet given in honour of the Chinese ambassador at Pandua. It is said: "(At the banquet) eating beef or mutton was forbidden nor could they drink for fear of trouble and because it is a breach of decorum, but they drank sweetened rose water".[13] This does not look like a Mahomedan banquet. Why should beef and mutton be forbidden in a truly Mahomedan banquet? Evidently Raja Ganesh had so much power that he was able to decide how the court should behave in a Hindu country on ceremonial occasions. He himself had made similar concessions to the Mahomedans of the country by his avowed leanings towards Islam. Had we possessed a true account of this period we would have probably found that a fusion of the two powers, Hindu and Mahomedan, into a harmonious one had taken place in the country and that it was a deliberate act on the part of Ghiyās-ud-din and Raja Ganesh. There was probably no question of usurpation of power by the latter. All accounts agree in saying that Ganesh rose to power between 1405 and 1409. Curiously enough this was the period when ambassadors from Bengal began to be sent to China. The initiative was taken by the court of Bengal. Their visits to China were made almost annually till 1414 when Ganesh died.

After that date ambassadors were sent only twice, once in 1420 and another time in 1138–39. The line of Raja Ganesh became extinct in 1442 and since then there was no attempt to resume relations with China. It therefore appears that the new foreign policy was decided upon by Ganesh and was pursued so long as his successors were in power. The rival state of Jaunpur had become powerful and the Sultanate of Delhi, however weak it might have been, was always looking on Bengal as a rebel province. There was necessarily an anxiety in the mind of Ganesh who was responsible for the new Hindu-Moslem regime in Bengal to secure assistance if possible from China, against any possible aggression either by the Sultans of Delhi or by the Sharqis of Jaunpur. In fact this help was asked for at least once in 1420 against the repeated attacks of Ibrahim Sharqi who had dislike for the new regime.

Social and Economic Condition

The Chinese records discussed here throw some light, however meagre that might be, on the social and economic condition of Bengal in the 15th century. The population was divided into two groups, Moslem and Hindu (Yin-tu). The customs of the two were different. About the Hindus it is said that they did not eat beef and that the women and men did not eat at the same place. It is also said: "When the husband dies the wife does not marry again nor the husband marry again when the wife dies". Unless we believe that the Chinese envoys were misinformed this piece of information is of very great importance for the study of the social history of Bengal of the earlier period. It shows that polygamy was still unknown amongst the Hindus of at least the metropolitan districts of Bengal in the 15th century. We are further told that the people were so generous as not to allow the destitutes of one village to seek food in another village. It was a duty of the co-villagers to maintain their own destitutes. The standard of honesty was very high as it is said that in business even involving such a big price as ten thousand piece of gold when one enters into a contract he respects it.

The language in universal use was P'eng-kie-li, i.e., Bengali, Persian was also in use most probably among the nobles. About the dress of the men we are told that they wore a white cotton turban and on their bodies long gown with a round collar and held around them by an embroidered sash. They also used leather slippers. This was evidently the dress of the rich people of the country whether Hindu or Muslim. The use of caps was reserved for the king and the Muslim nobles of the court. About the dress of the women it is said that they wore a short shirt, and wrapped around them a piece of cotton, silk or brocade. This was evidently the dress of the Muslim women of noble families. The ornaments in use were usually earrings of precious stones set in gold, pendants for the neck, bracelets for the wrists and ankles, and rings for the fingers and the toes.

Among the people were found various professional classes such as geomancers, physicians, diviners, artisans skilled in different branches of work, singers and dancers. There were also professional musical parties who used to go to the houses of nobles every morning to play on musical instruments specially the *sanai.* The custom of entertaining the guests with songs by dancing girls was already in vogue among the rich people. Tiger play was also a popular show among the public.

The country was rich and prosperous. We have already seen what Wang Ta-yuan, a writer of the 14th century writes about Bengal. He says: "The seasons of Heaven have scattered the wealth of the Earth over this kingdom, the riches and integrity of its people surpass, perhaps those of Palembang and equal those of Java". All accounts say that the soil was fertile and that it produced in abundance. The land used to yield usually two crops a year. There was no need of artificial irrigation and the crops grew by themselves in the proper season. Both men and women were diligent in works of the field. In seasons other than the sowing seasons, the people, were used to spinning and weaving. Among the agricultural products of Bengal the Chinese specially mention – rice which ripens twice a year, two kinds of millet, sesamum, beans, ginger, mustard, onions, garlic, cucumber, melons and brinjal. Among other native products the Chinese mention coral, pearls, crystals, cornelians and peacock feathers. The common fruits were banana, jack fruit, sour pomegranate and cocoa-nut. sugar-cane, sugar, honey, butter and ghee were also much in use.

The Chinese speak of the various industries of Bengal, paper, lacquer, sugar, cotton and silk. Paper used to be made from the mulberry tree. In one account it is said that the Bengal paper was white and that it used to be made out from the bark of a tree. It is probably the same tree that is meant. The paper was as smooth and glossy as the deer skin. The most important industry was however the cotton industry and the Chinese accounts mention a number of cotton fabrics of Bengal, all of which however cannot be identified. They mention six kinds of cotton stuff produced in Bengal:

(i) One kind is called *pi-pu* 篳布 or *pi-po* 篳泊 – it was of several colours. It was a cotton stuff which was according to one account over three feet broad and fifty-six feet long, and according to another over two feet broad and fifty-six feet long. It was fine and glossy like painted stuffs. It was identified with the stuff called betteela by Ibn Batuta,[14] but *pi-pu* could not have been the transcription of that name. *Pi-pu* would be in Cantonese *pat-pou* and this suggests a name like *bafta* which was in fact a general Persian name of cotton stuffs.

(ii) *Man-che-t'i* 滿者提 – it was a yellow cotton stuff, four feet broad and over fifty feet long. It was very closely woven and strong. The original of this name again is uncertain. The latter part of the name looks like *chite*. Tavernier mentions it as a painted cotton cloth which was also known as *calmendar (kalamdar)*.

(iii) *Sha-na-pa-fu* 沙納巴付 which was a stuff five feet broad and thirty feet long. It has been identified with Persian *Shanbaft* which is the name of cotton gauze. The identification may be taken as correct.

(iv) *K'i-pai-lei-ta-li*祈車白勒搭黎; this name occurs under various forms such as *K'i-pai-tung-ta-li* 祈白動搭黎 *K'i-pai-k'in-ta-li* 祈白勤搭黎, *Che-chu-hei ta-li* 者珠黑答立 etc. The correct form of the name seems to be *K'i-pai-k'in-ta-li*. Although it is difficult to say what is exactly meant by *Ki-pai* the latter part of the name *k'in-ta-li* evidently stands for *chanter* (Beng. chādar). The Chinese accounts give the measurement of these sheets as trove feet broad and sixty feet long. It is said that this stuff was a loosely woven and coarse one and was a cotton gauze.

(v) *Sha-ta-eul* 沙褟兒 was a stuff used for turbans. Its measurement is given in one source as 5 inches broad and 40 feet long and in another as 21/2 feet broad and 4 feet long. It is difficult to say which one is the correct one. The first measurement has the chance of being the correct one as for turbans usually very long pieces are needed. The original of the name is not known. It looks like chādar.

(vi) *Ma-hei-ma-lei* 馬黑馬勒 was a stuff four feet broad and twenty feet long. On the wrong side it was covered with a nap half an inch long. The Chinese say that it is the same as *tu-lo-kin* 禿羅錦 (var. *mien*). It is no doubt the same as the Malmal. *Tu-lo-mien* is described in the Buddhist texts as a very soft cotton stuff. In fact Malmal was also a stuff of the same quality. Tu-lo is a transcription of Sanskrit *tula*, cotton. *Tu-lo-mien* simply meant a fine cotton stuff.

Of other fabrics in use in Bengal the Chinese accounts mention silk, embroidered silk handkerchiefs, brocaded taffetas *sa-ha-la* 撒哈剌 i.e. shawl, etc.

The Chinese accounts tell us that the people had a big trade. The market place in the capital was full of different types of shops where all sorts of things were available. The Chinese trade with Bengal consisted of gold, silver, satins, silk, blue and white porcelain, copper, iron, vermillion, quick-silver and grass mats.

The Chinese visitors describe the people of Bengal as very generous and courteous and say: "To conclude, Bengal is rich and civilised. To our ambassador they presented gold basins, gold girdles, gold flagons, and gold bowls and to our vice-ambassador the same articles in silver. To our officials of the ministry of foreign affairs they presented golden bells and long gowns of white hemp and silk. Our soldiers got silver coins. If they had not been rich – how could they do it in such an extravagant way?"

A Note on K'i-lin

In some of the texts translated here, there is reference to an animal called K'i-lin which was presented to the Emperor by the king of Bengal. This was an animal not known in China and it aroused an unforeseen curiosity among the Chinese on its arrival. Hence a proposal was made by the officials to congratulate the Emperor formally on this occasion. Poems were written on K'i-lin. The commentary of the *Shu yu chou tseu lu* says that K'i-lin was presented by the Bengal court four times in the young-lo period. It further tells us that in the 7th year ch'eng-hua (1471 A.D.) a K'i-lin was born at Chang-to. It looked like a tiger and had the tail and hoofs of a cow. The people killed it.

In the 4th month of the 6th year kia-tsing (1525 A.D.) another was born at Wu-yang. It is not clear if these accounts have been mixed up with fables. But the K'i-lin presented by the king of Bengal was an African giraffe.

I. Ying Yai sheng lan

"The country is extensive, the population dense, the wealth and property abundant and great. Travelling by sea from Su-men-ta-la (Sumatra) and an island (i.e. the Mao-shan, Pu-lo-weh) and the Tsui-lan islands (Nicobars) are sighted, (whence) going northwestward for twenty li (sic. days) one arrives at Che-ti-kiang (Chittagong). Here one changes to a small boat and after going five hundred and odd li one comes to So-na-eul-kiang (Sonargaon) whence one reaches the capital. It has walls and suburbs; the king's palace and the large and small palaces of the nobility and temples, are all in the city. They are Musalmans.

The customs are pure and honest. The men and women are all black coloured, white ones are rare. All the men tie up (or cut off 祝) their hair and wear a white cotton turban and on their bodies a long gown with a round collar and held around them by an embroidered sash. On their feet they wear leather slippers.

The king and his highest officers follow in their caps and clothing the Muslim style. They are very clean and neat. The language in universal use is P'ang-kie-li (Bengali); there are also those who speak in Pa-eul-si (Farsi = Persian).

In trade they use a silver coin called Tangka, weighing three candareens, an inch and two-tenths in diameter and with writing on either side. With it they settle the price of goods according to weight. They have also sea-shells called k'ao-li (cowrie).

Their marriages and funerals are both according to the Muslim religion.

The climate is constantly as hot as in summer.

Their punishments include beating with heavy bamboo and banishment.

Their officials have seals and communicate by dispatches. Their army has pay and rations. The commander of the army is called *Pa-sse-la-eul*[15] 吧斯剌兒 (sipāh-sālār).

There are geomancers, physicians, diviners, all kinds of artisans skilled in every branch of work. There are people who wear a shirt with black and white patterns and held by a scarf with a fringe round their waists of coral and amber, coloured beads and with bracelets of beads fastened on their wrists. They are good singers and dancers to enliven drinking and feasting.

There are people called *Ken-siao-su-lu-nai* 根肖速魯奈 who are mountebanks. Every day at the stroke of five they come around the gates of the houses of high officials and of the wealthy people blowing *so-nai*[16] (*Surnā*-flageolets) and beating drums and then pass on to another. When comes the breakfast hour they go to each house to be rewarded with wine, food, money or other things. Besides these are also every other kind of players.

(Thus there are people who) go about the market places and to the homes with a tiger held by an iron chain. They undo the chain, and the tiger lies down in the courtyard. The naked man then strikes the tiger who becomes enraged and jumps at him and he falls with the tiger. This he does several times, after which he thrusts his fist in the tiger's throat without wounding him. After this performance he chains him up again and the people of the house do not fail to feed the tiger with meat and reward the man with money. So the tiger tamer has a promising business.

Their almanac has twelve months, without any intercalary ones. The native products are red millet, sesamum, beans, glutinous millets, and rice which ripens twice a year. The vegetables comprise ginger, mustard, onions, garlic, cucumbers and egg-plant. They have spirits made from cocoanut, from the nut of a tree and *kajang*[17] wine Betel-nuts take the place of tea (as with us in China).

The domestic animals comprise the camel, horse, mule, water buffalo, cattle, the marine goat, fowls, ducks, pigs, geese, dogs and arid cats.

Their fruits are the banana, the jack fruit, sour pomegranate, sugar-cane, suger and honey.

Of cotton fabrics they have *pi-pu* of several colours; it is called *pi-po* and it is over three feet broad and fifty-seven feet long. It is as fine and as glossy as if pointed. There is a ginger-yellow cotton stuff called *man-che-ti* which is four feet broad and over fifty feet long; it is very closely woven and strong. What is called *sha-na-pa-fu* is five feet broad and thirty feet long: it is like *sheng-lo* 生羅 (pongee) and is a *pu-lo* (? *tu-lo* cotton gauze). What is called *k'i-pai-lei-ta-li* is three feet broad and sixty feet long. (This) cloth is loosely woven and coarse: it is a cotton gauze.

The stuff for turbans is called *Sha-ta-eul (Chādar)*; it is five inches broad and forty feet long and is like our *san-so* 三梭. *Ma-hei-ma-lei* is a stuff four feet broad and twenty-feet long; on the wrong side it is covered with nap half an inch long; it is *tu-lo-kin*. They weave with silk, embroidered silk handkerchiefs. They have also brocaded taffetas. Their paper is white; it is made out with the bark of a tree and is as smooth and glossy as deers' skin.

Their household implements include lacquered cups and bowls, steel guns and scissors.

II. Sing ch'a sheng lan

"This country can be reached from Sumatra with a favourable wind in twenty days. This is a country in India of the West.[18] On the West, Bengal confines on the kingdom of the Vajrāsana called Chao-na-fu-eul[19] 詔納福爾 which is the place where Śākya attained spiritual wisdom. In the 13th year *yong-lo* (1415 A.D.) under the imperial orders twice issued the eunuch Hou-hien and others went with a fleet to present in his names presents to the king, his consort and chiefs.

The country has a sea-port on a bay called Ch'a-ti-kiang (Chittagong). Here certain duties are collected. When the king heard that our ships had arrived there, he sent high officers to offer robes and other presents, and over a thousand men and horses also came to the port. After "going 16 stages, we reached Suo-na-eul-kiang (Sonargaon) 'which is a walled place with tanks, streets, bazars and which carries on a business in all kinds of goods. Here servants of the king met us with elephants and horses. Going thence twenty stages we came to Pan-tu-wa[20] (Pandua) which is the place of residence of the ruler. The city walls are very imposing, the bazars well arranged, the shops side by side, the pillars in orderly rows, they are full of every kind of goods.

The dwelling of the king is all of bricks set in mortar, the flight of steps leading up to it is high and broad. The halls are flat-roofed and white-washed inside. The inner doors are of triple thickness and of nine panels. In the audience hall the pillars are plated with brass, ornamented with figures of flowers and animals, carved and polished. To the right and left are long verandahs on which were drawn up (on the occasion of our audience) over a thousand men in shining armour, and on horseback outside, filling the courtyard, were long ranks of (our) Chinese (soldiers) in shining helmets and coats of mail, with spears, swords, bows and arrows, looking martial and lusty. To the right and the left of the king were hundreds of peacock feather umbrellas and before the hall were some hundreds of soldiers mounted on elephants. The king sat cross-legged in the principal hall on a high throne inlaid with precious stones and a two-edged sword lay across his lap.

Two men bearing silver staffs and with turbaned heads came to usher (us) in. When we had taken five steps forward they made salutation. On reaching the middle of the hall they halted and two other men with gold staffs led us with some ceremony as previously. The king having returned our salutations kotowed before the Imperial Mandate, raised it to his head, then opened and read it. The imperial gifts were all spread out on carpets in the audience ball.

The king entertained the imperial envoys at a banquet and our soldiers were given many presents. (At the banquet to the envoys) eating beef or mutton was forbidden, nor could they drink wine for fear of trouble and because it is breach of decorum, but they drank sweetened rose-water (sherbet). When the banquet was over, (the king) bestowed on the envoys gold basins, gold girdles, gold flagons and gold bowls, all Assistant Envoys receiving the same articles in silver and each of the lower officials a golden bell and a long gown of white hemp and silk. All the soldiers (of the escort) got silver money. Of a truth this country is rich and courteous. After this (the king) had made a case (lit. tube) in gold in which he placed a Memorial to the Emperor, written on a leaf of gold and the envoys received it from him with due respect in the audience hall, together with various gifts to the Emperor.

The people of this country are most generous in character. The men wear a white cotton turban and a long white cotton shirt. On their feet they wear low sheep-skin shoes with gold thread. The smarter ones think it a correct thing to have designs on them. Every one of them is engaged in business, the value of which may be ten thousand pieces of gold, but when a bargain has been struck, they never express regret.

The women wear a short shirt, wrap around them a piece of cotton, silk or brocade. They do not use cosmetics, for they have naturally a white complexion; in their ears they wear ear-rings of precious stones set in gold. Around their necks they hang pendants, and they do up their hair in knot behind. On their wrists and ankles are gold bracelets and on their fingers and toes rings.

There is a clan of people called Yin-tu (Hindu) who do not eat beef, and the men and the women do not eat in the same place. When the husband dies, the wife does not marry again, nor does the husband marry again when the wife dies. If there are any very poor among them and with no means of support, the various families of the village will, in turn support them, but they are not allowed to seek their food in other villages. So (the people) are praised for their broad public spirit.

The soil is fertile and produces in abundance, for they have two crops every year. They do not weed on hoe their fields but men and women work in the fields or weave according to season.

Among their fruits they have the *po-lo-mi*[21] (jack fruit) which is as big as a bushel measure and wonderfully sweet; also the mango (*a-mo-lo*), though it has a sour flavour it is very nice. For the rest they have fruits and vegetables, cattle, horses, fowls, sheep, ducks and sea-fish. In their very extensive trade they use cowrie shells instead of coin.

The natural products are fine cotton cloths (muslins), sa-ha-la, rugs, to-lo-kin, cotton stuffs, rock-crystal, agate, amber, pearls, precious stones, sugar, ghee, king-fishers' feathers, and veils of sundry colours to veil the face.

The goods (used by the Chinese in trading here) are gold, silver, satins, silks, blue and white procelain, copper, iron, musk, vermillion, quick-silver and grass mats".

III. Si yang ch'ao kung tien lu

This country is to the north of the Nicobar islands at a distance of about 7000 li. It is called Eastern India. It is a thousand li square. Starting from Sumatra and going by Mao-shan and Tsui-ian (Nicobar) in a North-Westerly direction with a favourable wind one reaches Chittagong in 20 days. It is also known as the port of Ch'a-ti-kiang (Chittagong). After reembarking in small boats and travelling about 500 li one comes to Suo-na-eul-kong (Sonargaon). It has city walls, tanks, streets and markets. Again starting from there and travelling for 20 li one reaches Pandua which is the capital. Both the suburbs and the city itself are large and elegant. The king has a very big palace which is flat roofed and white-washed. The inner doors are of triple thickness and of nine panels. All the pillars of the palace are ornamented in brass with figures of flowers and animals, carved and polished. Both the king and his officials follow the Mahomedan style in their turbans and dress. They all are Mahomedans and observe also the Mahomedan marriage and burial customs. The people of Bengal are good tempered, rich and honest. They are famous in commerce. All men cut off their hairs and wrap their head with a cotton turban of white colour. They wear long gowns with a round collar with a coloured sash on the lower part of their body, and put on leather slippers on their feet. The women dress their hairs in knot on their heads. They wear a short shirt and wrap their body with a piece of coloured cloth, silk or brocade. They wear ear-rings of precious stones set in gold. Around their necks they have pendants, on their wrists and ankle gold bracelets and on their fingers and toes rings.

The climate in that country is always hot. Their almanac has twelve months without any intercalary month. The heaviest punishment is limited to banishment only. All officials have seals and communicate by despatches. The commander of the troop is called Sipāh-sālar. There are in the country physicians, astrologers, diviners and all kinds of artisans who are skillful in hundreds of crafts. They gather in the market and hold different shops there. Their language is Bengali but they are experts also in Persian. There is a class of musician called *Ken-siao-su-lu-nai.* They go to the houses of the wealthy people and the high officials and always play their musical instruments every morning. One beats a small drum, another big one and the third blows a *pi-li* (flageolet). Their music begins in a low and slow tone but ends swiftly and in a high pitch. When they finish their musical performance the hosts reward them with wine, food and *taṅgka.*

They use betel nuts to entertain their visitors but when they invite guests to a formal feast there is dancing and songs by actresses and dancing girls for the amusement of the guests. The actresses wear lined cloth in light red colour with decorations of flowers. They wrap the lower part of their body with coloured silken sash. They hang pendants and necklaces of either five coloured precious stones or coral or amber on both the neck and the shoulders and blue and red precious stones on their wrists.

Tiger play is much appreciated by the public. A man drags a tiger held by an iron chain and walks along the street. While the play begins the man loosens the chain and the tiger lies down on the ground. The man is naked. He strikes the tiger which becomes enraged and jumps at him. He then falls on the ground and fights with the tiger several times. After which he thrusts his hands into the tiger's mouth without wounding it. When the play ends the tiger lies down on ground again. The people then feed the tiger with flesh and give tangka to the man.

In trade they use either a silver coin which is called tangka or sea shells which are called cowrie. Their main industry is the manufacture of cloth. Their soil is very fertile and can produce every kind of crops. There are two crops a year. Besides, the country is good for feeding all kinds of catties and domestic animals. Their silver coins weigh 3/10 of a tael official weight, and are one inch and 2/10 in diameter with designs on the obverse. The cowries are taken by weight.

There are four kinds of wine, one is made from cocoanut, one is made from rice, another is made from the acquatic plant *kajang* and the last one from *t'ung* seeds. They manufacture six kinds of cloth: one kind of cotton stuff is called pi-pu. It is over two feet broad and 56 feet long. It is fine and white. There is a yellow cotton stuff called man-che-t'i which is four feet broad and 50 feet long. It is very closely woven and is strong. Cotton gauze is called *shanbaft*. It is five feet broad and 30 feet long. It is like pongee. Another kind of gauze is called *ki-pai-kin-ta-li* which is 3 feet broad and 60 feet long. It is used as turbans for the head. Another kind of cloth which is like our san-so and 24 feet broad and 4 feet long is called *sa-ta-eul*. The malmal is a stuff 4 feet broad and 20 feet long. On the wrong side it is covered with a nap 1/2 inch long. It is our *tu-lo-kin*. The native products are coral, pearls, crystals, cornelians and peacock feathers. As regards fruits they have banana, jack-fruit, pomegranates, sour prunes, sugarcane etc. There are much butter, ghee, and honey. There are different kinds of melons, onion, ginger, custard, brinjal and garlic. They have camels. Paper is made of mulberry tree. There is a tree which bears slender branches and green leaves. It blossoms in the morning and fades at night, similar to our *ye-ho* 夜合(magnolia pumila). Its fruit resembles our plums 李. It is called *an-mo-lo* (āmalaka). It is also called *yu-kan*[22] 餘甘 (lit. sweet remainder). It can cure the poison of cinnabar 丹 and stone 石.

When the king of Bengal receives the mandate of the Emperor of China there are long rows of over a thousand soldiers in shining armours, riding on horses in the right and the left verandahs of the palace. Besides there are warriors in bright helmets and armours with swords, bows and arrows in their hands, standing there as guards, looking martial and lusty. There are hundred men holding umbrellas of peacock feathers in the courtyard and hundred men mounting on elephants in the principal hall. The king sits on a high throne inlaid with eight kinds of precious stones and a two edged sword lies across his lap. Two officials bearing silver staffs come to lead the Chinese ambassador, at every five steps they make a salute and stop in the midway. Again two other officials with gold staffs come forward and lead the ambassador with the same ceremony as before. The king politely and reverently receives the imperial mandate and salutes by placing his hands on his forehead. When the reading of the imperial mandate and the list of presents end, carpets are spread on the floor and the king entertains the Chinese mission with a feast of both smoked and roasted beef and mutton, rose water and sweetened water of different kinds of perfumes.

Their tributes are not regular. In the 6th year yong-lo (1408) king Ngai-ya-sse-ting (Ghiyās-ud-din) sent ambassador with tribute. The ambassador reached T'ai-ts'ang in the 9th year yong-lo (1411). An official of the ministry of foreign affairs was sent there to receive him. In the 12th year yong-lo (1414) an ambassador named Pa-yi-tsi[23] (*Bayazid*) was sent to China with a tribute of k'i-lin and other things. Another ambassador was sent in the 3rd year cheng-t'-ong (1438) with the same tributes as sent on the previous occasion. The letter which was written by the king of Bengal was written on golden leaf. Their tributes consisted of horses, saddles, ornaments in gold and silver, gold engravings, leou-li vases, white porcelain with blue decoration, *sa-ha-la* (shawl), *cho-fu-he-ita-li* cloth, *tu-lo-kin*, crystallised sugar, skull of buceros, unicorn's horn, peacock feathers, parrots, frankincense, raw gharu wood (aguru), guggula, khadira, purple glue, dragon's blood incense (*karpūra*), ebony, sapan and pepper.

To conclude Bengal is rich and civilised. To our ambassador they presented gold basins, gold girdles, gold flagons, and gold bowls and to our vice-ambassador the same articles in silver. To our officials of the ministry of foreign affairs they presented golden bells and long gowns of white hemp and silk. Our soldiers got silver coins. If they had not been rich how could they do it in such an extravagant way?

IV. Shu yu chou tseu lu

Bengal is the ancient province of Sin-tu (India). It is India of the west. India has five Yin-tu (Indies). This is the Eastern Yin-tu country. This is also called the country of Si yin-tu (India of the west). This is the place where Śākya-(muni) attained enlightenment. Tsa-ti-kiang (Cātigāon) is at the mouth of the sea. Merchants from foreign countries come from outside and anchor there. They assemble and divide the profits of their merchandise at this place. During the reign of Ming-ti of the Han dynasty the religion of Buddha came to this country (China).[24] The custom in India is to burn the dead body on the pyre which is called *ch'a-pi* 茶毗 (*t'u-pi – stūpa*). This custom is prevalent even now. The disciples of Buddha also follow this custom. The ordinary people of China also imitate this and their dead bodies.

In the 3rd year yong-lo (1405 A.D.) of the present Ming dynasty Ngai-ya-sse-ting (Ghiyās-ud-din), the king of this country (i.e. Bengal) sent an ambassador to the Imperial court. The emperor ordered for the presentation of four sheets of each[25] (of the four varieties of silk): *chu*, *sse*, *sha*, and *lo*, eight sheets of *ch'uan* to the king, and three sheets of *chu*, *see*, *sha* and *lo* and six sheets of ch'uan to the queen. He ordered an ambassador to go to India and to invite some Buddhist monk. A Buddhist monk came to the capital.[26] His name was Mahāratna Dharmaraja 大寶法王. He stayed in the Ling-ku-sse. He had miraculous powers called *ṛddhi* 神通. He taught the people to recite *oṁ maṇi padme huṅ*-(Ch. *yang mo ni pa mi hung*). Then all those who believed in him began to recite it day and night. Then Li Ki-ting, a scholar of the Han-lin Academy said: "If he really possesses spiritual power, he ought to know the Chinese language. Why does he take the help of an interpreter to communicate? Besides what he says, the so-called *oṁ maṇi padme huṅ* simply means 'I have cheated you' – *Yang-pa-ni-hung*[27] 把你哄. People don't understand it".

In the 6th year yong-lo (1408 A.D.) the king of the count (i. e. Bengal) sent an ambassador who landed at T'ai-ts'ang anc brought tributes. The emperor ordered the minister of foreign affairs to go there and receive him.

In the 12th year yong-lo (1414) the king again sent his minister Pa-yitsi with tribute of K'i-lin and other objects. The Minister of the Rites handed a memorial of congratulation to the Emperor. The Emperor said in reply: "You only help me day and night in the administration of the affairs and the country is benefited by it. If the country is benefited it does not matter if there is K'i-lin or not. There is no need of congratulation". The Emperor presented to the king four pieces of kin 錦 and 60 pieces of ling 綾. The officers also were given presents befitting their ranks.

In the 13th year yong-lo (1115) the Emperor ordered the eunuch Hou-hien and others to carry his presents to the king, the queen and the ministers (of Bengal) in a ship accompanied by troops. When their king heard that our precious boat had reached their country, he sent the district officials with clothes and other presents with thousands of troops to welcome them. They landed at the harbour of Ch'a-ti (Cātigāon). Starting from there they reached Suo-na-eul-kiang (Sonargaon) after 16 stations. There are city, tanks, streets and markets. All goods are collected there and distributed. (The king of Bengal) again sent men to carry presents with elephants and horses for the reception. After twenty stations they reached Pan-tu-wa (Pandua). It is the capital of the king. Both the city and its outskirts are all decorated. There are streets, markets and innumerable shops. Hundred kinds of goods are collected there. The palace of the king is made of bricks and limes. The building is high and broad. The roof the palace is flat and polished in white. There are three inner gates and nine inner courtyards. The pillars are moulded in brass, with decorations of flowers, beasts and animals. There are long verandahs on the right and the left. In the verandah there were thousands of armoured horsemen. Outside there were giant-like men in bright helmets and armours holding swords, bows and armours. They had an appearance of grandeur. To the right and the left of the platform there were hundreds of fans of peacock feathers. Again in the front of the courtyard there are rows of hundreds of elephants. The king was on a high seat, decorated with eight precious things, sitting cross-legged. His sword was placed on his lap. Then he ordered two men holding silver sticks and in turbans to show the way. While advancing they saluted at every fifth step. They stopped on reaching the middle. Then two men came with golden sticks and received them as before. The king saluted by placing hands on the forehead and received the mandate. It was opened, read and handed over to the king. The king received it. Then woolen carpets were spread on the courtyard where our ambassador and troops were entertained. It was very ceremonious. They offered roasted beef and mutton but there is prohibition of drinking wine as it changes our nature. They offered instead water mixed with rose juice and honey for drink. When the feast was over, helmets, belts, vases and golden pots were presented to the ambassador. The Vice-ambassador was presented with helmet, belt, vase and pot in silver. The officers of lower ranks were presented with golden bells and long gowns of *jen*, *chu* and *sse*. All the soldiers were given silver coins. The country is rich and generous. Then the king with his own hands put his letter written on golden leaf in a golden casket and sent an ambassador with products of the country as present to the emperor. Since then ambassadors came occasionally from that country.

The customs of this country are very generous. The men put on white turbans on the head, use white long gowns and wear boots of goat's leather with golden lace. They have much culture. This is why the people in their business, even when the price of a thing is very high, never fail to respect their agreement. They mint silver coins called *tangka*. Each coin is 2.8. ounces (Chinese). It is the unit of money used in the country. The women put on short cloaks and scarfs of coloured cotton or silk with embroideries. They do not use any white cream but are naturally beautiful. They put on precious tiaras on the head, necklaces on the neck and dress their hairs in a knot behind. They use bangles on the wrists and ankles and rings on the fingers and toes.

The Hindus as a race do not eat beef and their man and women do not eat and drink in the same place. When the husband dies the wife does not marry and when the wife dies the husband does not marry. The orphans and widows who have none to support are fed by the houses of the village by turns and are not allowed to go to other villages to beg for food.

Their fields are very fertile and yield two crops in the year. There is no need of sowing the seeds (? irrigation) – the crops grow by themselves in the proper season. Both men and women are diligent in ploughing and weaving. They have melons, fruits, vegetables, cows, horses, cocks and hens, goats, goose, duck and sea-fishes. They use cowries in the market instead of coins. They have golden and silver goods, *tuan, ch'uan*, white porcelain with blue and white decoration, copper and iron, musk, vermillion, mercury, straw mat, etc. The mountain is called "Five-peak" (Pañca-śṛṇga).

The products of the country are cotton cloths, sa-ha-lo (shawl), woolen carpets, tu-lo-kin, crystal, *candrakānta* 水晶 *musāragalva* 瑪瑙, *pravāla* 珊瑚, pearls precious stones, opaque glass, sugar, honey, ghee, and peacock's feather. They also produce handkerchiefs of different colours, blankets, jack-fruits of big size and good and sweet to the taste and mangoes of which the smell is sour but which is good (to the taste).

Their tribute consists of horses, saddles of gold, silver and other metals, vases of opaque glass, porcelain with blue and white decoration, shawl, the cloth *che-chu-hei-ta-li, sien-po pi-pu, tu-lo-kin*, crystallised sugar, buceros, unicorn's horn, peacocks' feathers, parrots frankincense, raw gharu wood, guggula, khadira, purple glue, dragon's blood, ebony, sapan and pepper.[28]

V. Ming-she

Bengal is the same as Shen-tu of the Han period. It is the same as T'ien-chu of the later Hans. In later periods Central India sent tributes to the Leang emperors and Southern India to the Wei. In the T'ang period the country was divided into five T'ien-chu, also called five Yin-tu. Bengal is Eastern India. From Sumatra with a favourable wind one can reach there in 20 days.

In the 6th year yong-lo (1408) the king of Bengal (Ghiyās-ud-din) sent an ambassador to China with tributes. China also gave many presents in return. In the 7th year yong-lo (1409) their ambassador came again with 230 officers. The Emperor had just initiated a policy of communicating with foreign countries. So he sent many presents to Bengal. Since then they came every year. In the 10th year yong-lo (1412) just before the arrival of their ambassador to China the Emperor sent ministers to Chenkiang to arrange for their reception. When arrangements had been made the ambassador arrived with the news of the death of their king. Officials were then sent to attend the mourning ceremony of the dead king and the coronation ceremony of the Prince Sai-wu-ting 賽勿丁. In the 12th year yong-lo (1414) the new king sent ambassador with mandate to offer thanks and presents of a k'i-lin, famous horses and products of Bengal. The officials proposed to congratulate the Emperor (on this occasion) but the latter rejected it. Next year (1415) Hou-hien was sent to that country with presents to the king, the queen, and the ministers. In the 3rd year che-t'ong (1438) they sent a k'i-lin as present. All officials congratulated the Emperor on this country. The next year (1439) tributes again came from that country. Since then relations with that country ceased.[29]

Notes

1 *ibid.*, p.102
2 See Rockhill, *T'oung* Pao, p. 62.
3 *ibid.*, p. 435–436.
4 *T'oung Pao*, 1915, pp. 81 ff.
5 See Couvreur under *T'ien.*
6 See Lévi *I.H.Q.*1930, pp. 597 ff.
7 *The Cambridge History of India*, vol. III, p. 252.
8 The name of the new king was wrongly read by previous authors (especially by Mr. G. Phillips) as Kien-fuh-ting and Gien-fuh-ting (Bhattasali, *Coins and Chronology*, pp. 66, 97). Dr. Bhattasali accepted this reading and considered him as different from Saif-ud-din. He was led to the conclusion that the latter was dead by that time. But *Kien* or *Gien* 蹇 is a misreading for *Sai* 賽. This is clearly proved by the texts translated here.
9 Much light has been thrown by Dr. N. K. Bhattasali on the chronology of these rulers in his book *Coins and Chronology of the Early Independent Sultans of Bengal.* On the basis of new coins of Ghiyās-ud-din studied by him, he has been able to bring down the date of theat rlar up to 1410–11.The new coins of this rular discussed by him bear dates Hij. 811, 812, 813 (1410). Dr. Bahttasali thinks that Ghiyās-ud-din died in 1410 but the Chinese records show that he lived for a year more and that the news of his death was carried to China in 1412. Saif-ud-din ascended the throne that very year.
10 This was the reading of Blochmann but Dr. Bhattasali (ibid. p.100) expresses doubt on it. He has evidently been led to it by the complication in chronology but the arrangement which we have suggested by accepting the identification of Ganesh with Shihāb-ud-din obviates the difficulty. Coins in the Dacca Museum studied by Dr. Bhattasali have supplied the following dates for Shihāb-ud-din: Hij.817, 816, 815 and 814 (?) ibid. pp.102–4. The only sure date supplied by the coins of Saif-ud-din is also Hij. 814 (ibid. p. 92). We need not assume that Saif-ud-din died that year. It simply shows that the supreme authority definitely passed into the hands of Shihāb-ud-din after it had been exercised for a short time by Saif-ud-din just after the death of his father.
11 Dr. Bhattasali (ibid. pp. 107 ff.) has restored the name of another king Alauddin Firoz Shah Ibn Bayazid Shah who ruled for only one year. Three of his coins discovered so far either issued from Satgaon or Mu'azzamabad bear the date Hij, 817 (1414). He seems to have been another son of Shihāb-ud-din who after the death of his father wanted to usurp the throne. But evidently he did not succeed in getting possession of the capital where Jalal-ud-din established himself from the very next year (Hij. 818). Firoz either died or was simply removed. If we accept the identification of Shihāb-ud-din with Raja Ganesh, Firoz would probably be the Hindu brother of Jalal-ud-did with a Mahomedan name.
12 The coins supply names of two more kings named Danujamardana and his son Mahendradeva about whom no information is available from the Chinese records. All coins of Danujamardana discovered so far were issued from Chatgaon, Sonargaon and

Pandua and bear the dates Hij. 820 and 821 (1417–1418). Those of Mahendradeva were issued from Chatgaon and Pandua in Hij. 821 (1418). Dr. Bhattasali would identify Danujamardana with Raja Ganesh and Mahendradeva with the letter's son Jadu. This would be his name before his conversion to Islam (ibid. pp.113 ff.). But Raja Ganesh seems to have died or abdicated in 1414 and Jadu began to strike coins in his Mahomedan name Jalal-ud-din from 1415. There is no coin struck by him in 1417 and a part of the year 1418, and this was the period when Danujamardana and Mahendradeva were in power. Jalal-ud-din's coins again reappear from 1418. We have seen that the *de jure* ruler of the country was still Saif-ud-din and it is just possible that due to an intrigue in the court power had been seized temporarily by another noble.

13 There is some difficulty about the interpretation of this passage. This passage occurs in the *Sing ch'a sheng lan* as translated by Rockhill (infra p. 122). The *Sing ch'a sheng lan* is one of the oldest accounts and as we have already seen it was compiled by Fei-sin in 1436. There is no copy of the text in our Library and hence it is not possible to verify Rockhill's translation. Two other accounts – the *Si yang ch'ao kung tien lu* (infra, no. III) and the *Shu* yu chou tseu lu (infra, no. IV) give a different description of the banquet: "...the king entertained the Chinese mission with a feast of both smoked and roasted beef and mutton, rose water and sweetened water...". and "They offered roasted beef and mutton but there is prohibition for drinking wine as it changes our nature". The actual Chinese text in the last mentioned account is 燔炙牛羊禁不飲酒恐亂性而失禮 'fan chiu niu yang chin pu yin chiu k'ung luan hsing erh shih li' and it should be translated in the way in which we have done. But it is also possible though that would mean some violence to the Chinese text to punctuate it by putting a stop after *kin* 禁 in that case it may be translated as "Roasted beef and mutton were forbidden and nobody could drink for fear that it troubles our spirit and changes our nature". The *Sing ch'a sheng lan* is a contemporaneous account and if Rockhill's translation may be relied on it should be taken as the most faithful picture of the customs prevalent in the court.

14 Rockhill translates it as "This is also a country of western Yin-tu" but this would be meaningless in the present context. This should be taken in this sense of India of the West. India was always looked upon by the Chinese as a country of the west (si-yu).

15 Rockhill restores pa-sseu-la-eul as sipāh-salar- 'army leader'. Dr. Bhattasali (ibid, p. 171, n. 2) thinks that the original word was Fauzdar. This is not phonetically justified. Besides Fauzdar was an officer of much lower rank than the Commander of the Army.

16 Rockhill notes a different version from a separate edition of the text which runs as follows: "There is a clan of people called Ken-siao-su-lu-nai or musicians. Daily in the fifth watch they come and stand before the front doors of the chiefs and wealthy people, one of them blowing a so-na (flageolet), another beating a small drum, at first crescendo, then slowly, then in measured time. After that they gradually press the measure, then stop". So-na is no doubt Persian *zurna*, (Laufer, *T'oung Pao*, 1916: p. 480), Bengali *Sanai* but the original word for *Kensiao-su-lu-nai* is not known. Rockhill suggested that su-lu-na may be the same as so-na i. e. *surna* but *ken-siao* remains unexplained. Such musicians as a social class are still known in Bengal, but the Persian name by which they were known in the 15th century has been forgotten.

17 Kajang wine was a common drink in the islands of the Indian Archipelago (Rockhill – Chau Ju-kua), but its use in Bengal is not known. Probably it has been introduced here through mistake. This wine used to be prepared either from the leaves or seeds of the Kajang *(Kia-chang)* plant that grows in those islands.

18 Rockhill translates it as "This is also a country of western Yin-tu" but this would be meaningless in the present context. This should be taken in this sense of India of the West. India was always looked upon by the Chinese as a country of the west (si-yu).

19 Rockhill – "Precious Diamond Throne". This is Vajrāsana or Gaya. Rockhill did not suggest any identification for Chao-na-fu-eul. There is however no doubt that it is Jaunpur of which the District of Gaya formed a part.

20 Rockhill takes Pan-tu-wa to be Patna but this is certainly wrong Pandua, the capital of Bengal is meant.

21 Po-lo-mi as the name of jack-fruit is not known. It may be a mistake for Po-no-so i. e, *panasa.*

22 Rockhill takes an-mo-lo to be mango-*āmra,* but its description as yu-kan "sweet remainder" and its mention as a medicine show that *āmalaka,* myrabolan is meant.

23 The name of the ambassador Pa-yi-tsi (Cant. pa-iɐt-tsai) probably refers to his family name. It may be quite well restored as Bayazid.

24 A note added by the commentator mentions in this connection the Lie-tseu in which there is reference to the supernatural man appearing to Emperor Mu Wang of the Chou dynasty. The story runs that the emperor and built a very high platform in his honour. The note then relates the story of She-li-fang and his companions who are said to have come to the court of Shw-Huang-ti of T'sin dynasty and specks also of the golden image that was brought by general Ho-kiu-ping from the Lien-ki mountains. The commentator mentions all theses stories to prove that Buddism came to China in the Chou, Ts'in and the First Han periods and that the story of its introduction during the reign of Ming-ti of the Late Han dynasty is incorrect. But these legends are no longer believed to have any historical importance. They are pious forgeries of later times.

25 These are varieties of Chinese silk. Their names cannot be translated properly. The Chinese stuffs mentioned here and earlier are the following: *jen* which is a sort of silk stuff or tissues, *chu* 紵 is a hemp stuff, *see* 絲 is ordinary silk, *tuan* 緞 coarse silk stuff, *ch'uan* 絹 white silk gauze used either for writing or painting, *kin* 錦 different kinds of coloured silk stuff and *ling* 綾 fine coloured silk stuffs with floral designs on it.

26 There is evidently some confusion in the account. The Buddhist monk mentioned here must have been a Tibetan Lama. We learn from Hou-hien's Biography in the *Ming-she* that before being sent to India Hou-hien had gone to Tibet on an imperial mission in the 2nd year yong-lo (1404). In fact he was sent several times to Tibet and Nepal between 1403 and 1413 (Rockhill – *T'oung Pao,* 1915, p. 84). The *Ming-she* (chapter on Western Countries) tells us in connection with Tibet that a Bhikṣu called Ho-li-ma 哈立麻 came to the court from Tibet in the beginning of the yong-lo period. He is said to have possessed many super-natural powers. Of the many titles conferred on him by the Emperor one was Ta-pao-fa-wang *Mahāratna-Dharmarāja.* This seems to be the translation of a Tibetan name like *Rin chen po chos rgyal ba, Ho-li-ma* must have come to China with Hou-hien and seems to be the same a mentioned here.

27 The commentator refers to a similar case recorded in the history of the Song dynasty. The Si-hia Emperor Yuan-ho 元昊 called himself Wu-tsu 兀卒 which sounds in Chinese like Wu-tsu 吾祖 "I am the grandfather".

28 The Si-yu-lun 西域論 which is a sort of commentary on *Shu yu chou tseu lu* inserts an independent account of Bengal but it has nothing new. It is only a summary of the previous account.

29 The rest of the Ming-she is the same as the previous accounts.

Chapter 13

CHINESE COINS FROM TANJORE*

In September 1943 Dr. A. Aiyappan, the Superintendent of Madras Government Museum, very kindly sent me casts of 20 Chinese coins for examination and report. About the find-spot of these coins he wrote to me: "The coins form part of a find of treasure trove discovered at Vikraman village, Pattukottai Taluk, Tanjore District, – the other objects of the find being two small bronze images which have been identified as images of crawling Krishna. The treasure was discovered in October 1942 while digging the earth".

I wrote to him for further information on the weight and quality of the coins. In reply he supplied me with the following details: "The coins do not appear to be *pure* copper. A detailed analysis of the coins will be made later when we shall let you know. The approximate weight of each of the coins is furnished in the enclosed list. The twenty coins are put in 9 envelopes – (Nos. 1 to 16 in 8 envelopes – two coins each serially numbered and Nos. 17 to 20 in one envelop). The weight given against each number is therefore likely to being interchanged between the two numbers in each envelop. As the moulds of the casts have been washed away during the last floods here, we are not able in the absence of the casts to indicate the weights correctly against each number. The images of crawling Krishna are specimens of late work of about the 16th or 17th century A.D".

The following weights of the coins are serially given by Dr. Aiyappan:

Serial No.	Weight in Grammes	Serial No.	Weight in Grammes
1.	7.640	11.	3.43
2.	5.735	12.	3.09
3.	7.36	13.	4.51
4.	3.760	14.	3.415
5.	6.425	15.	2.925
6.	6.305	16.	2.415
7.	7.115	17.	3.41
8.	5.630	18.	3.045
9.	4.720	19.	2.97
10.	4.685	20.	1.86

* *Sino-Indian Studies* 1.1 (October 1944): 60–63.

An examination of the coins shows that most of them belong to the Song period and are of the 11th, 12th and 13th centuries.[1] Three coins belong to the T'ang period and are of the K'ai-yuan period (713–742). They are the oldest of the lot. The latest coins in the collection belong to the 13th century, the period *shun-yu* (1241 to 1253). The find of these coins in Tanjore is an additional proof of the fact that although relations between China and Northern India came to a close in the middle of the 11th century, commercial relations between China and Southern India continued for at least two centuries more.

The Chinese Buddhist records speak of relations between India and China up to the year 1053 when the last Indian monk named Che-ki-siang went to China. The only evidence of the last Chinese monk coming to India is the Chinese inscription of Bodhgaya dated 1033.[2] But the relations between Southern India and China which started in the T'ang period seem to have continued uninterrupted throughout the Song period. When Chau Ju-kua wrote his famous work, the *Chu fan che* in the beginning of the 13th century, the Chinese sailors were better acquainted with the Chola dominions than with any other part of India.

The coins had apparently been collected from the Chinese sailors but it is difficult to say how the coins of such varying ages as the 8th and the 13th centuries could be brought together. They might have belonged to the collection of some temple in which the coins of such a long period could be possibly preserved. The coins of the Song period, as may be seen from the following table form an unbroken series from 1008 to 1253 A.D. The Song dynasty came to an end in 1279. The coins represent practically the entire Song period (960–1279).

The *nien-hao* (regnal years) occurring in the legends of 18 of the 20 coins have been satisfactorily identified. Those occurring on the remaining two are too indistinct to allow such an identification. As the Chinese copper coins with square holes are more or less well known I have not thought it fit to give their photographic reproductions. An approximate idea of the weights of the coins may be made by referring to the weights given by Dr. Aiyappan. The serial numbers of his list and those of the following list are the same.

(15, 16, 17)	K'ai-yuan 開元	713–742 A.D.
(12)	Siang-fu 祥符	1008–1016 A.D.
(14)	King-yu 景祐	1034 A.D.
(13)	Che-p'ing 治平	1064–1067 A.D.
(20)	Hi-ning 熙寧	1068–1077 A.D.
(2, 9, 16)	Yuan-fong 元豐	1078–1085 A.D.
(3, 11)	Yuan-yu 元祐	1086–1093 A.D.

(1, 5)	Cheng-ho 政和	1111–1118 A.D.
(10)	Kien-yen 建炎	1127–1130 A.D.
(4)	Shao-hing 紹興	1131–1162 A.D.
(18)	Kia-hi 嘉熙	1237–1241 A.D.
(7)	Shun-yu 淳祐	1241–1251 A.D.

Notes

1 I take this opportunity of taking my friend Mr. Chou Ta-fu who helped me in identifying some of the coins.

2 Chavannes—*Les Inscriptions Chinoises de Bodhgayā*, p. 23.

Chapter 14

REPORT ON A NEW HOARD OF CHINESE COINS*

The present hoard of Chinese coins as reported by Dr. A. Aiyappan, Superintendent of the Government Museum, Madras (Vide letter No. 296/47-13-N) was discovered as a Treasure Trove in the Thalikettai village of Mannargudi Taluk, Tanjore District (Madras). The hoard was discovered in 1944 and was acquired by the Government by a public notification by the Collector of Tanjore on the 18th February 1944. The coins in the hoard are enumerated in the notification as follows:

Old	1/2anna	–	174
Old	1/4anna	–	1616
Bits	–		28
			1818

On examination we have found that these are Chinese Copper Coins of two varieties. The number of coins of the small variety (called in Chinese *hsiao-chien* – 'small coins') is 1601 and that of larger variety (called in Chinese *ta-chien* – 'large-coin') is 184. There are two coins (No. 26 of the list) which are very big and almost double the size of the second variety. Thus I have found in all 1787 coins. The remaining coins are in bits.

The marks on the coins allow us to place their issue in China in the periods mentioned against each class in the list from the Sui period (585 A. D.) to the end of the Song period (1275 A. D.). The legends except in the cases explained in the notes contain the *nien-hao* or regnal periods of emperors in which they were issued.

Ancient Chinese coins discovered in the Tanjore District on a previous occasion also belonged to about the same period – 713–1251 A.D.[1] As the present hoard contains a larger number of coins, it gives an unbroken series.

---

* *Sino-Indian Studies* 4. 3–4: 194–196.

The coins must have been acquired by some sailors or merchants towards the end of the 13th or the beginning of the 14th century and deposited most probably in a temple. We know from Chinese records that the commercial relations between the Chola Empire and the Far East was very brisk in this period[2] and that explains the prescence of so many Chinese coins in the South in the 13th and 14th centuries.

Mark	Period	I (Small Variety)	II (Large)	III (Larger)
1. Wu-Ch'u[3]	–585	3		
2. K'ai-yuan	713–756	114		
3. Kien-yuan	758–760	9		
4. T'ang-kuo	923–935	1		
5. Song-yuan[4]	960–975	6		
6. T'ai- p'ing	976–984	13		
7. Shun-hua	990–995	10		
8. Chi-tao	995–998	31		
9. Hsien-p'ing	998–1000	33		
10. Ching-te	1004–1008	37		
11. Hsiang-fu	1008–1017	68		
12. T'ien-hsi	1017–1022	39		
13. T'ien-sheng	1023–1032	73		
14. Ming-tao	1032–1033	8		
15. Ching-yu	1034–1038	23		
16. Hwang-song[5]	1038	190		
17. Chi-ho	1054–1056	18		
18. Chia-yu	1056–1064	67		
19. Che-p'ing	1064–1068	29		
20. Hsi-ning	1068–1078	150	19	
21. Yuan-fong	1078–1086	194	40	
22. Yuan-yu	1086–1094	160	4	
23. Shao-sheng	1094–1098	67	4	
24. Yuan-fu	1098–1101	25		
25. Sheng-song[6]	1102–1107	69	4	
26. Ch'ong-ning	1102–1107			2
27. Ta-kuan	1107–1111	21		
28. Cheng-ho	1111–1118	66	14	
29. Hsiuan-ho	1119–1126	11	15	
30. Chien-yen	1127–1129		13	
31. Shao-hsing	1131–1163	3	10	
32. Chien-tao	1165–1174	2		
33. Shun-hsi	1174–1190	3	11	
34. Ching-yuan	1195–1201	4	7	
35. Chia-t'ai	1201–1205	12	9	
36. K'ai-hsi	1205–1208		2	

(Continued)

Mark	Period	I (Small Variety)	II (Large)	III (Larger)
37. Chia-ting	1208–1225	1	11	
38. Ta-song[7]	1223	1		
39. Shao-ting	1228–1234	3	5	
40. Shun-yu	1241–1253		4	
41. Hwang-song	1254		2	
42. K'ai-ching	1259–1260		2	
43. Ching-ting	1260–1265		4	
44. Hsien-hsun	1265–1275		1	
		1601	184	2

Notes

1 CF. *Sino-Indian Studies I*, pp. 60–63.

2 CF. Dikshitar – *Southern India and China, Sino-Indian Studies II*, pp. 157 ff.

3 *Wu-ch'u* coins were current in China from the Han (206 B.C.) to the Sui period (585 A.D.). The Wu-ch'u coins of the present collection may be of the Sui.

4 *Song-yuan* coins were issued by T'a-tsu, the founder of the Song dynasty in the period 960–975.

5 *Hwang-song* coins with the legend *Hwang-song-t'ung-pao* were issued in the 5th year *Ching-yu*-1038 A.D.

6 *Sheng-song* coins were issued in the *Ch'song-ning* period 1102–1107 A.D.

7 *Ta-song* coins were issued in the 16th year Chia-ting 1228 A.D.

Chapter 15

KI-PIN AND KASHMIR*

The identification of Ki-pin, a country mentioned in the Chinese records of the Han period, has been a matter of controversy for many years. Prof. Sylvain Lévi was the first to suggest the identification of Ki-pin with Kashmir and to point out that there was no confusion in the Chinese records about the identity till 581 A.D. But since the T'ang period when a new transcription of the name of Kashmir as Kia-she-mi-lo came in use, the Chinese authors lost sight of the old identity and began to consider Ki-pin as another name of Kapiśa.[1] Prof. Chavannes with the help of other Chinese records endorsed the view of Prof. Lévi.[2] Since then the identification was accepted as conclusive but scholars not acquainted with the Chinese records reopened the discussion and summarily rejected the identification.[3] Some of them have identified it with Kapiśa and others more vaguely with Kapiśa-Kāśmīra without any qualification.[4] As the identification of Ki-pin is closely connected with the problem of the first Śaka invasion of India, the identification has been mainly actuated by their views on the Śaka invasion. The first country in India to be occupied by the Śaka invaders was Ki-pin and as most of the scholars believe that the Śakas came by the North-Western route through Afghanistan they are constrained to identify Ki-pin of the earlier period with Kapiśa or Kafiristan against the positive evidence of early records against it.

The Chinese accounts of Ki-pin, however, are so clear that they leave no room for confusion about the identity of Ki-pin and Kashmir so far as the early period (till 581) is concerned. As this identification is of great importance for the history of the Śaka period of Indian history, I propose to state the whole position again and collect such further information as had not been noticed before.

The oldest reference to Ki-pin occurs in the *Annals of the Former Han Dynasty*[5] where it is said: "The Great Yue-che went towards the west and made themselves masters of Ta-hia but the king of the Sai went southwards and made themselves masters of Ki-pin". It is generally admitted that Ta-hia was

---

* *Sino-Indian Studies* 2.1 (1946): 42–53.

the same as ancient Tokharestan and occupied the fertile valleys of the upper Oxus. It was formerly in the hands of Sai or Śaka people but when the great Yue-ches ousted them from that land the Śakas went southwards and occupied Ki-pin.

The same *Annals of the Former Hans* also contains a more detailed account of Ki-pin. It says: "The capital of the kingdom of Ki-pin is the city of Siun-sien which is 12,200 li distant from Ch'ang-ngan... The kingdom of Wu-ch'a lies 2,250 li to the east. The kingdom of Nan-tou is nine days' journey to the north-east. The country joins the kingdom of the Great Yue-che on the north-west and Wu-yi-shan-li on the south-west".

About Wu-ch'a the same account says that Nan-tou is to its west. Ki-pin is stated to be 330 li to the south-west of Non-tou. It further says that Wu-yi-shan-li joins Ki-pin on its east. The account contains the following description of the country:

> "The land of Ki-pin is flat and the climate mild and agreeable. They cultivate the five grains, grapes and other fruits. They manure their gardens and fields. In the low and damp ground they grow rice. In winter they eat raw vegetables. The people are ingenious in carving, ornamenting, engraving and inlaying, in building palaces and mansions, weaving nets, ornamental perforation and embroidery and excel at cooking".

The *Annals of the later Han dynasty*[6] says – "From P'i-shan one goes south-west through Wu-hao, crosses the hanging bridge, passes through the kingdom of Ki-pin and at the end of 60 days' march reaches Wu-yi-shan-li". In another connection it says – "K'iu-tsio-K'io attacked Ngan-si, conquered Kao fu, defeated P'u-ta and Ki-pin and subjugated their territories".

The next Chinese text to mention Ki-pin is *Wei-lio.*[7] It was composed by Yu-Huan in the Wei period between 220 and 265 A.D. The text is now lost but long quotations from it are preserved in the History of the Three Kingdoms (San kuo che). The text gives a description of the different routes leading from the frontier of China to the west. Of these routes the southern one after passing through different countries among which Yu-t'ien (Khotan) is mentioned, traversed the Ts'ong-ling (the Pamirs) and over the hien-tu or hanging passages reached the country of the Great Yue-che. Among the dependencies of the Great Yue-che the text mentions Ki-pin, Ta-hia (Tokharestan) and Kao-fu (Kabul valley).

This account of Ki-pin is faithfully reproduced in all later Dynastic Histories. In the Annals of the Northern Wei dynasty reference is made to an embassy sent to Ki-pin in 452 A.D. The same text also says that Ki-pin is to the south-west of Po-lu at about 14,200 li from the capital of the Northern Wei. The country is surrounded on its four sides by mountain ranges and has a length of 800 li from west to east and 300 li from north to south. The capital is called Shen-kien.

From the dynastic histories therefore we get the following indications on the location of Ki-pin:

1. Ki-pin was to the south-east of the kingdom of the great Yue-ches. The kingdom of Wu-ch'a also called Wu-sha or Wu-hao was 2,250 li to north-east, the kingdom of Nan-tou was at 9 days' journey to the north-east and Wu-yi-shan-li was to its south-west.
2. The valley of Ki-pin was surrounded by hill ranges on four sides; it was a flat country having a length of 800 li from east to west and breadth of 300 li from north to south.
3. The capital of Ki-pin was the city of Sun-sien or Shen-kien both of which meant, "beautiful, good-looking".

All these informations go back to the end of the Former Han period (202 B.C. – 8 A.D.) and the Later Han period (25–220 A.D.). During the first period, the Great Yue-ches were in possession of Ta-hia or Tokharestan comprising the upper valley of the Oxus. Even in the later Han period when they extended their territories up to north-western India after the conquest of kingdoms in Afghanistan, the ancient kingdom of Ta-hia continued to be considered as the proper kingdom of the Great Yue-ches. In fact, after their first conquest of India they began to govern India through a Viceroy. So the location of Ki-pin in these texts has to be studied with reference to Ta-hia. Ki-pin, if identified with Kashmir, would be exactly towards the south-east of the upper valley of the Oxus.

To the north-west of Ki-pin at a distance of about 2,250 li the Han annals place the kingdom of Wu-sha, Wu-ch'a or Wu-hao. Wu-sha was probably the correct form of the name. The distance is indicated in the *Annals of the Later Han dynasty* "60 days' Journey" up to Wu-yi-shan-li which was to the south-west of Ki-pin. The same Annals further says that Ki-pin was accessible from this region only by hanging bridges (*hien-tu*). Wu-sha has been identified with the kingdom of Tash-kurghan.

The kingdom of Nan-tou which was at a journey of 9 days to the north-east of Ki-pin is the country of Darada in the upper valley of the Indus. The ancient pronunciation of Nan-tou would correspond to something like Dar-du. This is the country which later Chinese writers from the time of Fa-hien mention as To-li or To-li-lo (Darada, Darel).

Wu-yi-shan-li which is placed to the south-west of Ki-pin is identified with Kandahar. Hirth was the first to show that the name is a transcription of Alexandria founded by Alexander in Afganistan. Wu-yi-shan-li of the Han Annals would best correspond, according to these scholars, to Kandahar.

The kingdom of Kashmir probably included Gandhāra just before the Yue-che conquest and extended in the south-west up to Kandahar.

The area of the valley of Ki-pin as given in these texts is also to be noted. It was surrounded by hills on all sides. The length from east to west is given as about 800 li which would be a little over 200 miles and the breadth, from north to south about 300 li which would be a little less than 100 miles. This seems to agree roughly with actual area of Kashmir.[8]

The capital is called Sun-sien or Shen-kien both of which mean something like "beautiful or good looking". Such a name may be very well restored as Śrī nagara. In fact the *Rājataraṅgṇī* (I, verse 104) would have us believe that the city of Śrī-nagara was founded by king Aśoka.[9]

These indications almost clearly show that the Ki-pin of the *Annals* of the Former and Later Han dynasties cannot be anything but Kashmir. Its external boundaries might have been varying but they never included Kapiśa. Kao-fu of the Han-Annals seem to have included the ancient Kapiśa. The four kingdoms which are mentioned in connection with the Yue-che conquest are Ta-hia (Tokharestan), Kao-fu (Kabul-Kapiśa region), Ki-pin (Kāśmira-Gandhāra) and T'ien-chu i.e. India proper. The boundaries of Ki-pin discussed above do not agree with those of Kafiristan. We have also seen that the *Annals* of the Later Han dynasty while mentioning the conquests of Kuzulo Kadphises says: "he attacked Ngan-si, conquered Kao-fu, defeated P'u-ta and Ki-pin and subjugated their territories". The direction of the campaign was evidently from west to east. Ngan-si is Parthia, Kao-fu – the Kabul region, P'u-ta – Paktha or Paktues of the Greek writers corresponding to the territory of the Pathan tribes and Ki-pin – Kāśmira-Gandhāra. If Ki-pin is identified with Kapiśa then it will have to be admitted that the conquest of Kuzulo Kadphises was confined to Afghanistan and never extended to India proper.

A host of other documents belonging to the post-Han period clearly speak of the identity of Ki-pin and Kashmir. These documents are of three kinds: (1) Biographical accounts of some Chinese monks who had come to India; (2) Geographical and historical texts in Chinese and (3) Translations of Buddhist texts in Chinese.

(1) Biographical Accounts of Chinese Monks Who Came to India

(a) *Che-mong*[10] – The Bhikṣu Che-mong came to India in 404 A.D. His original account of India is lost but a short summary is available from the Chinese sources. It runs as follows: "From Yu-t'ien (Khotan) he went south-west over a distance of 2000 li. When the ascent of the Ts'ong-ling (the Pamirs) was begun, nine of his companions went back Che-mong with the rest went forward over a distance of 7500 li and arrived at the kingdom of Po-luen (Bolor). Then his Indian companion Tao-seng died ...Then gathering all their energy they advanced. Che-mong himself and four of his remaining companions then *crossed the Indus (Sint'ou) and reached the kingdom of Ki-pin*".

(b) *Fa-yong*[11] – The monk Fa-yong came to India in 420 A.D. His route to India is described as follows: "He passed through different countries such as K'ieu-tse (Kuci) and Sha-lei (Kashgar). They ascended the Ts'ong-ling mountains and crossed the Snow Mountains. Vapour which blinds the eyes is very thick there, the glacier rises up to ten thousand li. Down below was a large river of which the current was quick as a shooting arrow. From the sides of the two mountains (on either side of the river) on the east and the west a rope was fixed which held a bridge. Ten men could pass together over it ... Going for three days after crossing the bridge. Fa-yong crossed still another snow mountain ... and *going further reached the kingdom of Ki-pin*. He worshipped there the bowl of Buddha, stayed there more than a year and learnt the language and the writing of India ... Then again *going westwards he reached the river Sin-t'ou-na-t'i ... crossed the river, went westwards and entered the kingdom of the Yue-che. He worshipped the Usnisa of Buddha there*".

(c) Song-yun[12] – Song yun *came* to India in 520 A.D. His account runs thus: "From Mong-kie-li (Manglaur, capital of Uḍḍiyāna) he went south-eastwards for eight days and reached the place where the Bodhisattva had offered his body to a tigress (Mahāban). Song yun learnt that the king of Gandhāra was then fighting with the king of Ki-pin on the Indus. He therefore crossed the Indus to see him. After five days journey he came to Takṣaśīlā (Taxila), then he recrossed the Indus, visited Fo-sha-fu (Shahbazgarhi), and the mount T'an-to (Viśvantara), then went to Puṣkalāvatī, crossed the Kabul river and reached Puruṣapura (Peshawar)".[13]

(2) Geographical and Historical Texts in Chinese

(a) A famous *geographical* text in Chinese called Shui-king, compiled in the later Han period speaks about the course of various rivers including that of the Indus, In chapter I while speaking of the course of the Indus it says: "*The river flows south-wards by the north of Ki-pin*". A commentary of the same text, the *Shui king chu*[14] was compiled by Li Tao-yuan towards the end of the 5th century. It quotes from various works compiled before its time but now lost. Two of these works the *She-she-si-yu-ki* and the *Kuang-che* by Ko-yi-kong speak of the location of Ki-pin and the course of the Indus. The former says: "*The river Sindhu after passing through Ki-pin, Kien-yue (Gandhāra), Mo-ho-la (?) and other countries enters the southern sea*". The latter says: "*The river flows by the north of the Nan-tou (Darada ?) country ... 340 li to its south-west is the country of Ki-pin*".[15]

(b) Hui-yuan in his *Fan yi ming yi tsi*, a work of the 12th century, says that Ki-pin is an altered pronunciation of the name of Kia-she-mi-lo (Kāśmīra). This note is reproduced from the *Si-yu-ki* of Hiuan-tsang which both Julian and Beal have dropped through mistake in their translations of the latter work.[16]

(c) The *Fo-tsu-t'ong-ki*, a Buddhist Encyclopaedic compilation of the 13th century reproduces in Chap. XXXII an old map to illustrate the route followed by Hiuan-tsang in course of his journey. The map includes the geographical data not only of the time of Hiuan-tsang but also of the earlier period. To the south of the Ts'ong-ling (Pamirs and Hindukush) it locates almost in the same latitude from east to west the following countries : Fan-yen-na (Bamiyan), Kia-pi-she (Kapiśa-Kafiristan), Lan-po (Lampāka), Kien-t'o-lo (Gandhāra), *Ki-pin*, Ho-sho-lo (? mistake for Ho-lo-sho – Rājapura), Sho-lan-to (Jālandhara) and Kiu-lo-to (Kulata). In his comment the author notes that *Ki-pin is the old name of Kia-she-mi-lo (Kāśmīra)* and that it is to the south-east of Wu-la-she (Urasā).[17]

(3) Translations of Buddhist Texts in Chinese

Saṅghabhadra in his Chinese translation of the Sāmanta-pāsādika always renders the name *Kāśmīra* of the *original as Ki-pin*. Saṅghabhadra translated the texts in 489 A.D.[18]

The Chinese translation of the *Milindapañha* belongs to the Tsin period (317–420 A.D.). In this translation too Kāśmīra of the original text is always rendered as Ki-pin.[19]

The *Abhidharmakośa* of Vasubandhu was translated for the first time into Chinese by Paramārtha of Ujjayinī in the second half of the 6th century A.D. The second translation of the same text was made by Hiuan-tsang towards the middle of the 7th century. Paramārtha always *renders Kāśmīra of the original text as Ki-pin but Hiuan-tsang as Kia-she-mi-lo.*[20] *The Biography of Kumārajīva*[21] – The famous Buddhist monk Kumarājīva was born in Kucha in Central Asia. His father was an Indian and mother a Kuchean princess. He went to China towards the end of the 4th century and worked there till his death in 413 A.D. His biography in the Chinese Buddhist collections tells us that when he was a boy, his mother took him to Ki-pin for his education. While coming to Ki-pin they crossed the Ts'ong-ling mountains and further on crossed the river Sin-t'ou (Sindhu) in order to reach the country. Their route was from the west to the east.

The texts discussed above are clear enough and need no comment. Che-mong, Fa-yong, Kumārajīva, all coming either from the west or from the Bolor side cross the Indus in order to reach Ki-pin. A westward march from Ki-pin brings Fa-yong to the capital of the Yue-ches i.e. the capital of Gandhāra, Puruṣapura, in order to worship the Uṣṇīṣa bone of Buddha. From Song-yun's statement also it is clear that the dominions of Ki-pin were confined to the eastern bank of the Indus. The king of Gandhāra was fighting with the king of Ki-pin in the latter's territories. Song-yun in order to reach the headquarters of the king of Gandhāra evidently took the following route from Manglaur. He went south-east along the valley of the Swat river, after eight days march reached Mahāban, crossed the Indus and met the king. He recrossed the Indus at Taxila and then directed his steps towards Puruṣapura.

The *Shui-king*, its commentary and all the sources from which the latter quotes, give a clear idea of the upper course of the Indus and the location of Ki-pin. Near about the source in the Darada country the Indus flows by the north of Ki-pin and then through the territories of Ki-pin and of Gandhāra flows southwards to the sea.

Ki-pin in all these cases could not have been anything but Kashmir. The Buddhist sources such as the *Fan-yi-ming-yi-tsi*, the *Fo-stu-t'ong-ki* and the translations of Buddhist texts mentioned above, all speak of the identity of the two names Ki-pin and Kāśmīra. The ancient pronunciation of the name Ki-pin also confirms the identification. In the pronunciation of the Han period *Kī* was pronounced *Ka* followed by some consonant which might have been an s. *Pin* was pronounced almost certainly *pir* or *wir*. Thus Ki-pin seems to have stood for *Ka* (s) *pir* or *Ka* (s)-*wir*. This form of the name is also found in the old Greek accounts in which Kashmir is mentioned either as Caspiri or Kaspera.[22] Ki-pin was thus a correct phonetic transcription of the old name of Kashmir.

In the 4th and 5th centuries Ki-pin (Kāśmīra) was famous in the Buddhist countries of Central Asia as a great centre of Sanskrit culture. This was the reason for which Kumārajiva's mother brought her son to Ki-pin (Kāśmīra) for a perfect education in the Sanskrit lore in the third quarter of the 4th century. Kumārajiva while in China seems to have attracted many Buddhist scholars of Ki-pin (Kāśmīra) and between 381 and 442 A.D. it was the Buddhist scholars of Ki-pin (Kāśmīra) who played the most important part in the translation of the Buddhist texts into Chinese. The names of some of the most eminent of them who went from Ki-pin (Kāśmīra) were: Saṅghabhūti, Dharmayaśas, Punyatrāta, Buddhayaśas, Gautama Saṅghadeva, Vimalākṣa, Buddhajīva, Guṇavarman and Dharma-mitra.[23] They all are mentioned in the Chinese texts as *natives of Kī-pin*. It is also said that some of them were personally acquainted with Kumārajiva during the latter's stay in Ki-pin and that they went to China at the latter's request. Besides, all of them belonged to the Sarvāstivāda school of Buddhism of which Kashmir was the only great centre in those days.

From the beginning of the 7th century the Chinese official records begin to distinguish Ki-pin from Kashmir and locate it in Afghanistan. The reason of this confusion is not quite clear. It seems that the name of Kashmir began to be transliterated more faithfully as Kia-she-mi-lo. Hiuan-tsang also gives this transliteration but he was evidently following an established custom. The pronunciation of Chinese characters had also considerably changed since early times and it was impossible to recognise Kāśmīr in Ki-pin in the 7th century. It was therefore thrust upon the name of Kapiśa (Kia-pi-she), a country which had then attained political ascendency. From the account of Hiuan-tsang we know that all kingdoms from Bamiyan up to Gandhāra were dependencies of Kapiśa in this period.

This confusion is exhibited for the first time in the *Annals of the Sui-dynasty* (581–617 A.D.) in which it is said that Ki- pin is the country of Ts'ao.[24] The country of Ts'ao is the same as Ts'ao-kiu-ch'a of Hiuan-tsang, Jāguḍa of the Sanskrit texts and Ghazni of modern times.[25] In the Sanskrit–Chinese Dictionary called *Fan-yu-tsa-ming* which was compiled by Li-yen in the 8th century there is a small geographical section in which both Ki-pin and Kāśmīra are mentioned side by side. The Sanskrit name of Ki-pin is given as Karpiśaya which is evidently a mistake for Kapiśaya or Kapiśa. Kāśmīra is Kia-she-mi-lo.[26]

The Annals of the T'ang dynasty mentions Ki-pin and Kāśmīra as two distinct countries.[27] The name of Kāśmīra is transcribed either as Kua-she-mi or as Kia-she-mi-lo. Ki-pin sent envoys with presents to the T'ang court several times between 619 and 758 A.D. In 750 a Chinese envoy named Wu-k'ong was sent to Ki-pin to escort the ambassador of the latter country. Wu-k'ong says: "Gandhāra is the eastern capital of Ki-pin. The king passes the winter there and in the summer he resides in Ki-pin. The respective climates of these two places prove good for his health". Hiuan-tsang also refers to the custom a century earlier while he says: "The kings of different kingdoms of India come to Kia-pi-she in the summer; in the spring and the autumn they come to the country of Gandhāra".[28] These kings were evidently the kings of the countries that were dependencies of Kapiśa in this period.

It is therefore quite clear that Ki-pin mentioned in the *Annals* of the two Han dynasties and those of other dynasties up to the advent of the Sui in 581 and other contemporary records was identical with Kāśmīra. Ki-pin of the Sui and T'ang periods (581–907) is identical with Kia-pi-she i.e. Kapiśa.

Notes

1 Lévi – J. As. 1895, pp. 371ff.
2 B. E. F. E. O., III, pp. 415, 417, 432, and 435.

3 Sten Konow – *Kharoṣṭhi Inscriptions*, Corpus, p. xxiii; *Cambridge History of India*, I, p. 567; Tarn – Greeks in Bactria and India and H. C. Rai Chaudhuri, *Political History of Ancient India* – all editions since 1923 – 2nd edition, p. 274.

4 Cf. Rapson, *Cambridge History of India*, I, p. 567 – "Ki-pin is a geographical term which is used in various senses by Chinese writers but which in this case would most naturally mean Kāpiśa (Kafiristan)". Tarn – *Greeks in Bactria and India* – "the Chinese mixed up Kāpiśa and Kashmir in their Ki-pin"; Tarn would identify Ki pin with Kophene (Kabul). Sten Konow identifies Ki-pin of the Han period with Kāpiśa Cf. besides his *Introduction* to the *Kharoṣṭhi Inscriptions* (Corpus) his article – *Notes on Indo-Scythian Chronology* (J. of Indian History, XII, pp. 8–14). While commenting on Sten Konow's views Pelliot says (J. As., 1934, n.) – "I take this opportunity of saying a word on another Chinese name discussed in the article of M. Sten Konow. In this article M. Sten Konow speaks of a country to be identified 'with Kāpiśa i.e. the country which the Chinese called Ki-pin'. Is it necessary to remind him once again that the identity of Ki-pin with Kāpiśa is not self-evident? On the contrary it is certain that prior to 600 A.D., Ki-pin always stands for Kāśmīra and not Kāpiśa in the translations of Buddhist texts whenever we have a parallel Sanskrit text. From the 7th century the old name Ki-pin was adopted by the Chinese to mean Kāpiśi but it is well-known that in this period the ancient denominations of the Han period and the periods of Six Dynasties were used topsy-turvy".

5 For the English translation of the account Cf. Hirth – *China and the Roman Orient.*

6 Chavannes – *T'oung-Pao*, 1907, pp. 191–192.

7 Chavannes – *T'oung-Pao*, 1905, p. 538.

8 This would give for Ki-pin of the Han period a circuit of 2200 li. This was the area of the valley alone. Hiuan-tsang (*On Yuan-Chwang*, I, p. 24) gives for Kāpiśa an area of 4000 li and for Kashmir 7000 li.

9 The Chinese name of the capital occurs in three different forms. The first two forms – *Sun-sien* and *Shen-kien* – mean "beautiful, good-looking" and seem to be translations of a name like Śrī-nagara. The last form given in the records of the T'ang period is Siu-sien. All these may also be imperfect transcriptions of the name Śrīnagara.

10 Chavannes – B. E. F. E. O. 1903, p. 432.

11 B. E. F. E. O., 1903, p. 435.

12 *Ibid.*, p. 415; p. 417, n. 8. Chavannes has summarised Song-yun's itinerary in this area as follows: "After visiting Mong-kie-li (Manglaor), capital of Udyāna, Song-yun and his companions went after 8 days' march to a place in the south-west where stood the stūpa commemorating the gift of his body to a tigress by the Bodhisattva. This stūpa, as we have said, is to be searched for in the region of Mahaban; Song-yun learnt that the king of Gandhāra was fighting on the western frontiers of Ki-pin (Kashmir). He therefore crossed the Indus and went to see him. When he left the latter, he went westwards and after five days' march reached Takṣaśīlā. He then recrossed the Indus and visited Fo-sha-fu (Shahbazgarhi) and the T'an-t'o mountain connected with the legend of Viśvantara. From there he went to the stūpa where the Bodhisattva gave his eyes (Puṣkarāvati), crossed the Kabul-rud and at last reached Peshawar".

13 Two more Chinese travellers came to Ki-pin (Kashmir) in this period. Their biographies are preserved in the *Chu san tsang ki tsi* (chap. 15) and *Leang kao seng chuan.* The first Che-yen came to Ki-pin in 427 A.D. He put up in the monastery of Mo-t'ien-to-lo (Madhyantara) and learnt dhyāna from Buddhabhadra. Che-yen died in Ki-pin. The other traveller was Hui-hien who came to Ki-pin between 457 and 464 and learnt

dhyāna from a teacher named Dharma. Ki-pin in both the accounts stands for Kashmir which had become famous for dhyāna traditions in this period.

14 The *Shui-king* and its commentary have not yet been translated into any European language. Pelliot and Chavannes have made extensive use of the text: Cf. B E. F. E. O. 1903, pp, 248 ff. and *Toung-Pao*, 1905 pp. 563 ff. I am now engaged in preparing an English translation of the first chapter of the text in collaboration with my friend Mr. Hsiao-ling Wu. The first chapter alone contains much information on India and Central Asia. It contains quotations from a number of ancient accounts which are now lost.

15 The she-she *Si-yu-ki* referred to seems to have been the *Si-yu-ki* or Record of Western India which had been composed by She Tao-ngan (313–385 A.D.) but was lost later on. The first Chinese travellers to India including Fa-hien must have been guided by the account of Tao-ngan.

16 Pelliot, B. E. F. E. O. III, p. 340.

17 *Fo-tsu-t'ong ki* Chinese text-Shanghai edition, xxxv, 9 chap. 32, pp. 36–37.

18 The text corresponds to Pali *Sāmantapāsādikā*. Wherever the *Sāmantapāsādikā* mentions Kāśmīra, the Chinese text gives Ki-pin. The Nidānakathā mentions Kāśmīra in connection with the journey of Majjhantika. The Chinese text mentions Ki-pin, Ch. Taisho, 1462, p. 685 (b), I. 19. It may be noted in this connection that the *Dīpavaṃsa* and *Mahāvaṃsa* refer to the various missions sent out to convert different countries. Madhyandina (Madhyantika or Majjhantika) was sent to Kāśmīra. He was the first to convert the country to Buddhism. The story of Madhyantika occurs in the *Aśokāvadāna.* There are two Chinese translations of this Avadāna, one the *A-yu-wang-chuan* which was translated by Fa-kin about 300 A.D. and the other, the *A-yu-wang-king* which was translated in 516 A.D. In regard to Buddha's prophecy on Madhyantika's journey to Kashmir, the first translation says: "They went to the kingdom of Ki-pin. When they arrived in Ki-pin Buddha told Ānanda – "One hundred years after me a Bhikshu named Mo-t'ien-ti (Madhyantika) will establish the law of Buddha in the kingdom of Ki-pin". The older translation says: "Ānanda, do you see these mountains and wooded country. One hundred years after my Nirvāṇa there will be a Bhikṣu named Madhyantika in the kingdom of Ki-pin". Przylusky, *La legende de Empereur Aśoka*, p. 311 and p. 340.

19 See Demiéville – B. E. F. E. O. 1924, pp. 79, 169 – where the Pali and corresponding Chinese texts are compared.

20 Comparison of the relevant passages of the original text of the *Abhidharmakośa* with the translations of Paramārtha and Hiuan-tsang was instituted by Lévi: J. As. 1895 p. 384.

21 Bagchi, *Le Canon Boudhique en Chine*, I, for the biography of Kumārajiva see pp. 178ff.

22 This was already suggested by Lévi (J. As. 1895, pp. 373–84) and Chavannes *T'oung-pao*, 1895, p. 538, n.4. Chavannes says: "the characters *Kī-pin* are the very transcription of the name which Ptolemy has transmitted to us under the form Kasparia and which was heard by the Chinese as Kaspir. From the Han period to the Northern Wei period the name Ki-pin is used only and always for Kashmir".

23 *Le Canon Bouddhique en Chine*, I, pp. 160, 174, 176, 200, 335, 338, 363, 370 and 388.

24 Lévi -J. As. 1895, p. 375.

25 *Ts'ao-ku-ch'a* is a faithful phonetic transcription of the name Jāguḍa, mentioned in the Sanskrit sources. Jāguḍa corresponded to the reign of Kandahar – Watters. *On Yuan-chwang*, II, p. 347 and Lévi – J. As. 1915, pp. 83ff.

26 Bagchi - *Deux Lexiques Sanskrit-Chinois*, II, p. 347.

27 Chavannes - *Les Tou-kiue Occidentaux*, p. 130–132, 166–168.

28 Lévi and Chavannes – J. As. 1896, p. 161.

Chapter 16

SINO-INDIAN RELATIONS — THE PERIOD OF THE UNITED EMPIRES (618–1100 A.D.)*

The accession of the T'ang dynasty in 618 A.D. marks a new era in the history of China. It may be compared in glory and majesty only with the period of the great Han rulers. It is characterised by progress in all aspects of Chinese life, political, intellectual, religious and artistic. So far as Buddhism is concerned it was a period of assimilation and new creation of the Chinese genius. The Chinese, with the restoration of their distinctive political and social life and the revival of their literary traditions began to see what use they could make of this foreign religion in building up their national life which had been so much disturbed since the fall of the Hans. This led to the creation of a Buddhist civilisation in China which was much more than a mere copy of the Indian Buddhism.

The founder of the T'ang dynasty, Li-yuan who belonged to a nobility of ancient descent, took advantage of the weakness of the Sui rulers and with the help of his able son Li She-min seized the throne in 617 A.D. Ch'ang-ngan, the capital of the Sui, was occupied and Li-yuan was declared Emperor in 618. Li-yuan is better known in history under his posthumous name, Kao-tsu. The dynasty founded by him continued to reign till 907 A.D.

Kao-tsu was succeeded in 627 A.D. by his son Li She-min who is commonly known in history as T'ai-tsong. T'ai-tsong reigned till 649 A.D. He was one of the ablest rulers of the dynasty. He restored to China her former political glory. China was still under the menace of Turkish invasion from the West and the North. This induced him to extend the sphere of China's political influence beyond the natural boundary of the country and establish friendly relations with distant lands. The Turks were won over either through military defeats or diplomacy. The supremacy was once again founded in different parts of Eastern Turkestan viz. Kucha, Karasahr, Khotan, Kashgar and Yarkand. Friendly relations were established with Samarkand, Bokhara and

* *Sino-Indian Studies* 1.2; and 1.4 (1945).

Kashmir. Tibet had risen into political eminence in this period. So an alliance was made with Tibet and it was cemented through the marriage of a Chinese Princess named Wen Ch'eng with king Srong-btsan Sgam-po.

The successor of T'ai-tsong, Kao-tsong (650–683) somehow retained authority over the conquered territories. He also annexed Corea to the Chinese Empire. His widow, Wu Tső-t'ien succeeded to the throne in 684 and reigned till 705. She was a very able ruler. She put down effectively the political troubles in Eastern Turkestan. The Emperor Hiuan-tsong succeeded to the throne in 712 and enjoyed a long reign till 755. He was as great a ruler as T'ai-tsong. He put down the political unrest in various parts of Central Asia and restored the political supremacy of China over those territories. He established political relations with the neighbouring kingdoms. After the death of Hiuan-tsong a political decadence started which ultimately led to the downfall of the T'ang dynasty.

Although relations with India remained uninterrupted during the T'ang period, the attitude of the Confucian literati towards Buddhism was not at all favourable. The T'ang Emperors, anxious to restore the former greatness of the nation, was often induced to adopt harsh measures against Buddhism. A leader of this campaign against Buddhism, Fu-yi (555–639) had a great influence in the court. He was one of the deadliest antagonists of Buddhism. He submitted a vigorous anti-Buddhist memorial in 624 to the Emperor Kao-tsu. He said in his memorial –

> "Buddhism infiltrated into China from the Tarim under a strange and barbarous form, and as such it was then less dangerous. But since the Han period the Indian texts began to be translated into Chinese. Their publicity began to adversely affect the faith of the Princes and filial piety began to degenerate. The people began to shave their heads and to refuse to bow their heads to the Princes and their parents. They began to roam and beg and became monks in order to evade the public duties. They studied the three *pāramitās* and the *gatis* and refused to pay respect to others on the pretext of strict observance of their religion and the work for higher perfection. Ever since they began to honour this foreign sage (Buddha) the country has been a prey to barbarian invasion. Real rulers disappeared, ministers became traitors, the Government became tyrannic and the sacrifices became neglected. The result is that the monks and the nuns now count by tens of thousands. I request to get them married so that the country may have a hundred thousand families. They will thus bring up children to fill the ranks of your army".

Fu-yi's campaign led to the persecution of Buddhism in 626 and 631 A.D. when an imperial decree was passed ordering the Buddhists to bow to their parents according to the Chinese usage. Although T'ai-tsong began his reign by persecuting the Buddhists his attitude towards them gradually changed in spite of the life-long anti-Buddhist campaign of Fu-yi. This change in the attitude of the Emperor was not a little actuated by political considerations. Turks had been converted to Buddhism. Buddhism was prosperous in various parts of Eastern Turkestan and also in the neighbouring kingdoms of Samarkand, Bokhara and Kashmir. The growing kingdom of Tibet was culturally linked with India.

The Confucian campaign however continued unabated throughout the T'ang period. Another important leader of the campaign was Han-yu (763–824). He submitted in 818 A.D. a memorial to the Emperor couched in the following words: "When the Emperor Kao-tsu succeeded the Sui, he thought of exterminating Buddhism. But the ministers who surrounded him were narrow-minded and little grounded in our national traditions. His project, therefore, could not be carried out when you ascended the throne you began by forbidding the conversion of new followers to Buddhism and the erection of new monasteries. But your orders were not carried out you have now permitted the Buddhists to bring in procession a bone of Buddha! I suppose you do not believe in their stories". The Emperor Hien-tsong (806–820) was sympathetic towards the Buddhists. Han-yu was disgraced.

The Taoists also joined the Confucian literati in leading the campaign against Buddhism. As a result of their campaign an Imperial decree was passed in 845 A.D. for the laicisation of the Buddhist monasteries. But the Emperor Yi-tsong (860–873) who was an ardent Buddhist rescinded the order.

The anti-Buddhist campaign on the whole was not successful in having the desired effect. Buddhism was too firmly rooted in China to be weeded out.

The enlightened policy of Emperor T'ai-tsong brought China in closer, touch with India. This was accelerated by the visit of the famous pilgrim Hiuan-tsang to India. Hiuan-tsang started from Ch'ang-ngan in 629 without the permission of the Emperor. On account of the uncertain political condition of Central Asia the Chinese subjects were discouraged to undertake any journey to the west. But Hiuan-tsang, who was a fervent Buddhist, was bent upon going to India and made all his preparations in secret. During his long stay in India he had seen and known India more than any other Chinese traveller, collected valuable information on the country and established personal contact with Emperor Harṣa and a number of smaller kings of India. His importance was not overlooked by the Emperor and so when Hiuan-tsang arrived at Ch'ang-ngan in 645 he was well received by the Emperor. "Never in the history of China did a Buddhist monk receive such a joyous ovation as that with which our pilgrim was welcomed. The Emperor and his court, the officials and merchants, and all the people made holiday. The streets were crowded with eager men and women who expressed their joy by gay banners and festive music". The Emperor pardoned the pilgrim for not taking his permission while leaving the country, received him in an inner chamber of the palace and listened there from day to day to his account of the foreign lands. Henceforth the pilgrim began to exercise a great influence on the Emperor. This explains the new Imperial policy towards India which consisted in the frequent exchange of embassies between China and different parts of India. This policy was carefully followed by the successors of T'ai-tsong till about the middle of the 8th century A.D.

In 643 the Emperor sent Li Yi-pao as ambassador to king Harṣa of Kanauj. This was in return for a mission which Harṣa had sent to the Chinese Emperor with presents. Hiuan-tsang was in Kanauj in 636 and the friendship which he contracted with Harṣa must have induced the latter to send a mission to the Emperor of China with presents. Li Yi-pao was ordered by the Emperor to accompany the Indian envoy on his way back and to carry a letter from the Emperor to Harṣa. Li Yi-pao was accompanied by another Chinese official named Wang Hiuen-ts'ö. They reached Magadha after a journey of nine months. On the completion of their official mission Li Yi-pao and Wang Hiuen-ts'ö visited a number of Buddhist holy places such as Rājagṛha, Gṛdhrakūṭa and Māhabodhi. They had two Chinese votive inscriptions engraved in 643 on the Gṛdhrakūṭa and the Māhabodhi temple. The original stones have not been discovered. The Chinese ambassadors returned to their country either towards the end of 646 A.D. or the beginning of 647 A.D.

The very same year (647) Wang Hiuan-ts'ö was entrusted with a second Imperial mission to Magadha. On his arrival at the capital of Harṣa, Wang Hiuan-ts'ö found that Harṣa had died and that his minister A-la-na-shuen (Aruṇāśava ?), the king of Tīrabhukti, had usurped the throne. The Chinese mission was not well received by the usurper, its escorts were murdered and the treasures plundered. Wang Hiuan-ts'ö saved his life by escaping overnight and fleeing to Nepal which was allied with China through Tibet. Wang Hiuan-ts'ö then secured military help from Nepal and Tibet, marched on Magadha, defeated the usurper, and took him a prisoner to Ch'ang-ngan in 648. Wang Hiuan-ts'ö this time returned to China by the route of Nepal and Tibet. The Indian usurper, Aruṇāśava (?) remained in China till his death and was given posthumous honours. His statue was set up by the side of the statues of king Srong-btsan Sgam-po and those of the kings of Kucha, Turfan etc. The statue was placed on the avenue leading to the tomb of Emperor T'ai-tsong. Wang Hiuan-ts'ö this time brought with him a Brahmin named Nārāyaṇasvāmin, who is said to have been a specialist in the drugs that give long life. This was because the Emperors of China as well as the eminent people of the country, through the influence of Taoism, had a craze for the research for long life. T'ai-tsong at first placed confidence in the Brahmin but the latter failed to give long life to the Emperor who died in 649 A.D. The new Emperor had no more any interest in Nārāyaṇasvāmin, who asked Wang Hiuan-ts'ö to take back the Brahmin to his native country.

Wang Hiuan-ts'ö started on his third journey to India in 657 A.D. He was also entrusted with presents of kaṣāya to be carried to Buddhist sacred places in India. This time also he passed by Tibet and Nepal. He visited Kapiśa and reached the Mahābodhi temple on the 5th November, 660. He set up another votive inscription in the Mahābodhi temple. He returned to the capital of China in March 661. He completed his account of India about this time. The work which is now lost contained 10 chapters of account and 3 chapters of illustrations.

Wang Hiuan-ts'ö was most probably sent to India for the fourth time in 664 to bring back from India a Chinese monk named Hiuan-chao whom he had met in India during his last visit. This time also he passed by Tibet and Nepal. He must have come back in 665 as it was then that an image of Bodhisattva which had been made after a model brought from India by Wang Hiuan-ts'ö was set up in the principal hall of the *Ki-ngai-sse*, a temple situated near the palace. Wang Hiuan-ts'ö himself directed the execution of the image.

The T'ang history has preserved systematic account of the political relations that were established in this period between China and different parts of India viz. Ceylon, Kashmir, Baltistan, Kapiśā, Uḍḍiyāna (Swat valley), Gandhāra, and kingdoms in the West, East, North, South and Central India.

It is reported that a king of Ceylon sent in 670 A.D. presents to the Emperor Kao-tsong. In 711 a king of Ceylon sent an embassy to the Emperor Jui-tsong with presents. In 742 a king of Ceylon sent presents of pearls, ivory etc. on two occasions through ambassadors to Emperor Hiuan-tsong. In 746 he sent through the famous Buddhist scholar Amoghavajra, who was then going to China, a palm-leaf copy of the *Mahāprajñāpāaramitā* as present to the Emperor. Presents were again sent in 750 from Ceylon and in 762 an ambassador was sent from Ceylon to the Emperor Su-tsong.

Baltistan and Kashmir in a way bordered on the Chinese Empire. The Chinese Emperors claimed a sort of suzerainty over those kingdoms although we do not know how far the actual political relations justified that claim. The Chinese official history gives the following account of China's political relations with those countries. [Baltistan] – In 717 (5th month) the Emperor awarded the title of "king of *Pu-lu* (Bolor)" to the local chief – *Su-fu-shö-li-che-li-ni* (Śubhaśrī). In 719 (7th month) the king of Bolor Śubhaśrī sent an ambassador to the Emperor to express his gratitude for the award. In 720 (10th month) the title of "the king of Bolor" was awarded by the Emperor to the local chief *Su-lin-t'o-yi-che* (Surendrāditya). In 731 (4th month) the title of "the king of little Bolor (Yasin)" was awarded to *Nan-ni* by the Emperor.

In 733 (3rd month) the king of (little) Bolor *Mo-kin-mang* sent a noble named *Cha-cho-na-se-mo-mo-sheng* to thank the Emperor for the award. In 741 the king of little Bolor sent again an ambassador to China. In 745 (7th month) the king of little Bolor sent a Buddhist teacher named Kia-lo-mi-to (Kālamitra) to pay respects to the Emperor. [Kashmir] – In 720 (8th month) the Emperor awarded the title of the "king of Kashmir" to *Chen-t'o-lo-pi-li* (Candrāpīḍa). Official correspondence was exchanged between China and Kashmir again in 724. In 733 (3rd month) the king of Kashmir Mu-to-pi (Muktāpīḍa) sent a Buddhist priest named *Wu-li-to-nien* with presents to the Emperor. The priest was received by the Emperor in a banquet and sent back with presents. The same year (4th month) the Emperor awarded the title of the "king of Kashmir" to Muktāpīḍa.

The political condition of Kapiśā, Gandhāra and Uḍḍiyāna was uncertain in this period. The two latter kingdoms were certainly dependent on Kashmir. We know from the Chinese official history that in 720 (4th month) the title of the "king of Wu-ch'ang (Uḍḍiyāna)" was given to the local chief by the Emperor. The king of Gandhāra sent an ambassador to China in 758 (5th month) with presents to the Emperor. The title of "*tegin*" was awarded to the chief of Kapiśā in 720 (9th month). Official relations between Kapiśā and China were resumed in 738 and 758 (6th month).

So far we have discussed the notices on the relations of China with the frontier kingdoms of India. But official connection was not uncommon with other parts of India as well. As early as 692 (3rd month) a representative of King *Ti-po-si-na* (Devasena) of Central India came to pay respects to the Emperor. The envoy must have been the same as Brahma (Fan-mo) who assisted Bodhiruci in 693 in the work of translation. In 741 the son of the king of Central India came to pay respects and he was given a Chinese name Li Ch'eng-ngan. In 731 (10th month) the king of Central India *Yi-sha-fu-mo* (Yaśovarman) sent his minister, the Buddhist monk Pu-ta-si-na (Buddhasena) to pay homage. We know that Yaśovarman was the King at Kanauj. He was in constant war with the King of Kashmir and it is probable that he had appealed to the Emperor for intervention.

In 692 (3rd month) representatives of the King of Eastern India *Mo-lo-pa-mo* (Mālavarman?) and the King of Western India, *Sha-lo-yi-to* (Śīlāditya) came to China to pay homage. We do not know who Mālavarman was but the other King was certainly Śīlāditya III of Valabhī who reigned in the end of the 7th century. In 692 the King of Southern India, *Che-lu-ki-pa-lo* (Chālukya...) sent an ambassador to the Emperor. Official relations were resumed with South India in 719 and in 720 (8th month), the King *Sha-li Na-lo-seng-kia-pa-to-pa-mo* (Śrī Narasiṃha Potavarman) proposed to the Emperor to send elephants and cavalry to fight with the Arabs and the Tibetans. The Chālukya king who was reigning in 692 must have been the son of Pulakeśin II. Narasiṃha Potavarman was the Pallava ruler of Kanchi.

These scrappy notices show that for nearly one hundred years (643–758 A.D.) China tried to maintain regular political relations with different parts of India. The last great ruler of the T'ang dynasty, Hiuan-tsong died in 755; the political condition of Eastern Turkestan became uncertain and China lost her hold on the kingdoms in that region on account of the encroachment of the Arabs and the Tibetans. The promised help of Narasiṃha Potavarman was not enough to check the Arab advance towards India and the Chinese frontier. This was responsible for the cessation of the political relations between India and China since the middle of the 8th century A.D.

The cultural relations between India and China continued as before. This was mainly carried out since the beginning of the T'ang by the innumerable Chinese and Indian monks who defied all barriers, either natural or artificial, in order to contribute to the progress of the Law. The Indian Buddhist scholars kept on coming to China by the land and sea routes throughout the T'ang period. The names of at least 20 principal translators have been preserved in the Chinese accounts.

One of the principal Indian translators was Prabhākaramitra. He was born in a royal family of Central India. He left the house at the age of ten and took up Buddhistic studies under able teachers. He made so much progress in course of a few years that he could easily recite hundred thousand gāthās of the Mahāyānasūtras. He was then given *upasampadā* and took up the study of the Vinaya. He was however of a meditative temperament and began to practise *samādhi* under the direction of great teachers. He settled in the monastery of Nālandā. He studied the *śāstras* with famous Śīlabhadra and soon showed great aptitude in the study of Abhidharma. He was at last appointed a teacher of Abhidharma at Nālandā. He had soon a number of disciples who later on became famous teachers in India.

Prabhākaramitra had a great desire to travel in foreign lands. He heard that the "Northern Barbarians" (Tibetans?) had not yet been converted to Buddhism. He started for the Northern countries with ten disciples. Travelling towards the north by stages he reached the camp of the chief of the Western Turks (Yabghu Kagan). He took the opportunity of explaining the Buddhist law to him. The Kagan felt interested in this foreign religion and at last accepted it.

On the invitation of the Chinese ambassador at the court of the Turks in 626 Prabhākara decided to go to China. But the Kagan would not leave him. Afterwards at the request of the Emperor of China, Prabhākara was allowed to start for China. He reached the capital towards the end of the year 627. He settled in the monastery of *Hing shen sse*. The Emperor was very much attracted by his intelligence and scholarship. He requested Prabhākara to translate in 629 three texts into Sanskrit, the most important amongst them being the *Mahāyāna Sūtrālaṁkāra-śāstra* of Asaṅga.

The Confucian literati however could not tolerate the great respect and admiration which the Emperor showed towards Prabhākara. They carried on a vehement propaganda against him before the Emperor which had its effect. The Emperor soon ceased to take any interest in him. Prabhākara had no more enthusiasm for work and died in 633 at the age of 69.

Another great Indian teacher who went to China in the T'ang period was Bodhiruci. He was a Buddhist monk of Southern India. He left his family at the age of twelve and at first joined the Brahmanical school of Parāśara. He studied all the literature of this school and specialised in *Sāṅkhya*, *Śabda-vidyā* and other sciences such as, astronomy, astrology, mathematics, medicine etc. He then went out in the world in order to discuss religious matters with Buddhist scholars. There was at that time a Mahāyāna Sthavira named Yaśaghoṣa. While carrying on religious discussion with the latter Bodhiruci was greatly impressed by the superiority of the Buddhist religion. He adopted the Buddhist faith and began the study of the Buddhist literature.

The Chinese envoy Po-yun, most probably came to the Chālukya king who had sent an ambassador to China in 692 to return the compliments paid to the Emperor. He requested Bodhiruci to go to China. Bodhiruci reached China in 693. The very same year Bodhiruci translated the *Ratnamegha-sūtra* in the monastery of *Fo-shou-ki*. Śramaṇa Brahma (*Fan-mo*) the envoy of the king of Central India took part in the explanation of the Sanskrit text. The Śramaṇa Canda (Chan-t'o) and Brāhmaṇa Li-wu-ch'an translated the words. The Chinese monk Hui-che verified the translation. Ch'u-yi and others took down the translation, Sse-hiuan and others put it in good style and Yuan-ts'ie, Chen-ying and others controlled the meaning. Thus a full-fledged board was' set up to help Bodhiruci in his work. Bodhiruci translated 19 texts during his stay in the *Ta chou tong sse* and the *Fo-shou ki sse*.

Bodhiruci came to the capital in 706 with Emperor Ho-ti. He stayed in the monastery of *Si-chong fu sse* where he translated the most important and voluminous Mahāyāna sūtra, the *Ratnakūṭa*. Hiuan-tsang had brought a copy of this work from India and began to translate it. Bodhiruci had brought a copy of the Ratnakūṭa with him. So the Emperor Ho-ti requested him to continue the work started by Hiuan-tsang. The portions already translated were collected and revised. Bodhiruci translated the remaining portions of the text. The work was begun in 706 and completed in 713. The translation was begun in the Fo-kuang palace, and the Emperor came in person to copy the explanation of the text. It was a unique occasion in which all the great functionaries, the queens, and other women of the palace, were all present.

The Emperor Jui-tsong who ascended the throne in 710 A.D. continued to take personal interest in the work till it was completed.

The board set up for this memorable work was constituted as-follows, Īśvara, a chief of Eastern India who was then at the Chinese capital, and a few others rendered the Sanskrit words into Chinese, Dharma, a Buddhist monk of Northern India, Prajñāgupta of Southern India and a number of other monks explained the meaning of the original text, the Chinese monks, Hui-kio, Tsong-yi, P'u-kin, Liu-fang and others took down the translation, Sheng-cheng, Fa-tsang, Ch'en-wai, Wu-cho, Shen-leang, Huai-ti and others discussed the meaning of the text, Ch'eng-li, Shen-kien, Yun-kuang and others put it good style. The nobles of the court were present at the time of the work. Emperor Jui-tsong wrote a preface.

Bodhiruci translated 53 volumes consisting of 111 Chapters. The translation of the *Ratnakūṭa* was his last work. After the completion of this work he devoted all his energy to the practice of dhyāna. He was at this time more than 100 years old. In 724 he accompanied the Emperor to Lo-yang where he stayed in the monastery of *Ch'ang-shou-sse* (since then called *K'ai-yuan-sse*). He died in this monastery in 727 A.D. On seeing that his end was approaching he told his disciples: "My body is getting gradually weaker like the drops of water that evaporate. Although I have lived long I feel that my end is approaching. So long I have been taking food in order to remove weakness. Now that I have reached the end what is the good of prolonging my life". So saying he took to fasting which lasted for 55 days. He then asked his disciples to leave him alone. "I need an atmosphere of tranquility. Don't make any noise". He then quietly passed away at the age of 156.

Another great Buddhist scholar who went to China in this period was Śubhākarasiṁha. He claimed descent from Amṛtodana, the uncle of Śākyamuni. He was at first in the monastery of Nālandā where he studied the various branches of the Buddhist literature. He was desirous of preaching the law in foreign countries and undertook a hazardous journey. He at first went to the country of the "Eastern Barbarians" (Turks?). Subsequently at the request of the Emperor he went to China. He reached Ch'ang-ngan in 716 A.D., with a large collection of Sanskrit manuscripts which he presented to the Emperor. Śubhākara put up in the monastery of *Si-ming.* Śubhākara went to Lo-yang with the Emperor in 724. It was at this time that he translated 5 works into Chinese. He died in 735 A.D. at the age of 99 and was buried in the mountain in the west of Long-men. Although he did not translate many works into Chinese his reputation as teacher was very great in China. He introduced a special school of mysticism in China. The last great Indian teachers to be in China were probably Vajrabodhi and his disciple Amoghavajra. Both of them were great personalities both at home and in

China. They firmly established the mystic school of Vajrayāna in China. Vajrabodhi was the third son of Īśānavarman, the king of Central India. He left the house at the age of 10 and joined Nālandā for his studies. He was at Nālandā for five years. He then went to Western India where he stayed four years for his studies. He came back to Nālandā where he continued his studies for six years more. He then went to South India where he most probably became the teacher of king Narasiṁha Potavarman of Kāñci. He then went to Ceylon and subsequently accompanied the Ceylonese mission to the Chinese Emperor. The mission was to present to the Emperor a copy of the *Mahāprajñā-pāramitā-sūtra*, precious objects, perfumes etc. He reached Canton in 720 A.D. In China he made a number of disciples, amongst whom the most famous were Amoghavajra and Yi-hing. He translated 11 Vajrayāna works between 723 and 730 A.D. The propagation of his mystic doctrines was entirely successful. Many studied them in the two capitals of China and the Buddhist laymen and monks did not escape the influence of the new doctrines. Vajrabodhi died at Lo-yang in 732 A.D.

The principal disciple of Vajrabodhi, Amoghavajra, was commonly known in China under his Chinese name Pu-k'ong. He belonged to a Brahmanical family settled in Ceylon. He was converted to Buddhism by Vajrabodhi at the age of 15. He accompanied his teacher to China. He studied the *Siddhaṁ* and the *Śabdaśāstra* with his teacher and was initiated by the latter into mystic practices. He reached Lo-yang with Vajrabodhi in 724 and stayed in the temple of Kuang-fu. He worked there till 731 when he was asked by Vajrabodhi to go back to India and make a collection of Sanskrit texts. Vajrabodhi died in 732. Amoghavajra left China in 736 and after a year of difficult voyage came to Ceylon. He stayed in *Daritavihāra* of Ceylon for three years studying the mystic doctrines of five different schools. It was at this time that he was entrusted by the King of Ceylon to carry presents of Sanskrit texts to the Emperor of China.

He returned to China in 746. Since then up to his death in 774 he worked incessantly and translated 119 works into Chinese. He wrote to the Emperor in 771 – "From my childhood I followed my teacher Vajrabodhi for 14 years (719–732) and was initiated by him in the practice of yoga. I then went to India and made a collection 500 texts which I brought back to China. I returned to China in 746. Since then up till now I have translated 77 texts consisting of 120 Chapters".

The account of these great Indian teachers who had gone to China shows the great effort which the Indian scholars were making in propagating Buddhist literature in the T'ang period. All of them received from the Chinese Emperors and people, the respect they deserved and were given facilities for their work in

China. We get the names of at least 21 Indian or Indianised foreign teachers who translated a large number of Buddhist texts into Chinese:

Prabhākaramitra of Nālandā	(627–633)	3
Bhagavaddharma (?) of Western India		2
Atigupta of Central India	(652–654)	1
Nandī of Central India	(655–663)	3
Jñānabhadra of Java	(664–676)	1
Divākara of Central India	(676–685)	19
Buddhatrāta of Kapiśā	(?)	1
Buddhapāla of Kapiśā	(683)	1
Devaprajña of Khotan	(589–691)	7
Śikṣānanda of Khotan	(695–710)	24
Mitraśama of Tukhāra	(705)	1
Ādisena (?) of Kāśmira	(693–721)	9
Bodhiruci of South India	(693–727)	35
Parāmiti (?) of India	(705)	1
Vajrabodhi of Central India	(720–732)	26
Śubhākarasiṁha of Magadha	(716–735)	21
Utpalavīrya (?) of Kucha	(790)	3
Dharmacandra of Eastern India	(730–43)	1
Ajitasena of Northern India	(732)	3
Amoghavajra	(720–771)	177
Prajñā of Kapiśā	(781–810)	8
		289 Works

But the Indian scholars were not alone. The help they received from their Chinese collaborators was not insignificant. But for their sympathy and active help the colossal work done in this period could not have been accomplished. The Chinese Buddhist pilgrims and scholars not only took part in the work of translation but also helped their countrymen to know India and Indian culture better. The pioneer in this task was the famous pilgrim Hiuan-tsang, whom we have already mentioned more than once.

Hiuan-tsang was a devout Buddhist. In his travels he "cared little for other things and wanted to know only Buddha and Buddhism. His perfect faith in these, his devotion to them, and his enthusiasm for them were remarkable to his contemporaries". He like all other Buddhists of his times followed a syncretic type of Buddhism. He was very rigorous in keeping the rules of his order according to the Vinaya principles. He was a staunch follower of the Yogācāra School of Mahāyāna but he also believed in the efficacy of magical formulae, invocations and worship of the Mahāyāna deities.

He had visited almost all parts of India, lived in the principal monasteries of the land and established personal contact with the great personalities. His principal teacher in India was Śīlabhadra, the great abbot of the Nālandā monastery. He made a deep study of the Yogācāra philosophy with him. The personal friendship which he had contracted with scholars in India is best exhibited in the following correspondence which passed between him and some teachers at Mahābodhi after his return to China. In 654 a monk of the Mahābodhi temple was sent to China with the following letter to Hiuan-tsang. The letter was written by Sthavira Prajñādeva (Hui-t'ien) "who knew well the doctrines of the 18 Schools of Hīnayāna".

> "The Sthavira Prajñādeva who is surrounded by men of great knowledge in the temple of Mahābodhi near the Vajrāsana of the Bhagavat sends this letter to Mokṣācārya [= Hiuan-tsang] of Mahācīna, who knows well and have penetrated well into the Sūtra, Vinaya and numerous Śāstras. He respectfully wishes him to be ever free from illness and pain. I Bhikṣu Prajñādeva, have now composed an eulogy of the great divine transformations of Buddha (= trikaya?) and a comparative study of the Sūtra and Śāstras etc. I hand them over Bhikṣu Fa-ch'eng who will carry them to you. Amongst us the Ācārya has numerous acquaintances and one of them, Venerable Jñānaprabha (Che-kuang) joins me in enquiring about you. The Upāsakas always continue to offer their salutations to you. We all send you a pair of white clothes to show that we are not forgetful. The road is long. Do not mind the smallness of the present. We wish you may accept it. As regards the Sūtra and Śāstras which you may require please send us a list, we will copy them and send them to you. This is all, Mokṣācārya, that we want to let you know".

Hiuan-tsang sent the following reply:

> "I learnt from an ambassador who recently came back from India that the great teacher Śīlabhadra was no more. This news overwhelmed me with a grief which knew no end. Alas! the boat on the ocean of suffering has sunk, the eye of men and gods is shut. How can I express the sorrow that his death has caused us. When Buddha passed away Kāśyapa continued and enlarged his noble work. When Sānavāsa died Upagupta continued to preach his fine doctrines. Now that a general of the Law has gone back to his own place may the teachers of the law acquit themselves of their task. My only desire is that the pure explanations and subtle discussions may extend in large waves like those of the vast ocean, that the blessed knowledge and the glory of the law

> may be eternal like the five mountains. Amongst the Sūtras and Śāstras that I, Hiuan-tsang, had brought with me, I have already translated the *Yogācāra-bhūmi-śastra* and others in all 30 volumes, large and small … I should humbly let you know that while crossing the Sindhu I had lost a load of sacred texts. I now send you a list annexed to this letter. I should request you to send them to me if you get the chance – I am sending some small objects as present. Please accept them".

The copies of these letters, preserved in a solitary corner of the Chinese Buddhist collection, bear testimony to the personal relationship that was established by Hiuan-tsang with his Indian friends. His example was followed by other Chinese pilgrims of the T'ang period, Wang Hian-ts'ö, Hiuan-chao, Yi-tsing and others. But Hiuan-tsang contributed even more to a better understanding of Indian Buddhism. After Kumārajīva he was certainly the most able translator of Sanskrit texts. He possessed a profound knowledge of Sanskrit and did not require the help of any interpreter. Seventy-six works are attributed to him, some of them are voluminous. The 76 works consisted of about 1250 chapters, amongst which were, the whole of the *Mahāprajñāpāramitā* in 600 chapters and the *Yogācāra-bhūmi-śastra* in 200 chapters. Hiuan-tsang was a great scholar of Buddhist philosophy and so he translated first the fundamental works of the Mahāyāna philosophy as well as the Abhidharma works of the Sarvāstivāda school which represented the Hīnayāna philosophy. He also translated a work of the *Vaisesika* philosophy – the *Dasapadartha-sastra* which was of great value for the study of the Yogācāra philosophy. All his translations bear the stamp of his deep scholarship.

His personal work, the *Ta t'ang si yu ki* – "The Memoirs of the Western World of the great T'ang period" is by far the best account of the foreign lands in Chinese. All previous accounts were either scrappy or one sided. For example from the account of Fa-hien practically nothing can be learnt about the political and social conditions prevailing in Eastern Turkestan and India. But Hiuan-tsang's account is a creditable performance from various points of view. Although he places greater emphasis on Buddhism he does not ignore the Indian life in general. He gives an account of the political condition, learning, society etc. of all the countries he visited. Even on Buddhism we know much more from his work than from the works of others. His account of the condition of Buddhism in India is of great value for the history of Buddhism in general.

Hiuan-tsang's influence was exercised in all fields of Buddhist studies. Amongst his disciples Tao-siuan became a great exponent of the Vinaya principles and the Vinaya school which flourished in China and Japan regarded him as the founder. The *Kośa* school which was based on the Abhidharma literature translated by Hiuan-tsang and which flourished in Japan also goes back to him. The Chinese and Japanese disciples of Hiuan-tsang were responsible for the foundation of the school. Another important school, the Yogācāra, called Hosso in Japan, was founded by one of his great disciples, Kui-ki and was based on the Yogācāra works translated by Hiuan-tsang. Many other Buddhist writers of the T'ang period drew their inspiration from Hiuan-tsang.

The example of Hiuan-tsang aroused in the heart of many a pious Buddhist in China a longing for visiting India. Wang Hiuan-ts'ö who visited India four times (643–663), although sent on official mission, did not fail to visit the principal places of Buddhist pilgrimage in India. He set up votive tablets at Bodhgayā and on the Grdhrakuta as an act of piety and took drawings of images to guide the artists of his own country.

Yi-tsing has given short accounts of 60 Buddhist monks who had been to India during the 2nd half of the 7th century A.D. These monks had come to India either by the sea-route or the land-route. Some of them did not go back to their native country and remained in India till their death. One of them, Hiuan-chao was educated in the *Ta hing sheng sse*, the place where Hiuan-tsang was residing, during the *Chen-kuan* period (627–650). We do not know exactly when he left for India but that was not before 650. On his way to India he visited Tokharestan, Sogdiana and other countries and then passed through Tibet which was then an ally of China. From Tibet he came to Jālandhara and after visiting different holy places at last came to Nālandā where he settled down for the study of the Yogācāra doctrines. Wang Hiuan-ts'ö met him in India at the time of his third visit and gave good report about him to the Emperor. The Emperor sent Wang Hiuan-ts'ö to take him back to China. He returned to China with Wang Hiuan-ts'ö. They passed by the route of Nepal and Tibet and completed the journey in 5 months. The Emperor received Hiuan-chao in audience. Emperor then ordered Hiuan-chao to escort a Brahmin named Lokāditya to Kashmir. This man is said to have known the medicine that could give long life and had gone to China on an invitation from the Emperor. On reaching the frontier of Kashmir Lokāditya met his own countrymen and left Hiuan-chao to follow the route to India. Lokāditya told him that the medicine which gives long life was available in Lāṭa country and advised him to go there. Hiuan-chao visited Balkh, Kapiśā, Sindhu and at last reached Lāṭa where he stayed for 4 years. He then passed to the South where he collected different kinds of medicine. Before starting for China he went to Bodhgayā and Nālandā. It was however impossible for him to go back to China, as Tibet had declared war on China and it was no longer possible to pass through Central Asia where the Arabs were barring the way Hiuan-chao died in India.

It is needless to give a more detailed account of all the 60 travellers who had been to India in this period. Some of them were Corean. But they all had the same pious zeal and came to India after overcoming many difficulties in the way, some of them not even caring to go back to their native land but to die in the holy land of Śākyamuni.

The last great Chinese pilgrim to come to India was Yi-tsing. He started from China by the sea route in 671 and after travelling in different parts of the South Sea Islands and in India went back to China in 695 A.D. In India he had been to Tāmralipti, Nālandā, Gṛdhrakūṭa, Vaiśāsalī, Kuśīnagara, Mṛgadāva etc. He spent 10 years at Nālandā in the study of Buddhist texts. When he returned to China he had with him a collection of 400 Buddhist manuscripts. He was not by temperament a philosopher like Hiuan-tsang his main interest being in Vinaya. As such his principal work was the study of the stupendous Vinaya of the Mūlasarvāstivāda school which he translated into Chinese. His translation of this Vinaya consists of a little more than 163 Chapters, almost the three quarter of the works he translated into Chinese (230 Chapters). His personal work, the *Nan hai-che-kui-nei-fa-ch'uan* "A record of the Buddhist Practices sent from the Southern sea" is entirely based on the *Mūlasarvāstivāda-Vinaya.* He died in 713 A.D. From the nature of his work it is evident that he was not a scholar to impress his disciples and countrymen so deeply as his predecessor, Hiuan-tsang. He did not go deep in his study of Buddhist religion and was contented more with the study of its formal aspect. This is just what could be expected. When Yi-tsing came to Nālandā, the great Yogācāra professor Śīlabhadra the teacher of Hiuan-tsang was already dead and there was nobody to take his place. Mysticism was gradually ousting the healthy philosophical schools at Nālandā. In fact Yi-tsing translated a number of *dhāraṇīs* but his heart was not in it. He did not take up any of the fundamental texts of the Buddhist mystic schools.

The last Chinese pilgrim to India was Wu-k'ong. He was sent to Kapiśā in 751 by Emperor Hiuan-tsong on an official mission. He did not return to China before 790 A.D. He passed long years in the monasteries of Khotan and Kucha. He did not visit any of the Buddhist holy places in India and came away from the frontier of India after visiting Kapiśā. The pious zeal of the earlier travellers no more inspired the Buddhists of this period and gradual worsening of the political condition of Central Asia on account of the Arab encroachment was already much interfering with the religious predilections of the travelling monks in this period. It is for this that the rest of the T'ang period appears as barren from the point of view of the Buddhist activities which were so long binding India and China together.

All through the T'ang period the Chinese Buddhist scholars took an active part in the work of translation. Numerous translations and also compilation works and commentaries are attributed to them. The following list will give a clear idea of their contribution in this respect:

1.	Hiuan-wan	... 9
2.	Hui-tsing	... 2
3.	Fa-yun	... 2
4.	Hiuan-tsang (645–664)	... 76
5.	Hiuan-ying (649)	... 1
6.	Hiuan-yun (656–660)	... 9
7.	Hiuan-fan	... 2
8.	Che-t'ong (653)	... 4
9.	Tu Hing-yi (676–679)	... 1
10.	Hui-li	... 1
11.	Huai-su	... 4
12.	Hui-che	... 1
13.	Hiuan-yi	... 1
14.	Yi-tsing (695–713)	... 71
15.	She Ngai-t'ong	... 1
16.	Hui-yuan (730)	... 1
17.	She Che-yen (705–721)	... 4
18.	She Hui-ti	... 1
19.	She Yen-tsong	... 3
20.	Fa-ts'iuan	... 4
21.	Yi-hing (683)	... 9
22.	Shen-k'ai	... 1
23.	Hui-Kuo (776–777)	... 1
24.	Kiong-sho (774)	... 1
25.	K'ong-ki	... 1
26.	Wu-ch'e	... 1
		212 works

Besides these translations and compilations we get a large number of original works on Buddhism written by Chinese scholars during the T'ang period. The official list mentions 68 Chinese authors who had written about 70 works, either commentaries or original discussions on Buddhism. A certain number of Japanese and Corean monks also had come to China in this period for study under able Chinese and Indian teachers. They also wrote a number of works which have been preserved in the Chinese Buddhist collection.

In short the work for the better understanding and propagation of Buddhism during the T'ang period was colossal. The Buddhist scholars from India, Central Asia, the South Sea Islands, Cambodia, Corea and Japan, all ran to China to collaborate with the Chinese Buddhist scholars in this work. The Nālandā monastery in India and the principal monasteries of China served as the important seats of learning where, flocked from all parts of the

Eastern Asiatic continent pious Buddhists who were inspired by great ideals of the Buddhist civilization.[1]

Sino-Indian Relations – The Period of the United Empires (II)

The political decadence that started towards the end of the T'ang period continued even after the assumption of power by the Song dynasty. The loss of control over Central Asia, the internal strifes and constant menace of foreign invasion gradually contributed to the weakening of the central power. The very same factors brought about the disruption of political life in contemporary India and removed the possibility of its unification under a suzerain ruler. These are the reasons for which we do not hear of any official contact between India and China in this period.

But religion was still an important and powerful factor in the life of the people of the two great countries. The Chinese and the Indian monks were still inspired by an indomitable zeal for keeping the light of the law burning. This zeal alone kept the Buddhist churches in China and India united for a few centuries more in spite of the unfavourable political and. social conditions in both the countries.

Five Chinese inscriptions were discovered from Bodhgayā. The first of these inscriptions was engraved by a Chinese Buddhist monk named Che-yi who had come to India towards the end of the 10th century. Che-yi probably did not go back to China. The other four inscriptions belong to the eleventh century. The second is due to a Chinese monk named K'o-yun, the third to Yi-ts'ing and Yi-lin and the fourth to Shao-p'in, all dated 1022 A.D. The last bears the name of Hiuan-wen who was sent by the Song Emperor T'ai-tsong to set up a votive stūpa near the Vajrāsana at Bodhgayā. It is dated 1033 A.D. They are indicative of certain activities of the pious Buddhists in China to keep up the relations with the Buddhists of India. There are a few other references to such activities in the Chinese records of which Chavannes made a special study in his now famous article – *Les Inscriptions Chinoises de Bodhgayā* (Revue de l'histoire des Religions, 1896). We are giving below translations of extracts from his article to show to what extent the Buddhists were active in China in this period.

> "The Chinese pilgrims who went to India in this period were numerous. As early as 964 A.D. when the Song dynasty had come into power only for five years, 300 monks started for the Holy Land. They travelled for twelve years. One of them named Ki-ye has left a short account of his travels. The year following their departure, the monk Tao-yuan came back from the west after an absence of 18 years. In 966, 156 persons

among whom there was one Hing-k'in responded to an invitation from the Emperor who wanted to send a mission to India. In 978, Ki-ts'ong and his companions came back from India, Kuang-yuan came back in 982, Fa-yu came back in 983 and left again for India just after his return, Ts'e-huan came back between 984 and 987 and Ch'ong-ta who was away from China for ten years returned in 989 (990?). Last of all in 1031, Huai-wen who had gone to India twice, left for India for the third time. He came back in 1039 and it was during this mission that he set up in 1033 an inscription which has been preserved at Bodhgayā.

"Besides these men there were certainly others of whom the historians have kept no account. None of the authors of the inscriptions of 1022 is mentioned either in the *Fo-tsu-t'ong-ki* or in the history of the Song dynasty. If they could be forgotten, there is no knowing how many others had shared the same fate. We know besides that there were in 982 a number of Chinese monks at the Imperial court who knew Sanskrit. It is probable that they had been to India for their studies.

"The most important thing is that a good number of these monks did not travel as common men. Some of them had been entrusted by the Emperor with quasi-official missions. The 157 men who left in 966 A.D. were furnished with letters patent ordering all the kings of Central Asia and Northern India to help them with guides. Similarly Fa-yu who was to follow the route passing by Sumatra about 983 A.D. had received credentials for the principal kingdoms in thalws land. On their arrival in India the pilgrims had often to carry out certain religious duties in the name of their Emperor. Kuang-yuan who came back in 982 could prove by a letter from an Indian Prince that he had given on behalf of the Emperor a kasaya to the Buddha at Bodhgayā. Huai-wen was acting directly on behalf of the Emperor Jen-tsong and the Empress in building a stūpa at Bodhgayā in 1033 A.D. The Indian monk Kio-kie who came to China in 1010 A.D. was given by the Imperial order a gold embroidered kasaya for presentation at the Vajrāsana. Even in the T'ang period, the pilgrims were not entrusted with such missions. The first Song emperors alone utilised the services of the monks for their personal religious duties.

"While the Chinese Buddhists were being drawn to the Holy Places by their pious beliefs, the Indian monks were also streaming into the Chinese court where they were assured of warm reception. We have probably too much ignored the considerable role that the Indians played in the propagation of their faith. The interest aroused by the Chinese pilgrims has thrown into the background the work accomplished by their Indian coreligionists. In fact the Chinese translations of texts belonging to the Tripiṭaka was as much the work of the one as of the other. The foreign monks came to China not in the T'ang period only. In the 10th and the 11th centuries Buddhism was still flourishing enough in the country of its origin to enable those missionaries who wanted to preach their religion to go abroad. It was perhaps the last ray of the light that was on the point of being extinguished. But till then divine flame was always burning and exerting its vivifying influence up to North China. In 972 A.D. the Śramaṇas K'o-che, Fa-kien, Chen-li, Su-ko-t'o and forty other monks of Western India arrived at Ch'ang-ngan. In 973 the Emperor received Fa-t'ien, a Śramaṇa of Nālandā with great honours. Fa-t'ien assumed the name Fa-hien in 982. He lived in China till his death in 1001. In 971, Mañjuśrī, the son of a king of Western India and in 977 Ki-sang, a Śramaṇa of Western India, also settled in the capital for sometime. T'ien-si-tsai a native of Kashmir, She-hu, a native of Uḍḍiyāna and Hu-lo, a Śramaṇa of Central India came to China. Emperor T'ai-tsong made a project of undertaking the work of the translation of sacred texts which had been stopped for two centuries. In 982 he appointed a board of translation at the head of which were placed three Indians, Fa-t'ien, T'ien-si-tsai and She-hu. It was probably due to their activity that the Chinese Tripiṭaka was enriched by a large number of works translated between 982 and 1011. The number of Sanskrit works on which they worked seems to have been numerous. The *Fo-tsu-t'ong-ki* tells us that each of the travellers coming from India or returning to China used to bring some palm-leaf manuscripts of Sanskrit texts with him. It is possible that one day some of these manuscripts of which we have only the Chinese translations will be discovered from the monasteries of Shan-si. The appointment of the board of translation and the redoubling of interest by the Emperor for Sanskrit studies was not without effect in attracting numerous Indian monks in China. They came in numbers. They were the following: Yong-she between 984 and 987, Pu-t'o-k'i-to a monk of Nālandā in 989, Kia-lo-shan-ti of Central India in 995, Ni-wei-ni of Central India and Fo-hu of Western India in 999, Fa-hu of Western India and Kie-hien of Northern India in 1004, Mu-lo-she-ki of Kashmir and Ta-mo-po of Western India in 1005, Chong-to of Western India and Kio-kie of Central India in 1010, Tsi-hien of the kingdom of Pan-ni in 1011, Che-hien of Western India, T'ien-kio of Uḍḍiyana, Miao-to of Ceylon, T'ong-sheu of Central India, Pu-ts'i of the kingdom of Varendra in Eastern India and many others in 1016. The author of the *Fo-tsu-t'ong-ki* tells us that there were never so many Indian monks in the Chinese court. Then came to China Ngai-hien-she, Sin-hu and their companions from Western India in 1024, five monks including Fa-ki-siang in 1027 and Shan-ch'eng and eight other Śramaṇas in 1036.

"This era of prosperity was however going to end suddenly. The history of the Song dynasty terminates its notice on India from 1036 A.D. although the Song dynasty continued to remain in power for two centuries and a half more. If the chronicler has stopped, it is because he had nothing more to report and because the relations between India and China ceased from 1036 A.D. The *Fo-tsu-t'ong-ki* also confirms it. It mentions the arrival of Che-ki-siang, a Śramaṇa of Western India in 1053 but after that date it does not mention either any Chinese pilgrim or any Indian missionary. There is still another indication which reveals a great crisis through which Buddhism passed in the middle of the 11th century. The number of monks and nuns in China in 1021 A.D. were respectively 397615 and 61240; in 1034, 385520 and 48740 but in 1068 only 220660 and 34030.

"The cause of this turn of fortune is not evident. Buddhism was not at all persecuted in China in the 11th century. No edicts of proscription were passed as during other periods. But however hidden, influences which undermined Buddhism were quite strong. The enemy of Buddhism was not the temporal power. The conflicts of ideals brought about its downfall. In the second half of the 11th century the literati started the offensive movement of rationalism which vigorously reacted against all principles of foreign importation. The leaders of this movement were Han K'i (1008–1075), the famous historian Sse-ma Kuang (1009–1086), Ch'eng Hao (1032–1085) and his brother Ch'eng Yi (1033–1107) and in the twelfth century the famous commentator and philosopher Chu Hi (1130–1200) – in short all the glories of this powerful school which like the Confucian literati vehemently attacked the Buddhist beliefs, incessantly and mercilessly. When we take into account how much the mind of the cultured class in China is even now imbued with the doctrines of the Song literati; we can understand what immense influence they must have exerted during their life-time. There is nothing to be surprised if Buddhism had been incapable of resisting such cruel enemies.

"In the same period Buddhism was passing through a still more serious crisis which had a fatal consequence. The Mahomedan invasion is not probably its immediate cause. The conquests of Mahmud of Ghazni (1001–1030) coincide on the contrary with the period during which the monks travelling between China and India were the most numerous. However in an indirect way the Islam had some influence on the destiny of Buddhism. By checking the formation of powerful native dynasties in the north and the centre of India, it removed its legitimate protectors which during so many centuries had helped it with princely gifts".

The activities of the translators during the Song period were not without importance. Although the texts translated into Chinese are not of much use for the study of early Buddhism they are of fundamental importance for the study of the later phases of Buddhism in India. Buddhism in India in this period had changed considerably and had given rise to mystic schools much influenced by the Brahmanical schools of Tantra. A large majority of Buddhist texts translated into Chinese in this period therefore belonged to these Tantric schools of Buddhism. The number of texts translated was considerable. About 285 such texts have been preserved in the Chinese Tripiṭaka. It will not be quite out of place to give a short description of Indian translators who worked in China under the Song.

The first and foremost of these translators was Fa-t'ien (法天). This might be either a Chinese name adopted by him or a Chinese translation of his Indian name which might have been Dharmadeva. He assumed a new name in 982 which was Fa-hien (法顯) or Dharmabhadra. He was originally a monk of the Nālandā monastery in Magadha. He came to China in 973 and was held in much esteem by the Emperor. He died in China in 1001 and was awarded posthumous honours by the Emperor. He translated in all 118 Sanskrit texts into Chinese. Another Indian monk who worked in China in the same period was She-hu (施護). This was probably the Chinese translation of his original name –Dānapāla. He was a native of the country of Wut'ien-nang (Uḍḍiyāna) in Northern India. He came to China in 980 and translated 111 texts into Chinese. The most important of these was a translation of the *Daśasāhasrik Prajñāpāramitā*.

There was another translator named T'ien-si-tsai (天息災) but his original name is not known. He was according to one source a native of Kia-she-mi-lo (Kāśmīra) but according to another source a monk of the monastery of Mi-lin in Jālandhara. There is however no contradiction as the kingdom of Jālandhara was a dependency of Kashmir. T'ien-si-tsai came to China in 980 and died in China in 999. He translated in all 18 works which include a translation of the *Mañjuśrīmūlakalpa*, in 20 chapters.

Another translator, Fa-hu (法護) or Dharmarakṣa came to China in 1004 with relics of Buddha and palm-leaf manuscripts. He was a monk of Western India. He worked in China till his death in 1058 and translated 12 works. All these were Mahāyāna works with the exception of one that was a Sarvāstivāda Abhidharma text. Other translators of this period were the following:

Che ki siang (知吉祥) or Jñānaśrī of Western India who translated 2 works about 1053 A.D.

Kin tsong che (金總持) or Suvamadhara who translated 2 works! about 1113 A.D.

Maitreyabhadra (慈賢) of Magadha who was in China till 1125 and translated 5 works.

Sūryakīrti (日稱) translated 7 works.

Besides, we get the name of three Chinese translators named Wei-tsing, Shao-to and Wang Je-hieu who translated altogether 10 Sanskrit texts in the 11th century. The number of Chinese, works on Buddhism by Chinese Buddhist monks as well as laymen that were compiled in the Song period was considerable. Seventy-six such works of varying importance by 43 authors have found place in the Taisho collection of the Chinese Tripiṭaka. This shows that the literary activity of the Buddhist scholars both Chinese and Indian in the Song period was not at all insignificant.

Note

1 Some portions of this account have been used in my recent book – *India and China*. An exhaustive reference to the principal authorities on this subject will be found in that book.

Part Two

SHORT ARTICLES

Compiled by Mrs. Ratna Sinha

SINO-INDIAN SPHERES OF INFLUENCES*

In ancient times, as now, there were certain spheres of influences. But these spheres were not determined so much by political or economic conditions as by cultural factors. The exploitation, in the modern sense, of smaller countries by bigger ones was wholly unknown and modern methods of colonisation had not evolved. Slow and gradual expansion of culture had brought into existence certain zones but has also an unconscious process and not a deliberate imposition which is generally fraught with subversive reactions.

In Eastern Asia two such zones had come into existence of which one was the Chinese and the other the Indian. The cultural expansion had produced what may be called a Greater China (Maha-Cina) and a Greater India (Maha-Bharat). These zones, however, were not exclusive and in certain areas they penetrated each other and produced cultural buffers. Some of the modern geographical terms, such as Indo-China, Indonesia, Ser-India (for Eastern Turkestan) still faithfully perpetuate the traditions of old cultural contacts.

There were two cradles of civilisation in Eastern Asia – China and India. The old Chinese civilisation was evolved in the province of Kan-su about 4000 years ago and thence it was carried to the fertile valleys of the Hwang-ho and its effluents. It gradually spread to other parts of the country and the aboriginal tribes slowly came under its influence. But the civilising process was so slow that the Chinese culture had reached only the banks of the Yang-tse kiang in the south by the 7th century B.C. Even in the 2nd century B.C. the Chinese influence was very feeble in the south-western provinces – Sse-chuan and Yun-nan. The powerful Central Government of China did not find it feasible to open a proposed route to India through Yun-nan on account of the unfriendly attitude of local tribes. The region was still beyond the sphere of civilising influences of China and military expeditions were not enough to turn the local tribes into friend of the Chinese empire.

---

* *Hindustan Standard, Puja Annual* 1944.

From about the beginning of the Christian era, the Central Government of China adopted a forward policy in regard to the small kingdoms in Eastern Turkestan, drove away the nomadic hordes that were barring the way to the west and brought almost all the kingdoms in that region as far as the Pamirs within the sphere of its political influence. The main interest of China was to guard the trade routes that connected China and the west. In the 7th century these kingdoms were converted into protectorates under a Chinese Governor with his headquarters at Ngan-si (Kuchar). The Chinese cultural influence, however, remained confined to the eastern part of Central Asia bordering on the Chinese empire.

The policy of expansion brought Corea and Japan within the sphere of Chinese culture. It was under Chinese influence that the civilisation of those two countries were developed and all aspects of their culture – script, literature, art, religion and philosophy still bear the stamp of Chinese civilisation. In the south, in the northern part of Indo-China and specially in Tonkin, the Annamese people although of a completely different racial stock adopted the Chinese civilisation and carried it further south along the coast into the country which we now call Annam on the decline of the Hindu colony of Champa. The Chinese Government was not, however, equally successful in the western part of Yun-nan where the autochthonous T'ai people maintained some sort of independence till the middle of the 13th century when it was brought under the central government. The T'ai people, however, had adopted many elements of the Chinese civilisation.

Thus China in the period of her highest prosperity had brought under its sphere of political and cultural influence not only the entire Chinese empire but also Corea, Japan, Tonkin (Annam), and Eastern Turkestan. She also maintained friendly relations with Kashmir, Tibet, Burma and the various kingdoms of Indo-China. The Mongol Emperor, Kublai Khan, entertained the grandiose idea of uniting all these elements by closer links and founding an empire not only political but also cultural. But he failed to realise through his invincible military strength what China had achieved in course of about one thousand years by a method of peaceful penetration. A cultural dominion had been already established over all these countries and that fact was only to be recognised. The various elements had already been brought together by closer and more durable links than an Emperor like Kublai could think of.

Ancient India's Influence

Ancient India extended her sphere of influence by a method quite unique in the history of the world. No military expedition was needed by her to guard any possible trade route, no army of conquest was required to safeguard the interest of her people abroad. Asoka had shown the way of *Dhamma Vijaya* or "conquest by law" and it seems that was the way followed by those Indians who carried their civilisation to the foreign lands. It was a slow and gradual expansion by the mountain passes of the north to Eastern Turkestan and Tibet and across the seas to Burma, Indo-China and Insulindia.

Indian culture had spread to Bactria already before the Christian era and it was established in different parts of Eastern Turkestan during the first few centuries of the same era. Small colonies of Indians were founded in various places in the southern part of Eastern Turkestan as far as the frontier of China. The Buddhist religion and art, Indian script, Indian sciences etc., were adopted in all the small kingdoms of that region. Sanskrit was studied by learned people and in some parts, most probably among the Indian colonisers, some Indian dialect was the current speech. Some of the local rulers even claimed Indian origin. But still there is not the slightest proof of any military expedition led by the Indians in that region. The Buddhist missionaries who had carried the Indian civilisation there and the Indian merchants trading with the local people had no need of any help from their mother country for their protection.

Tibet came within the sphere of Indian civilisation in the 7th century, of her own accord. The first emperor of the united Tibetan empire sent scholars to India for education and they were the first to raise the Tibetan dialect to the status of a language of culture. For the first time a script modelled on the Indian script was adopted for the Tibetan language. A grammar of the Tibetan language was written, based on the principles of Sanskrit grammar. Numerous texts were translated from Sanskrit into Tibetan. Buddhism became the national religion of the people and for several centuries frequent exchange of scholars between the two countries established closer and more durable links between them.

Indian civilisation was carried to Indo-China and Insulindia by merchants and Hindu priests and established in those countries during the first few centuries of the Christian era. Indian colonies soon grew up in different parts of the peninsula on the Annamese coast, in Cambodia, Java, Sumatra and Malay peninsula. Some of the Hindu kingdoms founded were Champa in what we now call Annain, Kambuja (Cambodia), Srivijaya (Sumatra and Malay peninsula) Yavabhumi (Java). The smaller islands of the Indian archipelago too accepted the Hindu culture. The wave reached in the east the islands of Bali and Lombok and the southern coast of Borneo. In the first period it was Brahmanism which became the accepted religion of these countries; Hindu temples dedicated to Siva and Vishnu were set up and the sacred literature of the Hindus began to be studied. The kings claimed descent from India, bore

Indian names and published their edicts in Sanskrit. Indian script was adopted in the entire region.

India's Cultural Colony

Nearer home, Burma also became a cultural colony of India. Brahmanism as well as Buddhism were adopted by the people very early. Indian script was adopted and Indian literature began to be studied. The wave of Indian culture had reached as far as Yun-nan and the T'ai state of Nan-chao founded in the 7th century had come to certain extent within the pale of Indian civilisation. Indian geographical names were transported to this region. Thus Yun-nan came to be called Gandharakuta and its rulers assumed the title of *Maharaja.* Under the influence of Buddhism, some places in that region were given the names of Buddhist holy places such as Rajagriha, Gaya, Gridhrakuta etc. The rulers of Nan-chao claimed descent from Asoka.

Thus about the 9th century the entire region including Burma, Yun-nan, the Malay-Peninsula, Indo-China, Sumatra, Java, Bali and small islands of the Indian archipelago constituted what is now called Greater India. Yun-nan was called Gandhara, the upper valley of Menam Kasambi, Upper Burma Arimardanapura, Siam Sukhodaya, the moutainous region to its north Yonarastra, Cambodia Kambujarastra, the region of modern Annam Champarastra, and the mountainous region to the north-west Atavirashtra. In the Malay peninsula there were the-kingdoms of Sri-Dharmaraja, Tambralinga and Lankasuka, in Sumatra and Java kingdom of Srivijaya and various other small kingdoms with Indian names in other parts of the archipelago.

We can therefore clearly see that the sphere of Indian influence extended in the west up to the Hindukush and in the east up to the China sea; in the north it had brought under it Eastern Turkestan and Tibet and in the south the whole of Insulindia. The southwestern portions of China, specially certain parts of the province of Yun-nan had also come under it and the T'ai tribes had adopted some elements of Indian civilisation. That is the reason why the various branches of the T'ai people, on their migration to Burma, Assam and Siam, did not take long to adopt the local culture and merge into the local people.

Two Cultural Influences

Thus was Eastern Asia divided into two zones of cultural influences, one the Chinese and the other, the Indian. These zones were not however water-tight compartments as none of them was determined by imperialistic motives. The people of Sino-Tibetan speech as in Tibet, Assam and Burma willingly adopted Indian civilisation without changing some of their racial characteristics, language, social customs and nobody interfered with their autonomy in these matters. On the other hand, elements of Indian culture had been a deep influence on the Chinese civilisation. Indian Buddhism, art, and sciences became part of the national culture of China.

History may not repeat itself but it can certainly impart many useful lessons to the posterity. Institutions that are imposed, friendship that becomes an infliction and plans for co-prosperity which hide subtle methods of exploitation of one by other were hardly known in the past. The methods adopted by China and India to bring innumerable groups of people within the spheres of their respective civilisation in the past, were so effective that artificial geographical and political boundaries set up during the last few centuries have not succeeded in destroying the links that connected the various groups in the past.

KHOTAN AS THE CULTURAL OUTPOST OF INDIA*

Forgetfulness would have been a bliss, if the subconscious had not retained the memories of the past to unloose them at the crucial moments. Past would have been a dead past, if the earth had not preserved in its bosom the ancient foot-marks to help its recovery. The desire of the modern scholar to dig out these marks has been as insatiable as that of the treasure-hunter of the olden days and there has often been an unprecedented competition among different nationalities in this search. This competition among scholars and archaeologists of various European countries led to the discovery of an enormous mass of materials from the deserts of Eastern Turkestan and within a short period of less than 25 years brought into focus lights from different quarters on the past history of this arid land.

The ancient Chinese records as well as the archaeological discoveries made in different places in Eastern Turkestan have unmistakably shown that the small kingdoms and principalities in this region had adopted Indian culture and preserved it as their own for about one thousand years. Buddhism was the accepted religion of the local people and script, literature, art and all other elements of culture had been mostly borrowed from India. The Tarim desert, situated as it is in the centre of this region, separates the populous localities of the north from those of the south. The Tarim river, known to the Indians in ancient times as Sita with all its branches watered these localities. Some of the ancient kingdoms have now disappeared in the sand-dunes, but the principal ones still exist. Kashgar or Shaila-desha, Yarkand or Cokkuka, and Khotan were the principal kingdoms of the south, and Kuchar (Kuchirajya) and Karasahr (Agnidesha) were those of the north. All these kingdoms once formed a sort of "Greater India" of the North. The dominant culture in those countries was Indian. They had also received some elements of Chinese culture specially because the local people served as active intermediaries of trade and culture between China and India.

---

* *Hindustan Standard, Puja Annual* 1945.

Military outposts had also been set up in some of these areas by the Chinese in very early times for safeguarding the principal routes of communication between India and China. Some of the modern archaeologists would, therefore, revive the name Ser-India which had once been given by the Greek geographers to this region.

Khotan's Role

Of all the ancient kingdoms in this region Khotan must have played the most important role in the dissemination of Indian culture. In fact it served as an advanced post for the colonisers and the missionaries from India. This was mostly due to its contiguity with Kashmir. The road from Kashmir to Khotan, though difficult was not long. It passed along the upper valley of the Indus up to Darel and then proceeding north-westward along the Yasin valley it went over hills and valleys up to Task-Kurghan. From Task-Kurghan to Khotan it was a westward journey over the Bolor Tagh range. This has been the usual route to Khotan from Kashmir even in recent times. It was also followed by the first Chinese traveller, Fa-hien, while coming from Khotan to India towards the end of the 4th century. His example was also followed by other Chinese travellers to India as well as by Indian travellers to Central Asia and China.

Khotan is mentioned as Godana or Godaniya in ancient Sanskrit cosmographical texts. Godana and Apara-Godana or Outer-Godana were the two northern countries known to the early Indian authors. This is the name under which the Chinese writers of the first and second centuries mention the country. The Chinese write "Yu-t'ien" but the old pronunciation of the name as current in the first century A.D. was Gu-dana. The pronunciation of the name had deteriorated through centuries into Kho-tan and in the 7th century the great Chinese pilgrim Hiuan-tsang tried to correct it in the light of his knowledge of Sanskrit as Kustana and explain it as the "Teat of the Earth." But this was evidently wrong. The Tibetans used to call it Gosthana or "the Land of Cows." The neighbouring mountain was known as the Goshirsha mountain and the principal Buddhist monastery in the capital of Khotan had the name of Gomati-vihara. The name of the country was thus a Sanskritic one – "The land of the cows" which must have been given by the Indian colonisers of ancient times.

But when did this colonisation start? No definite proof has been as yet found for fixing the date of the first colonisation. There is no doubt that it had taken place long before the Christian era. Asoka's emissaries might have gone up to Khotan, but there is no positive proof of this. A local tradition picked up and recorded by Hiuan-tsang says that when Asoka banished the officials who had blinded his son, Kunala at Takshashila, these men left the country and settled in the region of Khotan. In the course of time one of them was set up as their king. The corresponding Tibetan account which is rather contradictory says that when Kunala was blinded at Takshashila, his ministers and followers left the country in disgust taking him with them, went to Khotan and settled there. They placed Kunala on the throne and for many centuries the descendants of this Prince sat on the throne of Khotan. The historicity of this tradition has not been established, but it is permitted to believe, on the strength of records belonging to the period immediately succeeding it, that contact had been established between North-Western India and Khotan sometime in the Maurya period. Archaeological finds which unmistakably go back to the beginning of the Christian era clearly show that powerful Indian colonies had been already established not only in Khotan, but also in all its neighbouring principalities along the southern fringe of the Tarim desert extending almost up to the frontier of China.

The ancient documents unearthed in this area are written in what is known as the Kharosthi script which was prevalent in North-Western India since the time of Asoka till the Saka-Kushan period. The language of these documents is closely connected with the Indian dialect that was spoken in North-Western India in the same period. Many of the names of the local kings, officers and other dignitaries of the court are also Indian names. All these evidently presuppose a strong Indian infiltration in this region at least a century before the beginning of the Christian era.

The Sakas and Kushans after their conquest of India brought about a closer contact between India, and Eastern Turkestan. The Sakas had strong affiliations with the local people of the Khotan region. The tendency was strong among some modern scholars even to take the ancient language of the local people of the region as a Saka dialect. This however was not quite justified as the local people spoke not a Sakish language, but what is known as Eastern Iranian. The Sakas almost in every region merged into the Iranian people and if they ever left any influence whether racial or linguistic it was in the substratum.

The Kushans had already founded a strong empire before their conquest of India. This Empire included not only Bactria but also a considerable portion of Transoxiana. Various branches of their race were to be found settled in different parts of Eastern Turkestan and it is possible that when their political power attained its apogee after their conquest of North-Western India and Kashmir, they tried to extend their sway over the Khotan region. In fact the ancient Chinese records bear testimony to the establishment of a Kushan dominion in Eastern Turkestan during the reign of Kanishka. The contest of power that went on for several years between the Kushan emperor and the

Chinese army in this region was decided unfavourably for the Chinese who were defeated and ousted from this region.

Fruitful Era

This was the beginning of a most fruitful era in Indian colonisation and missionary activities in the whole of Central Asia. The Kushans who adopted Indian culture and religion took the lead and showed the way to other nationalities. Their own missionaries were the first to carry Buddhism to different parts of Eastern Turkestan as well as to China. The Indian monks followed suit. This era of prosperity in the history of Buddhist propagandism continued till the 8th century in an uninterrupted manner.

Centre of Learning

Khotan appears as a great centre of Indian learning throughout this period. A large number of Buddhist monasteries came to be founded in its capital and in the neighbouring hills. Indian Buddhist scholars settled in those monasteries became a source of attraction for the Buddhist monks from other parts of Central Asia and China. As early as the 3rd century A.D. Chinese scholars began to come to Khotan to study the Indian lore from competent Indian scholars settled there, instead of coming to India. The principal monastery in the capital of Khotan was called Gomati-vihara. Fa-hien who visited the country towards the end of the 4th century A.D. tells us that there were fourteen large monasteries in Khotan and besides a multitude of smaller ones. The account of a Buddhist Yatra of Khotan given by him reminds one of the Yatras still prevalent in India. The account runs thus:

> "At a distance of 3 or 4 li from the city, a four-wheeled image-car is made, over thirty feet in height, looking like a movable Hall of Buddha, and adorned with the seven preciosities, with streaming pennants and embroidered canopies. The image of Buddha is placed in the middle of the car with two attendant Bodhisattvas and Devas following behind. These are all beautifully carved in gold and silver and are suspended in the air. When the images are one hundred paces from the city gate, the king takes off his cap of State and puts on new clothes; walking barefoot and holding flowers and incense in his hands with attendants on each side, he proceeds out of the gate. On meeting the images, he bows his head down to the ground, scatters the flowers and burns the incense. When the images enter the city, the queen and Court ladies who are on the top of the gate, scatter far and wide all kinds of flowers which flutter

down and thus the splendour of decoration is complete. The cars are all different; each monastery has a day for its procession, beginning on the first of the fourth moon and lasting until the fourteenth when the processions end and the king and the queen go back to the palace".

Sarvastivada Buddhism

The form of Buddhism prevalent in Khotan was fully Indian. It was the Buddhism of the Sarvastivada school of which the chief centre was then Kashmir. The Mahayana Buddhism of which the chief centre was then in Gandhara was also current in Khotan. The fragments of ancient Buddhist texts discovered in this region fully substantiate this, contention. There are fragments of the Sarvastivada literature as well as those of Mahayana. There is also evidence to show that new Sanskrit Buddhist texts were being composed in those days in the monasteries of Khotan by Indian scholars. Fragments of a lot of other Sanskrit texts such as the medical texts, drama etc., have also been discovered from the region of Khotan. The Buddhist cave temples in the hills of Khotan, the wall paintings still found in them, the remains of Buddhist sculptures unearthed from the sand-dunes all go to prove that Khotan was a centre of Indian culture in those days. The cave temples are in all respects like those of Ajanta, Bagh und Bamiyan, the paintings in spite of the local influence have the same affiliation, while the sculpture mostly belongs to the Indo-Greek school that was prevalent in North-Western India. The account of Khotan as given by Hiuan-tsang is of interest in this respect. He says: "The system of writing had been taken from that of India, but the structure had been altered by a sort of successive changes. The people were Buddhists and there were above 100 monasteries, with more than 5,000 brethren, chiefly Mahayanists. The reigning sovereign was Buddhist and claimed Vaisravanadeva as his progenitor". The local traditions picked up by the Chinese pilgrim refer to numerous associations of Khotan with India and especially with Kashmir.

A discovery of the greatest importance in the history of our literature was made by Sir Aurel Stein a few years ago in a dilapidated monastery of Gilgit, midway between Kashmir and Khotan. While coming back from his last expedition in Eastern Turkestan some old leaves of Sanskrit manuscript fell into his hands. This led to his discovery of a stupendous hoard of Sanskrit manuscript in the debris of an ancient Buddhist monastery. The hoard was subsequently brought to Kashmir and immediately recognised as a Buddhist collection of about the 6th century A.D. The script in which most of the texts is written is a variety of North Indian writing of Gupta period as current in the region of Khotan. The largest and the most important text of the collection is the Vinaya of Mula-Sarvastivada school of Buddhism which was prevalent in Kashmir. It is written in Sanskrit and constitutes one of the most important contributions of Buddhism to Sanskrit literature. Most of the works of the Gilgit find was long lost in original. It was brought back from the Khotan region by some unknown monk of Kashmir long long ago to be preserved for us in the monastery of Gilgit.

The study of the ancient history is far from complete. Archaeological work in Eastern Turkestan is not yet exhaustive. Search for the lost links of history in ancient Chinese annals has been barely started. Indian scholars are not yet in the field, but yet our interest in this history is the greatest. The interest lies not merely in ascertaining what we did for other peoples and how we collaborated with other great countries of Asia in the task of evolving a common civilisation for Eastern Turkestan, but also in restoring what was lost to our own civilisation in the past.

> God grows weary of great kingdoms, but never of little flowers.
> Wrong cannot afford defeat but Right can. – Tagore

INDIAN SCIENCES IN THE FAR EAST*

Science was international in ancient times as now but while in modern times the transmission of knowledge from one part of the world to the other is quick, in ancient times it was a slow process. Nevertheless the progress of knowledge depended then as now on the co-operation of diverse nations. It is well known that scientific notions in astronomy and medicine were developed by the ancient Egyptians and the Chaldeans but with the fall of Babylon in 539 B.C. it was the Greeks and not the Persians who took up the tradition. The Greeks henceforth went on perfecting the knowledge and building up what is known as the Greek science.

In India the Vedic Aryans had developed a scientific knowledge in identical branches (astronomy, mathematics and medicine) between 2000 and 600 B.C., the period during which the Babylonian science was also developed. The Vedic literature mentions the star-gazers (*nakṣatradarśa*), calculators (*gaṇaka*) etc. Already in the period of the *Ṛgveda*, the year was a solar year of 360 days and a quinquennial cycle with an intercalary month had been elaborated. Twenty-seven or twenty-eight lunar zodiacs (*nakṣatras*) and the phases of the moon also were known. The planets came to be discovered slightly later in the Āraṇyaka period about the 8th century B.C. Certain technical geometrical knowledge was also acquired in course of construction of the altars. The solution of the theorem of the square of the diagonal (Pythgorean Theorem) was known in the Sūtra period (600–400 B.C.). The fundamental bases of medical science (*Āyurveda*) were also established in the Vedic period.

Indian indebtedness to the Chaldean knowledge has not been proved. It was maintained by some scholars when our knowledge of the Chaldean science was imperfect that India derived her knowledge of the lunar mansions from them. But authentic Babylonian sources show that the Chaldeans from early times distinguished 12 zodiacal constellations or certain definite stars in them in order to speak of the position of the planets. These stars or star groups were 36 or probably in earlier times 24. But there is no reference to 27 or 28 as the

* *The Indo-Asian Culture* 11.1 (July 1953).

counting was in a duodecimal system. As the Chaldeans knew the solar zodiac with 12 signs, they had no need of lunar zodiacs. The Indian lunar zodiacs were therefore of independent origin. The notions of medical science which we find in the Vedas have no analogy with the Babylonian system. So those notions also in India were of independent origin.

The rise of the Achaemenians was very important in the history of science. Darius founded an empire which extended from the frontiers of Greece up to the banks of the Indus. This empire existed till 331 B.C. when Alexander destroyed it. But during a period of nearly two centuries before Alexander appeared on the scene, the Greeks who inherited the science of ancient Egypt and Chaldea and Indians who inherited the scientific knowledge of the Vedic period had occasion to meet in the capital and big cities of the Persian empire. There was then a great exchange of scientific ideas between these two people and that explains many of the similarities between the Greek and Indian sciences: it is now known that the "Treatise on Winds" by Hippocratius and the "Timeus" of Plato were based in theories that went from India. That explains also the similarities in some of the philosophical ideas of the two people e.g. the presence of the doctrine of transmigration in the system of Pythagoras. The influence of Greece on India in this period is not quite evident but in a later period a number of astronomical notions of the Greeks with Greek names were taken over by the Indian astronomers in order to perfect their own system. Division of the heavens into zodiacal signs, decani, and degrees, rectification of the order of the lunar asterisms which no longer accorded with reality and along with that the knowledge of the precession of the equinoxes came from the Greeks.

Thus the Greeks and the Indians were the only two peoples who continued to develop scientific knowledge and sometimes in collaboration after the fall of the ancient civilisations of Egypt and Babylonia. They were also responsible for the dissemination of scientific knowledge among different people. The Greeks transmitted it to the Christian world and later to the Arabs while the Indians transmitted it to Eastern Asian countries – Central Asia, China, Tibet, Mongolia, Korea, Japan and to the countries of South-East Asia – Indo-China and Indonesia.

Geography, Mathematics and Astronomy

We do not have any records of the Scythian nomads of Central Asia in the early period. But as they peopled the whole area between the Achaemenian empire and China, they seem to have carried a lot of Indian knowledge to the Chinese in the 4th and 3rd centuries B.C. Indian influence on Chinese civilisation in this period is marked by the adoption by the Chinese of the Indian geographical knowledge: the conception of the Central Mountain (Meru) from which arises the four rivers, the theory that the earth consisted of 7 continents surrounded by seas and situated around the central mountain etc. The identification of this Meru with Kun-lun was done very early and since then attempts were made to search for the sources of the Yellow river in that mountain.

Along with this geographical knowledge also came the knowledge of astronomy. The ancient Chinese knew a few stars in the sky like the Pleides, Antares etc and with their help they calculated the duration of the seasons. It had led them to calculate the duration of the year as 366 days. The first scientific notions came to them in two waves: First came the Indian knowledge of the 28 lunar mansions which the Chinese call *sieu*, the knowledge of the distinction between planets and stars and the cycle of Jupiter. In the second wave came more precise mathematical knowledge which helped them to discover the connection of the sun with the lunar mansions, to fix the winter solstice, to begin the year with the vernal equinox and to intercalate the month in the cycle of five years. This led to the compilation of the first calendar called T'ai chu li in 104 B.C. by Chuan-hsiu which became the basis of all future calendars. As the precession of the equinoxes was not yet known, the solsticial points were taken as fixed in this calendar.

China came in direct contact with India with the arrival of the Buddhist monks in the 1st century B.C. This enabled the Chinese to have more accurate knowledge of Indian science and to build up their system on the borrowed data. They soon became acquainted with the gnomon and clepsydra. Towards the end of the 1st century B.C. a mathematician, Liu-hin, fixed great periods of time on the basis of Indian *kalpa*s. For the next two centuries the most important problem that taxed the Chinese astronomers was how to make the lunar calendar agree with the solar one and how to determine the exact duration of each lunaison. Solar years were not yet known.

In 196 A.D. Liu-hung, a great mathematician, calculated the solstice with the help of gnomon and declared that the solsticial points were not fixed, that the equator and the ecliptic were not the same. This was an advance on the previous knowledge and the new calendar prepared by Liu-hung remained in force for nearly three centuries. It was in the 6th century that more precise knowledge was imparted by the Indian missionaries and the uncertainty in the calendar and consequent quarrel among the astronomers came to an end.

This new knowledge was imparted through Indian texts which were translated into Chinese in the 6th century. The texts are now lost but Chinese history tells us that they were in use till the 17th century. These texts were:

(i) *Po-lo-men t'ien wen king* – Sūtra on the astronomy of the Brahmins in 21 chapters by a Ṛṣi called She.

(ii) *Po-lo-men Kie-kia sien t'ien wen shuo* – discourse on the astronomy of the Brahmin Kie-kia in 30 chapters.

(iii) *Po-lo-men t'ien wen* – a book of Brahmanical astronomy in one chapter.
(iv) *Mo-teng-kie king huang tu* – a map of the sky in the *Matangi sūtra.*

A direct acquaintance with the Indian texts led to certain improvements in the calendar. In 576 A.D. Chang Tze-sin discovered that the orbits of the planets were elliptic and not circular. In 566 A.D. a new calendar was made which became the basis of all future official calendars.

The prestige of Indian astronomy was thus established in China and in the 7th century Indian astronomers were officially appointed to help in the preparation of the calendars. In the 7th century we find in Ch'ang-ngan, the Chinese capital, three different Indian schools of astronomers: Gautama, Kāśyapa and Kumāra. In 684 A.D. a member of the Gautama family prepared a calendar called *Kuang tse li* "the calendar of the bright house" which was in force for three years. Another member of the same school presented a new calendar in 718 A.D. It was practically the translation of an Indian calendar. The book is called *Kiu-che-li–Nava-graha-siddhānta.* It was in use for four years and is still preserved. It contained calculations of the moon's courses and also the eclipses. In 721 A.D. a Chinese Buddhist scholar, Yi-hing, undertook to prepare a new calendar based on Indian sources. This calendar which is known as the *Ta yen li* was completed in 729 A.D. after Yi-hing's death. The work used much of the old Indian materials and introduced in the Indian fashion nine planets – the sun, the moon, the five planets and two new ones – the Rāhu and the Ketu by which the Indian astronomers represented the ascending and the descending nodes of the moon.

As astrology was inseparable from astronomy in those days, it will be worthwhile to note some translations of Indian astrological texts into Chinese in this period. Amoghavajra, an Indian Buddhist scholar who was in China from 724 to 774 A.D. translated four astrological texts:

(i) *Fan t'ien huo-lo kiu yao* – The Horā and the Navagraha of the Brahmins.
(ii) *Tsi yao sing chen pie king fa* – The different influences of the seven stars and lunar mansions.
(iii) *Ts'i yao jang tsai kiue* – Mantras for averting the evil influences of the seven planets.
(iv) *Wen shu she li p'u sa ki chu sien so shuo ki hiong she je shan ngo su yao king* – Sūtra spoken by Bodhisattva Mañjuśrī and the sages on the auspicious and evil days and the good and evil planets and lunar mansions.

In Mathematics also there was a considerable influence of India on China. Certain mathematical and geometrical notions went with astronomy. It was in the 3rd century A.D. when Buddhism had been well established in China that the Chinese mathematicians produced special mathematical treatises.

The first attempt is a book of Mathematics which was compiled by Sun-tseu called *Sun tseu suan king* – "the Classic of Mathematics by Sun-tseu." The title betrays an Indian influence and may be rendered as *Gaṇita-sūtra* by Sun-tseu. Among other things the text states the solution of indeterminate problems. This was not understood for many centuries till it was taken up by Ts'in Tao-ku in the 13th century and explained algebraically.

In the 3rd century another important work on Mathematics was compiled by Liu-hui. The work is called *Hai tao suan king.* In this case also the word king (sūtra) is used. It is an elaboration of a classical treatise on Mathematics called *Kiu-chang suan shu,* "Art of calculation in 9 sections" which goes back to the 2nd century B.C. The last section is on Trigonometry and deals with 24 problems of what is known as the Pythagorean theorem. The work was further commented on in the Ts'ing period by Li Shang-che. The solution of this theorem, as we have seen, was known in India in the Sūtra period (600–400 B.C.), the period when Pythagoras also lived. Leaving aside the question of the original discoverer, it may be said without fear of contradiction that the Chinese derived their knowledge of this theorem from India and further elaborated it.

One of the sections of the *Kiu-chang suan shu* deals with algebra which is called in Chinese Ta-yen. The unknown quantity is described as *t'ien-yuan,* "monad" which seems to be a translation of Sanskrit *vīja.* Algebra as elaborated in China in later times shows definite Indian influence. The numbers are given contrary to the Chinese practice from the left to the right. The solution of the indeterminate problem is literally called atomisation, pulverisation. This again is a translation of the Sanskrit algebraical word *kuṭṭikāra.*

A number of Indian treatises on Mathematics were translated into Chinese in the 6th century A.D. viz,

(i) *Po lo men suan fa* – Brahmanical methods of calculation in 3 chapters.
(ii) *Po lo men yin yang suan li* – Brahmanical method of calculating time in 1 chap.
(iii) *Po lo men suan king* –Brahmanical mathematics in 3 chaps.

When a more detailed study of Chinese mathematics is available, it may be possible to make an exact estimate of the Indian influence. But so far as we can see, the influence was very profound. From the 13th century when contact between India and China ceased, the Chinese developed their own science on the bases supplied by India. China again transmitted the Indian sciences to Korea and Japan along with Buddhism from the 6th century onwards.

So far as the Hinduised countries in the Far East are concerned – Cambodia and Champa in Indo-China and Śrī-vijaya and Yavadvīpa in Indonesia – the

Indian sciences of mathematics and astronomy (*gaṇita* and *jyotiṣa*) were studied in Sanskrit original.

Medicine

Indian medicine played a still greater role in the history of the scientific activities of Eastern Asian people as it had a greater humanitarian appeal. The Buddhist missionaries like the Christian missionaries of later times were also medical men and carried with them medical literature wherever they went. The archaeological explorations in Eastern Turkestan have brought to light a number of documents on Indian medical literature which was generally current from the 4th to the 8th century A.D. in different parts of that region. The famous Bower manuscripts which were discovered in an old stūpa near Kucha contain three medical texts. "One of these texts speaks of the origin of garlic which, according to the author, is able to cure many diseases and can extend the life to 100 years. Besides, the manuscript speaks about digestion, about an elixir for a life of 1000 years, about the correct mixing of ingredients, about other medicines, lotion and ointment for eyes etc. A second fragment contains 14 medical formulas for external and internal use. The 2 biggest portion is the *Navanītaka*, i.e. 'cream' which contains an abstract of the best earlier treatises and which in 16 sections deals with the preparation of powders, decoctions, oils and also with injections/elixirs, aphrodisiacs, nursing of children, recipes etc. Many authorities on medicine are quoted in *Navanītaka*, particularly, *Agniveśa, Bheḍa, Hārīta, Jātukarṇa, Ksarapani, Parāśara* and *Suśruta*". Apart from these texts in Sanskrit original, there are also fragments of ancient translations of Indian medical texts in local languages. Thus we have a Kuchean translation of the Yogaśataka which is a medical text attributed to Nāgārjuna. We have besides Kuchean translations of various other Sanskrit texts on names of drugs which cannot be identified. Texts on the preparation of medicine were also translated into Kuchean. These translations clearly show that even the local people who did not know, Sanskrit were taking interest in the Indian medical texts.

The Chinese also had borrowed numerous elements of the Indian medical system. Although we do not find translations of the classical texts of Indian medicine into Chinese, the Chinese medical texts contain a large number of names of Indian drugs and besides the Indian "theory of wind". There are Chinese translations of a few minor medical texts:

(i) *Bhaiṣajyarāja-sūtra* translated in 230 A.D.
(ii) *Avalokiteśvarakrta-cikitsā-śastra* translated in the 7th century.
(iii) *Kumāratantra* of Rāvaṇa translated in the 10th century.
(iv) *Kāśyaparṣiprokta-strīcikitsā-sūtra* translated in the 10th century.

There are besides sections on medicine in various other Buddhist texts that were translated into Chinese.

Thus a text on meditation which was translated in 455 A.D. by a Chinese nobleman (*Che ch'an ping pi yao fa*) gives a description of the nervous system and deals with the diseases of the heart and the nerves. We know also that one of the important occupations of the Chinese pilgrims who came to India in different periods was to collect Indian medicinal herbs.

In Tibet and Mongolia

Tibet which became an important cultural colony of India from the middle of the 7th century, borrowed from India along with Buddhist culture: Indian grammatical science, Indian astronomy with the Jupiter's cycle of 60 years and besides Indian medicine. We have a number of Indian medical texts in Tibetan translation. The principal amongst them are – *Yogaśataka*, *Jīvasūtra* and *Avabheṣajakalpa* of Nāgārjuna, *Aṣṭāṅgahṛdayasamhitā* of Vāgbhaṭa with five different commentaries, Vaidyaka-siddhasāra, Mahauṣadhibala, Āyurvedasārasaṃgraha and *Aśvāyur-veda* of Śālihotra. There is besides a large number of texts on *Rasaśāstra* or *Rasāyana* i.e. Chemistry and Alchemy. The Indian medical system was transmitted to Mongolia by the Tibetans after the conversion of Mongolia to Lamaism in the 13th century.

In South-East Asia

In Cambodia, Champa and Java, so far as we can see from ancient Inscriptions, Indian Āyurveda was studied in original and applied. It was the custom among the rulers to found hospitals for the treatment of men as well as domestic animals, and services of competent medical men were retained for the purpose. This was in imitation of the prevalent Indian custom.

THE VISVA-BHARATI CHEENA BHAVANA*

It was well known to the great founder of the Visva-Bharati that the history of India could not be properly studied without reference to the history of other Asiatic countries. India in the past gave her civilization to millions of Asiatics. She also did not close her doors to the foreign people, such as the Greeks, the Persians, the Scythians, the Turks and to many others. This great exchange in the past brought about a community of ideas and ideals and established links between various peoples of this continent in spite of their racial and linguistic differences. Tagore wanted to have the past of India studied against this wide canvas when he started his Visva-Bharati.

The first visiting Professor of this new institution was Professor Sylvain Levi, Professor of College de France and a member of the French Academy. He was just the scholar who could inaugurate studies on lines required for the purpose. He started by teaching the Tibetan and Chinese languages and drawing the attention of the Indian scholars to the remains of Indian civilization in Central Asia, Indo-China and Indonesia. It was expected of the students that they would collect materials from all these sources in order to build up slowly the history of the great past of India.

The start once given, the materials for work came gradually pouring in. Various foreign Governments came to the help of the Visva-Bharati. The French Government made gifts of complete sets of the Research Publications of the French learned societies during successive years and in course of a short time a precious library was built up. In some respects the Visva-Bharati Research Library has still a unique character. Soon a complete set of the Tibetan Buddhist literature – the Tanjur and the Kanjur – was added to the Library and a number of Sanskrit manuscripts was collected. But a Chinese collection was still wanting.

This help came to the Visva-Bharati from the friends and admirers of the Poet in China about ten years ago. With contributions sent by them, the Cheena-Bhavana was founded and formally opened in 1937.

* *Visva Bharati Annals* 1947.

Apart from the building and the spacious rooms for study, the Cheena-Bhavana was provided with a valuable library consisting of rare Chinese publications, not only different rare editions of the Chinese Buddhist literature but also, Chinese history, classics, geography, encyclopædic compilations, poetical works of various ages, etc. In fact this library is the only one of its kind to be found in India. It is a very precious collection of over 100,000 volumes.

At the opening ceremony of the Cheena-Bhavana the poet said: "The most memorable fact of human history is that of a path-opening, not for the clearing of passage for machine or machine-guns but for helping the realization by races of their affinity of minds, their mutual obligations of a common humanity. Such a rare event did happen and the path was built between our people and the Chinese in an age, when physical obstruction needed heroic personality to overcome it and the mental barrier a moral power of uncommon magnitude. The two leading races of that age met, not as rivals on the battle-field each claiming the right to be the sole tyrant on earth, but as noble friends glorifying in their exchange of gifts. Then came a slow relapse into isolation, covering up the path with its accumulated dust of indifferences. To-day our old friends have beckoned to us again, generously helping us to retrace that, ancient path, obliterated by the inertia of forgetful centuries and we rejoice."

What was a matter of rejoicing for him is also one for the whole nation. This is an effort full of immense possibilities, not only in regard to the study of our great past but also, for establishing mutual understanding between the two biggest agglomerations of people on earth. Understanding between nations are not reached by mere words of propaganda, whether cultural or political, but through the patient collaboration of their best minds in the fields of literature, philosophy, history and other branches of human knowledge.

From the beginning of the Christian era up till the 12th century A.D., Indian scholars had been going to China almost in every period. They had, in collaboration with Chinese scholars, translated thousands of Indian texts into Chinese. The Chinese Buddhist collection at present consists of several thousands of translated Indian texts which are mostly lost in their original. Therefore an important section of Indian literature has been preserved for us in Chinese and unless we can make them accessible to our students and scholars the great past of India cannot be unfolded in its true perspective. This is again a task of patient collaboration between Chinese and Indian scholars which run be fulfilled after many years of painstaking work.

Moreover the Chinese historical literature contains much information hot only on various periods of Indian history but also on the history of those regions like Central Asia, and Further India where Indian civilization was predominating for more than one thousand years. These go to form important chapters of Indian history which can be recovered mostly from the Chinese annals. In this respect too the Sino-Indian Studies make its need imperative.

Part Three

ARTICLES IN BENGALI

Translated by Mrs. Ratna Sinha

INDIAN CIVILIZATION IN CHINA

It is quite unnecessary to remind the readers to take a fresh look at the close association that existed between India and China in the ancient period. The India-China contacts dating back to the second century before the Christian Era, occupies a major part of Indian history, though many of us are oblivious of this. Nevertheless, the knowledge of our past history contributes to a great extent towards the reconstruction of India by stringing together the lost links of our cultural ties.

The name *Cina* (*Chin*) attributed to China was introduced by India to the outside world. The Chinese people call their country by a different name. Even in the bygone days the Chinese used a different name for their country. Qin dynasty ruled China is the third century B.C. and according to the tradition the country was called Cinadesh after the name of the ruling dynasty. Despite the succession in the ruling dynasty and the subsequent change in the name of the country, the Indians maintained the previous name i.e., *Cina*. It is interesting to note that in the early Greek literature China has been referred to as *Sinae*, *Thinae*, etc.

Prior to the establishment of democracy in China, the elite class of China used to be called "Mandarin". The spoken language of the people living in Peking, the capital, used to be called "Mandarin". This word is a modified form of the Sanskrit word *mantrin*. Portuguese sailors and merchants spread this name "Mandarin" to the outside world.

Ancient Chinese literary sources throw light on the age-old Sino-Indian contact. Surprisingly there is very little record of the contact between there two nations in Indian literary sources. However there is reference of *Cinasi* and *Cinapatta* in Kautilya's *Arthasastra* and *Cina* in the Indian epic *Mahabharata* – we are not too certain about the date of their composition.

Sino-Indian interactions are recorded serially in the Chinese annals. Folklores have incorporated these annals, which should not be considered authentic. One such hearsay account is about seventeen Buddhist monks who went to China during the time of the Mauryan king Asoka. These Indian monks, being foreigners to the country of China were imprisoned and later on given freedom. According to another legend, a Chinese general while returning to China after vanquishing the Hunas in a battle fought in their land, collected a golden image of Buddha.

A long drawn battle was waged between China and the Hunas; the Hunas conquered the north and northwestern frontiers of China and began persecuting the Chinese people. The Great Wall of China was constructed to prevent the Huna aggression. In spite of this effort, the Chinese were not able to defeat the Hunas. In the third quarter of the second century of the Christian Era the emperor of China realised the need for immediate coalition with various countries of Central Asia which would enable him to root out the Hunas completely. Sakas and Takharians used to live in Khotan, Kashgar, Samarkand, etc. areas of Central Asia. The emperor of China with a view to establishing cordial relation with the neighbouring countries, sent an envoy called Zhang Qian to all these countries in 136 B.C. Immediately, as Zhang Qian crossed the borders of China, he was imprisoned by the Hunas. After staying in captivity for nearly ten years, he arrived in Tokharisthan, the capital of which lay on the other side of the Pamir, on the bank of Oxus river. Although Zhang Qian initiated an alliance with the Sakas and the Tokharians, they did not agree on waging a war against the Hunas.

However, plenty of Chinese goods at the capital of Tokharisthan drew the attention of Zhang Qian. On inquiry, he came to know that the Indian merchants brought those goods from India through southwestern regions of China. No sooner did Zhang Qian reach China than he suggested the emperor to establish trade relation with India. There were two routes to India – one through Central Asia by crossing the Pamir and Hindu Kush ranges and other was through Yunnan, the southwestern province of China.

It can undoubtedly be said from the accounts of Zhang Qian that a trade relation with India was established before the third quarter of the second century B.C. There is early reference to trade routes through Yunnan, though detailed description can be found only in the later Chinese literary sources. This route started from Yunanfu (that is, present-day Kunming), the capital of Yunnan province, crossed the hilly country and present-day Shan kingdom and ended at Bhamo, in the northern region of Burma. There were two land-routes for reaching India viz. one through the northeastern part of Assam and another through Arakan and Manipur. Both the routes met at Pataliputra, the capital of Magadha, the final destination.

In the first century B.C., the Chinese obtained full control over the trade route through Central Asia after defeating the Hunas and soon established contact with India through this route. That was the time when the Kushana kings seized power over northwestern part of India. Once this route came into use, the Kushana kings sent envoys along with Buddhist scriptures to the

Chinese emperor. The Kushanas had embraced Buddhism by that time. The envoy sent by the Kushana king arrived at the capital of China in year 2 B.C. In the meantime, Buddhist monks from eastern India came to Funan to spread the message of Buddhism. This time an important book highlighting Buddhism as a superior form of religion compared to other forms of religion in China, was published by a scholar named Mozi. This book influenced Chinese people profoundly. Some members of the royal family of China were converted to Buddhism. In the third quarter of the first century of Christian Era the emperor of China himself was drawn towards Buddhism. That was the time when two Indian monks Kashyapa Matanga and Dharmaraksa came to the capital of China laden with Buddhist scriptures. There is a popular legend that they came with a white horse laden with numerous Buddhist scriptures. The Chinese emperor extended a warm welcome to them at his capital. In 68 A.D. the first Buddhist monastery was founded in China which was named the White Horse Monastery.

From 68 A.D. to 220 A.D., the second Han dynasty ruled the country and patronized Buddhism, which spread rapidly among the people. Various foreign scholars from Parsia, Tokharisthan, Sogdiana, etc. established Buddhism on a firm footing. With their utmost efforts renderings of Buddhist scriptures were undertaken and this added to the growing popularity of the religion. These countries were drawn to the civilization of India and the Chinese sources corroborate this fact.

INFLUENCE OF INDIAN MUSIC IN THE FAR EAST

The rich Indian culture spread to various cultural spheres of the Far East. Indian philosophy, literature, science and art left their distinct marks through Buddhism. Over the ages the profound impact of the multifaceted Indian culture enriched these countries by enkindling their creativity in various spheres of culture. However, the influence of Indian music remains hidden behind the history of the music of these countries.

Many civilised nations and races inhabiting Central Asia adopted Indian music and, due to cultural contacts, the prevalent music of Central Asia was incorporated into Indian treatises on music. From the various references to Indian *raga*s (principal modes of Indian classical music) in our treatise on music, there are indications of this unique absorption of foreign music. Todi and Khambaj, two North Indian *ragas* and principal modes of Indian classical music, could have some connection with Turkey and Kamboj (i.e., ancient Iran) as the names of these *ragas* suggest. In the fifth and sixth centuries of the Christian Era, the Turkish people infiltrated into India. Similarly, an ethnic group of people from Central Asia called Kamboj also migrated to India and settled permanently on the northwestern frontiers of the country. It is quite likely that the infiltration of these foreigners had impact on the cultural life of people and music occupies an integral part of culture. In Kucha, situated in the northern part of Central Asia, people are known to have had a tradition of cultivation of music. The kingdom of Kucha developed a close contact with Kashmir by the second and third centuries of the Christian Era. The Sarvastivada Buddhism prevalent in Kashmir influenced the people of Kucha; treatises on Sarvastivada were translated into Kuchean language; and many Buddhist scholars from Kashmir came to Kucha and settled there.

The Chinese literature throws light on the cultivation of Indian music in Kucha. Music occupies a very high position in Chinese culture. Confucians emphasised the importance of music when performing ritual associated with religious or ancestral ceremonies. For this reason the Chinese emperors used to maintain a public orchestra. At times the emperor used to invite foreign orchestra and this led to the exposure to foreign influence.

In the last quarter of the sixth century A.D., a musician called Sujiva went to China from Kucha. He was skilful in playing *veena*, a popular instrument in India. Chinese music is based on five musical notes instead of seven musical notes as used in most other classical music. It was an amazing experience for the Chinese when they were introduced to the seven musical notes. Sujiva, the Kuchean maestro, actually was person of Indian descent. His ancestors were inhabitants of India and the family had a long tradition of music. The mention of seven notes, which were introduced by musician Sujiva of Kucha to China, can be found in Chinese sources. Out of these seven notes, four notes were undoubtedly absorbed from Indian treatise on music. For example, *sadja* (*shazhi*), *sahagrama* (*shahoujialan*), *pancama* (*banzhen*) and *rasabha* (*silishi*).[1] The three other notes referred to in the Chinese texts are little obscure to render the roots of these musical notes. It is probable that the distortion occurred due to the oversight of the Chinese scribes. Nevertheless, from the renderings of the notes viz., *sotuoli*, *zizhi*, *shala*, it is apparent that these notes were derived from Indian notes.

Another music composer from Kucha went to China in the last quarter of the sixth century A.D. According to the Chinese accounts, this maestro belonged to a Brahmin family, the name of which was Cao. It may be assumed that the word Cao is a Chinese transformation of Jha (Upadhyaya). The name of the Kuchean musician was Miaoda – this is probably a Chinese rendering of the Sanskrit word Suprakash or Subadh. The Jha family was cultivated musical tradition. Miaoda was so talented in music that with in a short time the king and other royal officials were attracted to his Indian classical music. The Chinese Emperor, realising the possible impact on Chinese music due to the increasing popularity of Indian music, made an earnest effort to stop the practice of Indian music. However, the attempt turned to be ineffective. Another musician called Mingda (Binda) from Kucha went to China in the beginning of the seventh century. With all probability he also belonged to the Jha family known for its musical tradition. The Chinese emperor was highly attracted by his music, so much so that on his request Mingda composed many songs.

It is said that these musicians originally from India were extremely gifted. On hearing a tune just once they could render it on their instrument. At the onset of monsoon, when the cascading falls resonated the earth, the musicians used to go to the hills to capture the vibrant notes in their own renderings. In this manner, music was enriched with the creations of the musicians. Their music received new dimensions with the absorption of melodious tune extracted from nature. Perhaps Indian classical music was a creative expression of sensitivity to the wonders of nature. It is possible that behind the composition of Indian classical *ragas* such as *desh*, *mallar*, *megh*, etc. the main inspiration had been the composers' communion with nature.

Along with the musicians and orchestra from Kucha, even gifted dancers used to go to China. In Chinese literature, names of some of the dance performances can be found – *Santinritya*, *pancha simha nritya*, etc. In the *simha nritya* dance, a number of lions were used. Each lion used to be choreographed by twelve dancers. A total number of one hundred and forty dancers were required for this special performance. It is not unlikely that these dancers began the use of mask in the Far East. However, choreography of dance performance using mask has been transported from India.

In 581 A.D., the emperor of China invited exponents of classical and instrumental music and groups of orchestra. These musicians came from countries like India, Kucha, Samarkand, Kashgarh, etc. In Chinese annals we find vivid description of these Indian musicians. It is written, "Indian musicians wear black cotton caps, white silk garments for the upper body, tight pants of purple brocade and long red overcoats. Each musical group consisted two dancers with neat hairdo and loose garment like Buddhist monks. They wore shoes made of jute ropes. For music they use gong, drums (*mridanga*, *baya-tabla*), flute in the shape of a pipe (could be *sanai*), a stringed instrument *veena*, the upper part of which is carved like a face of an animal, five-stringed *veena* (*tanpura*), cymbal and the conch". This vivid description depicting the costume and accompaniment resemble much of the present-day performance.

Chinese historians while narrating Indian music wrote: "There were seven kinds of note-array and there was a well balanced consistency among these seven kinds of notes". It may be presumed that the Chinese historians wrote about the major structure of Indian music and not about the *ragas* of Indian classical music. Apart from that there is little likelihood of the ragas flourishing in China in their complete form; perhaps Indian seven notes were considered as *jati* or precursors to the *ragas*. In the Indian treatises of music such as *Brihaddesi*, *Sangita ratnakara* and others there is a mention of seven *suddha jatis*, which is what the Chinese records seem to be suggesting.

Chinese sources refer to twenty musical tunes in Indian classical music. In spite of my earnest efforts, I have not been able to find any information about these musical tunes as they are recorded in an obscure manner. There are references to *kukkuter ladia* (cock fight), *fuler mela* (abundance of flowers), *Bogaila*, etc. In our ancient scriptures we find *talas* like *kukkut*, *mallikapramod*, *rayabankal*, etc. There is ample evidence to show that songs were attributed by their *tala*, which were measurements of beats. The names in Chinese records were perhaps derived from names of special *talas*.

From China, Indian music spread to Japan. Even today some of the hymns are sung in ancient Indian tune at old Japanese monasteries. This tradition has been carried on through generations of Buddhist monks. If these facts are collected, we may get some idea about the ancient musical notes prevailing in ancient Japan. In ancient Japanese literature there is a reference to a Brahmin named Bodhi, who introduced the Indian tradition of two kinds of notes in Japan in 800 A.D. The names of these two notes were "Bodhisattva" and "Bairo". Bodhi, a Brahmin, was a priest at a Buddhist temple at Nara. Hymns in his Indian tunes were sung along with rhythmic dance forms. Perhaps the note "Bodhisattva" was adopted and sung by the Buddhist monks. The Japanese did not record any detailed account of this Indian musical note. However, there is a clear hint of Indian influence in the sphere of music, in the record about the note "Bairo": "The chief composer of the Indian musical note "Bairo was the saint *Banlangduo*, i.e. Bharata. This song/tune used to be sung by the soldiers before they set out for war. While executing it seven times, if there the *sha-mo* sound, it indicates that the army will be victorious over the enemy." In Japanese language, the words have gone through transformation, such as Banlangduo is a modified name of Bharat. *Sha-mo* seems to be a modified form of the Sanskrit word *sama* (Hindusthani *som*). *Sama* indicates the starting point on the instrument of percussion which keeps the beat (*tala*). A lot of skill is required to retain the pace on the gap even after a tune is sung seven times. The name *bairo* could be a transformed form of the Sanskrit word *bhairava* (in Hindusthani *bhairo*). Perhaps *bhairava* epitomises vigour and brightness, which explains why this tune was sung during wartime. The treatise *Music by Bharat* is the oldest scripture on music and the fountainhead of melody. Bodhi, the Indian Brahmin musician, introduced the note *bhairava* and spread the legend of creation of music among the Japanese in the eighth century A.D. He went to Japan from China. Therefore, it is quite reasonable to assume that even in China this trend was introduced. The history of the evolution of Indian classical music is shrouded in oblivion even today. The history of the spread and influences of Indian music in China and Japan can only be unfolded if extensive research work is done through the study of ancient Chinese and Japanese literary sources.

Note

1 Simple and straight tone, consonant tone, fifth tone, and the tone of the bull respectively. See P. C. Bagchi, *India and China: A Thousand Years of Cultural Relations* (Delhi: Munshiram Manoharlal Publishers Pvt. Ltd., 2008), 167.—Translator

INDIAN HINDU CULTURE AND RELIGION IN CHINA

It was primarily through Buddhism that the Indian culture took its stronghold in China. This is the reason why in the history of Sino-Indian cultural relations, Hinduism occupies a negligible position. Most of the Indian scholars who went to China between the second century and the eleventh century of the Christian era were Buddhists. There is indeed mention of very few Hindu scholars who, in spite of being Hindus, worked extensively for the Chinese renderings of Sanskrit Buddhist scriptures as interpreters.

Nevertheless along with the dissemination of Buddhism among the Chinese people, an impact of Indian knowledge of science, astrology and medicine on them can be traced clearly. People were drawn to the study of Indian medicine enshrined in the *Atharvaveda* and Indian astrology. A few translations of the treatise on Indian medicine by the Chinese support this conjecture. Apart from these translations, it is interesting to note that there are references to Indian medicinal herbs in Chinese pharmacological books. There was a strong belief among the Chinese emperors that the Indian doctors knew about certain medicines which could enhance longevity of their apparently short mortal life. It was quite often that the Chinese emperors, with the hope to live longer, used to send their officials to India in search of Indian doctors. There is a reference to a Hindu doctor called Narayanasvamin, who treated the Chinese emperor with Indian medicines in the seventh century of the Christian era to improve his lifespan. However, despite all efforts the emperor had a premature death.

A number of books on Hindu astrology were translated into Chinese. The Brahmin astrologers were accorded high respect at the royal courts. The kings realized the necessity of astrological forecast prior to the performance of any royal function. Hence, public offices for the astrologers were maintained by Chinese emperors. The Indian astrologers were given due respect at such public offices for their knowledge of astrology. At the end of the seventh century of the Christian era, three different schools of Indian astrology viz. Gautama, Kasyapa and Kumar, were working in the capital of China. In the year 684 of the Christian Era, by the royal order, a lunar calendar was prepared by the

Gautama school of astrologers. This was in extensive use for three consecutive years. In the year 718 of the Christian Era, another astrologer of the Gautama school, called Siddha composed a lunar calendar named *Navagraha siddhanta.* This was in extensive use for four consecutive years. The Chinese rendering of *Navagraha siddhanta* is preserved even today in the archive.

At the close of the sixth century A.D., five compilations on Hindu astrology and mathematics were translated into Chinese language. Although there is no trace of the translations, yet the names of these books occur in Chinese historical annals. In front of each compilation we find the name *Brahaman sastra.* The Hindus were known to the Chinese as Brahmanas and this factor led them to name the books as *Brahmana jyotish sastra, Brahmana grantha sastra,* etc. Though these valuable treatises on Indian astrology and mathematics are lost, its marked influence can be traced in ancient Chinese astrology and mathematics.

The astrologers of the Gautama community went to China in the sixth century A.D. A Brahmin named Gautama Prajnaruci of Varanasi belonging to the Gautama community came to China in 516 A.D. He is referred to as a "lay Buddhist", whereas in other Chinese sources he is just called "Brahmin". Either he went to China with his wife and other members of the family or got married later in China. However, there is clear indication, in some Chinese references, of the birth of his son in China. At the instruction of the Chinese emperor he translated a Sanskrit text into Chinese. Actually, he was a high official working under the Chinese emperor. In the year 557 A.D., he was appointed as an official at Yecheng.

It may be assumed that Hindus came in groups to China to trade and in course of time settled there for good. Many Hindu families went to various places of Greater India like Java, Cambodia and Champa mainly to trade and gradually settled there permanently. Therefore, it is not improbable that small Hindu colonies grew up in China as well. It appears that it became convenient for the Indian Buddhist monks to go to China as the Hindu trading communities were already living there. Small Hindu settlements in China have left their trails behind.

In South China, in the city called Quanzhou near the seashore there are two huge pagodas belonging to tenth–eleventh centuries of Christian era. There are references to this city of Quanzhou in many foreign accounts and especially in Marco Polo's account as Zayton. In spite of several renovations, the pagodas have retained their marked characteristics of middle ages. These kinds of Buddhist temples are found in Japan and the construction method of this type of temples used to be called *Tenji kunyo* or "Indian method" by the Japanese. Though this type of temples with its different construction method was considered "Indian", in India this style of construction was never prevalent. However, this type of construction of temples after the style of pagodas – which requires extensive use of wood – can be found in Nepal and in the Malabar region of South India even today. It is not quite unlikely to assume that this style of temple construction may have been originated in India, but after the practice of using wood in temple construction became obsolete, this style of construction became defunct.

Once Zayton had the best monastery for the Buddhist monks living in China and outside India. Nevertheless there is ample evidence in the Zayton temple that there was also a Hindu community that lived nearby. This place was a large port and ships loaded with merchandise from various foreign countries used to anchor here for trade. Many Indian ships laden with Indian goods used to come to this post of Zayton to trade. Let me quote Marco Polo who, in the thirteenth century, wrote:

> "At this city is the haven of Zayton, frequented by all ships of India which bring thither spice and all other kinds of costly wares".

The conjecture about the existence of a Hindu community at the post is corroborated by some of the engravings in the Zayton temple depicting Hindu mythological stories. Surprisingly, on one particular pillar of this temple, a carving depicts the Indian mythological story of Lord Krishna destroying the terrible snake Kaliya that lived in the river Yamuna. Kaliya, the dreadful snake by stretching its numerous hoods encircled Lord Krishna, who is depicted playing his flute standing on Kaliya. On either side of Krishna, a conch and wheel, the symbols of Visnu, are engraved. Another engraving on the pillar depicts the Hindu mythology of the incarnation of Vishnu in the form of Narasimha annihilating Hiranya Kasipur, the demon. On this particular pillar, there is also a phallic image engraved with a devout cow shedding milk from her udder and cleaning the *Siva-linga.* On the bottom of the pillar there is a carving of a queer looking animal. This kind of image has only been found in a Hindu temple situated in Ponnapuram in Sri Lanka. A few more engraved *linga*s have been found from the large paved space on the approach to the temple in Zayton.

Surprisingly, there is no similarity what so ever between the carvings of this particular pillar and the rest of the pillars in the Zayton temple. The composition of these images has distinct Indian stamps, without displaying any Chinese influences. It is not impossible that this particular pillar was recovered from some vestiges of Hindu temple, which was constructed in the eleventh or twelfth century A.D. by the Indian sculptors and artists from the south India. With all probability the Hindu community living in this part of China used to be Tamil people. The Hindus of the Tamil countries of the south were pioneers in establishing trade relations with the outside world.

More evidence in favour of this conjecture can be found out if explorations are undertaken in various parts of China. It will be relevant here to mention that a Sanskrit manuscript, which was recovered from numerous Chinese Buddhist manuscripts, was unique in a sense that it has a compilation of some of the couplets from Kalidas's poetical works. Even the story narrating the stupidity of this great poet Kalidas had been partly incorporated in this Sanskrit compilation. This is the only instance where a Sanskrit book on some of the verses of Kalidas can be cited. Otherwise there is absolutely no evidence to indicate that Chinese Buddhist scholars or monks had any tradition of reading poetry composed by Kalidas or other Indian poets. Could the tradition of reading Sanskrit poetry be prevalent among the Hindu community living in China?

It may be concluded that not only China had age-old contact with Buddhist India or Buddhist culture, but also with the non-Buddhist Hindu culture mentioned as Brahmin culture by the Chinese people. Multifaceted Indian culture both Buddhist and non-Buddhist made its mark on the Chinese soil.

APPENDIX

IN MEMORIAM – PRABODH CHANDRA BAGCHI (1898–1956)*

Suniti Kumar Chatterji

The loss sustained in the domain of scientific studies and research in the Humanities, not only by India but also by the entire scholarly world, through the untimely passing away of the late Prabodh Chandra BAGCHI will for some time remain irrepairable, and for many years it will not be possible to make it good. He joined the majority at the age of 58 only, and if we consider what he did and what in comparison he did not find time to do, we would be forced to admit that it was certainly a case of untimely death for him. In our country scholars who have dedicated their lives to study and research and who have passed their 80th year and even more while remaining in full possession of their matured mental powers are not rare; and that is why when we think of this untimely death of Prabodh Chandra, we cannot but feel a great mortification, for both learning and research by themselves and also for our own people. His passing away is a national loss indeed; and in addition to this, there is the sense of loss which nothing can mitigate which his relations and the large circle of his friends are feeling.

In Bengal and in India there is no lack of scholars and research workers. But in the case of Prabodh Chandra BAGCHI's scholarship there was something quite remarkable, both in the subject of his researches and in the way in which these researches were given out to the world. Quite a number of scholars of the first rank have shown their great success, both in our country and abroad, through their work in Indology, and of course we can easily name Prabodh Chandra BAGCHI as one of the best of them. But the field in which Prabodh Chandra manifested his special competence has hitherto been

* Prabodh Chandra Bagchi, *Indological Studies: A Collection of Essays* (Santiniketan: Visva-Bharati, 1982), ix–xxi.

uncommon in India, and that is the relationship between India and China. Among modern Indian scholars, Prabodh Chandra's scholarship was a sort of a bridge between Indology and Sinology. In this matter he had followed the footsteps of his master, Prof. Sylvain LÉVI of Paris, and he was also the pupil, in spirit if not in actuality, of a number of eminent European savants in this line, like Paul PELLIOT, another great Frenchman. It is not always easy to find the competence and the mastery which is necessary in trying to trace out the lost history of the links between the two great civilisations of India and China by enquiry and research. For this, just as on the one hand a very deep acquaintance with Indian History and Indian Culture and along with it with Indian languages like Sanskrit, Pali and the Prakrit as well as their literatures is expected, on the other hand a really good working knowledge of the Chinese language is also a necessity; and when we think of the special character of the Chinese language and the difficulties of its script, we would have to admit that it would not be an easy thing to have a good working knowledge of Chinese, entailing an acquaintance with at least 2500 to 3000 different characters. Further, a close acquaintance with French and German, in addition, of course, to English, is necessary; and sometimes some knowledge of Japanese also becomes quite helpful as an ancillary, along with Chinese. To understand the history of the Mahāyāna Buddhism, a knowledge of Tibetan also is unavoidable. And further, along with the special competence in languages, a research worker in this field must also have an international as well as a scientific point of view, and ability to avoid the accidentals and get hold of the essentials, a mentality inspired by high culture. And after understanding everything oneself, the possession of a proper lucid style in writing, through which one can make others also understand easily and fully, is also necessary.

Prabodh Chandra BAGCHI's teaching and research was successful because he possessed not only all these qualifications necessary for throwing light on the question of the connexions between India and China and on the history of Asia, but also other qualities of head and heart which helped him in this work.

It may be said about Prabodh Chandra BAGCHI that he was the first Sinologue of present-day India. It was as early as 68 A. D. that two Indian Buddhist scholar-monks first arrived at Lo-yang, the capital of the Chinese Emperor of the Han Dynasty, Kāśyapa Mātaṅga and Dharmaraksha. They engaged themselves in translating Indian Buddhist texts from Sanskrit into Chinese. In this way, the literary and spiritual connexion which they established between India and China during the second half of the first century A.D. continued unbroken for nearly 1300 years. Within this tradition or scholarly sequence which they started, there came up quite a large number of Indian scholars and wise men who went to China and acquired the Chinese Language, and in collaboration with the scholars of China rendered Buddhist texts into

Chinese from Indian languages, and occasionally composed new works on Buddhism in the Chinese language. Most of them stayed on in China and finally laid bones in that country. On the other side, there were many Chinese enquirers who also came within this tradition. They, with the urge of acquiring as completely as possible the teachings of Buddha in his own language and in his own country, set at naught the most terrible difficulties of the journey from China and came to India, and learnt Sanskrit and other Indian languages, and in this way acquired the competence to translate Buddhist works into their own language, and finally returned home. After their return, they took it up as the main work of their lives to make Buddhist scriptures easily available in their mother-tongue, and like their Indian teachers and predecessors they spent their lives in this work. Kumārajīva from the city of Kucha in Central Asia, Bodhidharma from South India, Fa Hien, Hiuen Ts'ang and I-Tsing from China – their names are to be mentioned with all honour in this connexion. Gradually India was conquered by the Turks and the religion of the Prophet of Arabia was established in India; and the direct link between India and China was destroyed through this and other reasons. For some centuries interchange of and intercourse among scholars of India and China ceased completely. Our spirit, of enquiry about China gradually died out, and the study of Sanskrit in China too became almost obsolete. Nevertheless, through the intermediacy of the old Buddhist literature, some little knowledge and spirit of enquiry with regard to India continued in a thin stream in China. But in India we lost even all memory of the scholarship in Chinese which characterized many Indian learned men 1500 years ago.

Once again through the researches of the scholars of Modern Europe, the study of Buddhism as it was current in China formed a platform on which the old connexions between India and China were re-established. The European Sinologues began to translate Chinese works into European languages – in French, in German, in English; and a knowledge of the friendship between India and China in the olden days in a common quest through Buddhism slowly also reached India. The basic or primary knowledge of this Sino-Indian contact became established among enquirers in our country through the writings of these European scholars of Chinese and Chinese Buddhism, and a little interest in and desire for a closer acquaintance with the Chinese language manifested itself in the minds of some of our educational leaders. It was realized that we were to study Chinese for two reasons: first, to be able to understand ancient India much better through her great contribution in the cultural development of China and Asia; and secondly, to understand and appreciate our great neighbour, the ancient and highly civilized people of China.

In the present age in India, Sri Asutosh MOOKERJEE of Calcutta for the first time arranged for the teaching of Chinese in the University of Calcutta.

Round about 1917 he appointed a Belgian scholar who had studied Chinese in China to take classes in the language in that University. I was privileged to be one of the first students of this class for a short period. But unfortunately, owing to lack of interest among students, this Chinese class did not go on for long. Before this, i.e. before 1915, the great Linguistic Scholar Harinath DE, who may be described as an Indian Megliabecchi, had been learning Chinese from a Chinese teacher whom he had brought to live with him. That well-known student of Indian history, Kasi Prasad JAISWAL of Mirzapur and Patna, had obtained, during his student-days at Oxford, a scholarship for a year for studying Chinese, but he did not progress much beyond a little elementary knowledge. In 1921 Rabindranath TAGORE established his International University of Visva-Bharati at Santiniketan, and he was from the very beginning exceedingly eager to establish Chinese studies in his University. Prof. Sylvain LÉVI was invited by Rabindranath TAGORE from the University of Paris to come as a Visiting Professor at Visva-Bharati, and his arrival and stay at Visva-Bharati was of the greatest importance for the revival of Chinese studies in India. Teaching in both Chinese and Tibetan was started at Visva-Bharati by Prof. LÉVI. Pandit Sri Vidhusekhara SASTRI, who was in charge of the Sanskrit Department at Visva-Bharati, took up the study of these two languages with enthusiasm, and a number of his colleagues and pupils also joined in it, and in this way the foundations of a School of Chinese and Tibetan Studies were laid at Visva-Bharati. Prof. Sylvain LÉVI'S visit to India was most helpful in the career of Prabodh Chandra BAGCHI in directing his energies to the study of Chinese. The permanent result of it has been that in this present age, during the third decade of the 20th century, through Prabodh Chandra BAGCHI India's position in the comity of Sinologues of the world was rehabilitated, and as the first great Chinese scholar of modern India Prabodh Chandra BAGCHI came to the forefront. It was not merely, that – through his valuable researches, he was able to obtain from scholars of the world sincere praise and honour for Indian scholarship in this special field, and in this way brought kudos to India in a new field of scholarly endeavour.

Prabodh Chandra's life was just the life of an ordinary scholar who had dedicated himself to teaching and study, and there was nothing remarkable or sensational about his life, excepting for travels and sojourns in Europe and South-Eastern Asia and in China and Japan. Prabodh Chandra was born in 1898 in the village of Srikol in Jessore District in Bengal (now in Bangladesh). His ancestral home was in the district of Khulna (also in Bangladesh). After finishing school and college he graduated in 1918, and in 1920 he passed out from the University of Calcutta in the subject of Ancient Indian History and Culture, securing the first place with a first class. Almost immediately after this he was appointed by Sri Asutosh MOOKERJEE as lecturer in his own subject in the University Post-Graduate Department. In 1921 Sri Asutosh MOOKERJEE sent him to Rabindranath TAGORE's newly founded Visva-Bharati University to study Buddhist religion and the Chinese language, and in this way he became a disciple of Prof. Sylvain LÉVI. Prof. LÉVI was exceedingly pleased at finding a remarkably intelligent and industrious, as well as quiet, student in Prabodh Chandra, and Prabodh Chandra received because of his intellect and character, as well as amiability, the love and affection due to a son from Prof. and Madame LÉVI. I have some knowledge of the personal relationship which existed between Prof. LÉVI and his Indian students, both in Paris and in India although I did not have myself the privilege of being a direct student of Prof. LÉVI himself. Prof. LÉVI was greatly affectionate towards all his Indian pupils. But I felt that Prabodh Chandra BAGCHI was the most favourite and most intimate of all his pupils. I have on many an occasion seen plentiful evidence of this deep love which Prof. LÉVI entertained with regard to Prabodh Chandra, both when directly speaking to him or mentioning him before others. On the other side, Prabodh Chandra also had the deepest regard for his master. This affectionate relationship between Master and Pupil was certainly like that which we were in the habit of considering to be peculiarly Indian.

Through Prof. LÉVI'S eagerness, Prabodh Chandra went with him to Indo-China and Japan and in this way he found an occasion to travel through Cambodia, Annam or Vietnam, and Cochin-China or ancient Champa. During this travel and sojourn in the lands of South-Eastern Asia and the Far East, Prabodh Chandra had a unique occasion to study and discuss with his Master the history of Asia and of Buddhism as well as the Chinese language. He was thus privileged to have a direct knowledge of *Greater India.* After travelling through these parts of Asia, Prabodh Chandra returned home and shortly after he obtained a Government of India scholarship and found himself in Paris, and there with very great assiduity he studied with Prof. LÉVI and other savants of Paris University the Tibetan and Chinese languages and Buddhist religion and Buddhist texts, and carried on researches in the subject of his study, from 1923 to 1926. As a result of his researches he published in 3 volumes a very valuable work in French on the *Buddhist Canon in China*, and brought out annotated editions of his two Sanskrit–Chinese Dictionaries. These latter were published in facsimile from 18th century Japanese editions, giving the Chinese words and their Sanskrit equivalents in the 7th century script of North India known as the Siddha-Mātṛkā, with pronunciation in Chinese characters as well as Japanese *Kānā* Syllabary indicated beside each Sanskrit *akṣara.* He also wrote linguistic and other notes which were very valuable on these dictionaries. Thus the research work of Prabodh Chandra BAGCHI was of a unique character, particularly for India. He was awarded by the University of Paris its highest research degree, viz. that of a *Docteur-ès-Lettres* (D.-ès-L.). This degree immediately entitles a French citizen to obtain a high scholarly appointment in the State. Before Prabodh Chandra BAGCHI, there was only one Indian scholar so far who had obtained this degree – the late Dr. Subodh Chandra MUKHERJI, who had worked on Sanskrit Rhetoric; after Prabodh Chandra BAGCHI, recently another Indian scholar has obtained this degree on a thesis on the *Influence of Indian Thought on French Literature* – Dr. Taraprasad DASH.

In this way, after coming back home with high academic honours from France, Prabodh Chandra BAGCHI was appointed a lecturer in the Department of Ancient Indian History and Culture in the University of Calcutta. The University published his books in a series known as *Sino-Indica*, and through the publication of these works Prabodh Chandra's name as a scholar of note in Buddhism as well as Chinese became established. Years ago, the Japanese scholar Bunyu NANJYO had published from Oxford University a Catalogue of the Chinese Buddhist *Tripiṭaka*, in which all the various books which were translated from Sanskrit and Prakrit into Chinese were arranged systematically. This Catalogue has been recognised as one of the most important source-books for the study of Chinese and Japanese Buddhism. NANJYO who had studied Sanskrit at Oxford under F. Max MUELLER had given the original Sanskrit names of the various texts which were to be found in the Chinese *Tripiṭaka*, and this was the main reason for the usefulness of NANJYO's Catalogue. Prabodh Chandra BAGCHI's service to this branch of scholarship was in this, that he compiled a systematic history of this mass of Chinese translations; and by finding out the chronology of the Chinese and Indian translators and making brief studies of the works which they translated, gave a historical presentation of an entire mass of translation-literature which had spread over a thousand years. The Chinese Buddhist pilgrims used to come to India to study Sanskrit, and gradually they had also developed a method of teaching Sanskrit in China. As part of this method, they used to compile small vocabularies or dictionaries of Chinese and Sanskrit for the use evidently of beginners. Such dictionaries had been found in China and in Japan in printed editions. Prabodh Chandra BAGCHI obtained two dictionaries of Chinese and Sanskrit compiled by Chinese-Buddhist pilgrims, who used to come to India to study Sanskrit, going back to the 7th and 8th centuries, which were printed from wooden blocks in Japan in the 18th century, and, as said before, he first brought them to the notice of the average scholar outside China by giving a facsimile reprint of them and by writing full notes. His first researches in the domain of Sino-Indian studies were thus both valuable and significant.

From 1927 to 1945, for 19 years, Prabodh Chandra BAGCHI was on the staff of the Calcutta University. During this period he had built his own house at Baliganj in Calcutta. For all this long period I had the privilege of having Prabodh Chandra as a very valued colleague; and not only in the University, but also elsewhere, in Prabodh Chandra's own home and in my home and in the homes of other friends, I have been privileged to be honoured with intimate friendship of Prabodh Chandra BAGCHI. I was feeling greater and greater respect for Prabodh Chandra, the scholar, and at the same time no one could avoid loving Prabodh Chandra the man. Fortunately we had our mental attitudes almost identical or very similar in most matters.

In many matters relating to life and the world outside life, about the Ultimate Reality, there were points of agreement between Prabodh Chandra and myself. It was exceedingly difficult to find such a simple-hearted, straightforward and modest person who always maintained cheerfulness of spirit. Deep scholarship had not in any way acted as a load on his natural sweetness of temper. But one also noted that with all his simplicity, Prabodh Chandra had a vein of independence in him; and for that reason he was never inclined upon cultivating those in authority who had the gift of preferment and official favour in their control. It is for this reason that Prabodh Chandra was quite unjustly ignored in many matters – it was only because he had not come to the proper quarters and made representations on his own behalf; but Prabodh Chandra never cared for these things. I personally have a feeling that so long as he was in Calcutta University, we were not able to appreciate to the fullest the value of his personality and his scholarship.

In the linguistic science Prabodh Chandra had a special competence. This he had shown in his Introduction to his *Pre-Aryan and Pre-Dravidian in India*. He was intimately connected with the work of the Linguistic Society of India, both as Member of the Editorial Board of its Journal and as high office holder, for quite a number of years.

In 1945 Prabodh Chandra accepted the Directorship of the Vidya-Bhavana or Research Institute of the Visva-Bharati, giving up his Calcutta University appointment.

He built up a new Research Department as well as the Department of Chinese Studies at the Visva-Bharati, and work commenced in the Research Department in its various brandies with a considerable amount of enthusiasm. It was through his initiative that quite a respectable number of research publications and articles began to be published from the Visva-Bharati, and some young research workers came into the field; and what Rabindranath TAGORE had been hoping for the Visva-Bharati, it became one of the premier centres of both Western and Eastern Learning in India. The Publications of the Visva-Bharati under Prabodh Chandra's directorship embrace researches in Sanskrit, Tibetan, Chinese, Avestan, Old Persian, Persian, Bengali and Oriya, and these have established the reputation of the Visva-Bharati everywhere.

In 1947 the Government of India sent five young scholars to China to learn the Chinese language, history and culture, and two of them were from the Visva-Bharati, and they all acquitted themselves very creditably in China. Prabodh Chandra BAGCHI himself was sent to the University of Peking as Professor of Indology for two years. In this way once again he got an opportunity of being in China, and he came in touch with some of the best Professors in Peking, and came back home with a greater competence and experience in his subject.

Again, Prabodh Chandra was sent to China once again in 1952 as a member of a Cultural Mission, and he was enabled on that occasion to spend a few weeks there once more.

In the meanwhile the Indian Central Government took over Rabindranath's University of the Visva-Bharati as a University administered by the Government of India. Pandit Jawaharlal NEHRU himself became the Chancellor of the University and Rabindranath's son Sri Rathindianath TAGORE became the first Vice-Chancellor. He was succeeded by Prof. Kshitimohan SEN, and in 1954 Prabodh Chandra BAGCHI was elected to this responsible post. Prabodh Chandra took up his work in all seriousness, and with a remarkable spirit of enthusiasm and dedication. Immediately after becoming the Vice-Chancellor he offered a voluntary cut of Rs. 250/- from his monthly salary of Rs. 1500/-, directing that this amount might be spent for the benefit of poor students. In this way he took up his work for the promotion of Scientific Humanism in the Visva-Bharati and to make the ideals of Rabindranath effective through his creation.

Prabodh Chandra BAGCHI's family life was quite peaceful and happy. But about a year before his death Fate had decreed for him a terrible sorrow, and that was the death of his only son at the age of 16. This was a great blow, and his health, which was never of the best, and was also impaired by excessive labour in the work of the Visva-Bharati, gradually deteriorated and prepared the way for his early passing away. Prabodh Chandra had married in 1921 in the district of Pabna. His wife, Sm. Panna Devi, was an ideal Hindu lady and a real *Sahadharmiṇī* for him. After three daughters, his only son Pratip was born in 1938. Two of these daughters were married before Prabodh Chandra passed away and the third daughter died at Santiniketan in 1943. Two daughters were born after the birth of this son. Prabodh Chandra's son showed great promise, but during his 15th year the boy was affected with some incurable disease in the brain and it could not be properly treated. In 1955 the BAGCHIs had to suffer this great sorrow. Prabodh Chandra wanted to plunge himself still more in his work, but this proved too much for him, and as a result of a heart-attack he passed away on the morning of the 19th of January 1956.

Prabodh Chandra's books and articles and the research publications which he had edited or helped to bring out through the Visva-Bharati Research Department will be the best monument of his scholarship. I have mentioned about his book on the *Buddhist Canon in China* and the edition of the *Sanskrit-Chinese Dictionaries*. The Pre-Aryan Cultures of India – Kol or Nishāda and Dravidian – which form the basis of Indian civilization, were treated on the basis or the background of Linguistics by three eminent French scholars – Jean PRZYLUSKI, Jules BLOCH, and Prabodh Chandra's master Sylvain LÉVI in a number of very important articles published in different French journals. These papers were exceedingly important for a study of the beginnings of Indian civilization. Prabodh Chandra translated these from the French into English, and he published a work embodying these from the University of Calcutta, in 1929, entitled *Pre-Aryan and Pre-Dravidian in India*. In this work Prabodh Chandra wrote an introductory article giving a full account of the Austric family of languages and their place in India and in Asia, and by adding one article by himself on the same topic as those in the French articles, including also another article by the present writer, made it quite a useful compendium for the study of the Pre-Aryan beginnings of Indian civilization. This work has been exceedingly helpful in drawing the attention of Indian scholars to this very important problem. Among the various articles he wrote on Indian history in its Asiatic background, that on *The Role of Central Asian Nomads in the History of India* is a very important contribution, making quite clear the way in which the various peoples of Central Asia who came to India had helped in the evolution of its history. He also identified the dialect described as Culikā Paiśācī by the Prakrit grammarians with the Sulik or Sogdian speech of Central Asia, which was an Iranian dialect, and probably the original Culikā Paiśācī was on this basis. He also suggested that the beginnings of the Mahāyāna, in its theory of the Bodhisattva helping to bring about the spiritual regeneration of Man, are to be found in Aśoka inscriptions. In another article he has shown the intimate connexion between the Śaiva Tantrism of India as described in some texts preserved in Nepal with a similar school in Indo-China. Prabodh Chandra BAGCHI's researches were fruitful in another line – the study of the Old Bengali *Caryāpadas* by comparing them with their Tibetan versions. This was done to some extent in the case of some of the Śaurasenī Apabhraṃśa Dohās in relation to their Tibetan translations in a work which was published from Paris by Dr. Muhammd SHAHI-DULLAH. Prabodh Chandra BAGCHI made a thorough study of these old Bengali short poems in relation to the Tibetan, and discovered and published new material of the same type from Nepal.

Prabodh Chandra was not a mere researcher, but he was also literary minded. He wrote in a beautiful Bengali style, and his main work was in French and not in English. He has a number of very popular books which are exceedingly valuable, historically and scientifically in both Bengali and in English, on the relationship between India and China and on the spread of Indian Culture in Central Asia, China, as well as in South-Eastern Asia.

Prabodh Chandra sometimes would be impatient against injustice and dishonesty. But I have never found him angry against any person as such. It is needless to speak about his personal relationship with his friends.

If China has obtained Buddhism from India, she has also obtained from India her Philosophy, and Inspiration in many of the Fine Arts, from Architecture and Sculpture to Painting and the Dance and the Drama. Whatever Sciences India possessed in those times were also participated in by China. *Fan-Shu* or the Indian system of writing was taken to China with the Sanskrit language, and this brought in to the mind of the Chinese scholars a new spirit of enquiry about the Phonetics of Chinese, and a great impetus came to the Chinese mind for studying one important aspect of their language which was so far neglected by them. Indian Medicine and Astronomy are also believed to have influenced China. All these things have been brought to us by the European Orientalists and from this knowledge some of us in India are now feeling a sort of a new sense of pride, which I trust would be considered pardonable. The Chinese people also have acknowledged all this, and their respect for India has always been very deep and sincere. But then the question arises: is it that India alone has given to China, and a highly civilized nation like China had nothing to give to India? China certainly has been an incomparably great people; and in many walks of life, the Chinese contribution to human civilization has been unique and has been profound. If through twelve centuries of intimate contact with China, India has not been able to receive anything from this great country, that could not be something complimentary to India and it would only show the mental poverty of India – her inability to profit from contact with great nations. Everywhere the progress in a nation's culture is dependent upon its contact with peoples of high culture from outside. But unfortunately when we look into this matter, we find that the Sino-Indian relations have not been always a one-way traffic: we have also taken many things from China, as we have given to China. In this connexion, certain things had suggested themselves to me as to where we profited by our Chinese connexion, and received certain elements in our art and our literature from China. I need not dwell into all that in detail. There are scores, may be even hundreds, of Sanskrit words in Chinese, and the question arises – are there any Chinese words in Sanskrit? So far we have been able to find about half a dozen only: the name *Cīna* =China, (from the name of the Ts'in Dynasty of the 3rd century B.C.); *kīcaka*, 'a kind of slender bamboo (from which flutes are made)', which Dr. Sylvain LÉVI suggested was from the Chinese *ki-cok*; and Prabodh Chandra BAGCHI suggested that the Sanskrit word for 'vermillion' *sindūra*, was also from the Chinese (*ts'in-t'ung*), besides an old Sanskrit word for 'paper', *śaya* which is not found in current Sanskrit, was also from the Chinese (*tsieh*). I have suggested that the Sanskrit word *musāra*, meaning 'a kind of precious stone', is also from the Chinese (Old Chinese **mwa-sadh* or *mwa-sar*, Modern *mo-so*); and the Indian word *tasara* meaning 'a kind of silk', I thought was Chinese, and Prabodh Chandra suggested that a Chinese compound expression like *tai-sse*, *tai-sser* meaning 'great silk', may be the source from which this Indian word was taken. Prabodh Chandra was anxious to find out if there were other words of this type. He was also of the idea that even in the religious thought of India, as a sort of a backwash, some Chinese influences came in. The later developments of Taoism, Prabodh Chandra was convinced, had exerted a good deal of influence on the Buddhist as well as Brahminical Tantra, in both ideas and practices, from the 8th century onwards.

Through the untimely passing away of Prabodh Chandra BAGCHI, researches in this line have come to suffer a check – at least for the time being; and we can only hope that young Indian Sinologues of the present-day, who are studying the Chinese language, will carry on the work which has been left unfinished by Prabodh Chandra BAGCHI.

Within a few weeks, early in 1956, Bengal and India lost four great persons in the intellectual domain - Prabodh Chandra BAGCHI (who died on 19-1-56); Haridas BHATTACHARYYA, distinguished Professor of Philosophy and editor of the Ramakrishna Mission *Cultural Heritage of India* in its second edition (died on 20-1-56); Meghnad SAHA, eminent Scientist (died on 16-2-56); and Bijan Kumar MUKHERJI, eminent Jurist and Chief Justice of Supreme Court of India (died on 22-2-56). In their own special fields they were like towers of light. In Ancient Indian History and Culture and Sinology, in Philosophy, in science, and in Law – in these subjects these lights have become extinguished. But the light of what they have left behind them will never be dim.

Calcutta
20th July 1957

PRABODH CHANDRA BAGCHI (1898–1956): A MODEL IN THE BEGINNINGS OF INDO-SINIC BUDDHIST PHILOLOGY*

Akira Yuyama

Prefatory Note

Early in 1997 I was invited to contribute a paper to a volume in celebration of an eminent Bengali-born savant Prabodh Chandra Bagchi (1898–19.IX.1956) on the occasion of the centenary year of his birth. To my regret, however, my extremely busy schedule at that time prevented me from writing anything. A year after that I was instead asked to send a few lines of appreciative word on his works. I hurriedly wrote a short tribute in praise of this grand savant. I always feel much indebted to such pioneers in the field of modern Indian and Buddhist studies.

In that short notice I placed special emphasis on the background discussing how Bagchi's work on Buddhist culture in India had developed even beyond the boundaries of his country, particularly to Central Asia and China. His wide range of interests lay in cultural aspects of Buddhism all over Asia. Without his teacher Sylvain Lévi, he might have not decided to pursue this line of research work.[1] Bagchi was thus part of the lineage of French scholarship which began with Eugene Burnouf.[2] After all, the goal is the study of humanities across the globe.

However, my paper may have gone astray. I have since heard no direct information from the organs in question as to whether or not it was published. No reply to my query in this connection has ever reached me from them, and to my knowledge this memorial volume never appeared. I have therefore decided to bring it out here in a totally revised form.

* *Annual Report of The International Research Institute for Advanced Buddhology at Soka University* 5 (2002): 135–146; and 6 (2003): 342.

Bagchi in his Motherland

It is a matter of pleasure for me to write a brief remark in appreciation of Prabodh Chandra Bagchi, a scholar of international reputation in the field of Buddhist studies. I believe that he is to be remembered as a scholar who developed a fresh approach to the relevant fields of study. However, it is impossible to describe him and his work within the limited space. I will therefore confine myself to taking a brief glimpse at his scientific activities, which he carried out on an international scale. This grand savant has left a vast range of academic achievements for the world of knowledge during his regrettably short lifetime. If he had lived a few more decades he must have benefited us even more.

In his motherland he was not just an extraordinarily distinguished scholar but also thoroughly amiable to anyone who had direct or indirect contact with him. Those fortunate students, friends and colleagues were innumerable, though many more have now lost their chance to meet him or work with him in person.

Through his writings, however, Prabodh Chandra Bagchi still benefits immensely those who are engaged in related fields of study. I am no exception. He has fostered a great many brilliant scholars both at home and abroad. Indeed, there were scholars senior to him, who have derived great advantage from him and who regard him with real adoration, for example, Suniti Kumar Chatterji (1890–1977).[3] Bagchi's shorter writings have fortunately been brought out in a book together with an index.[4] One can witness the wide range of his interest. A number of his articles are written with full reference to Chinese source materials.

Bagchi's Scope Beyond the Subcontinent

V. Raghavan (1908–1979) remarked in a small booklet published on the occasion of the XXVI International Congress of Orientalists held in New Delhi in 1964: "One of the drawbacks of Indian Indology in the past has also been lack of exploitative original work in regions outside the country, i.e. in Greater Indian regions".[5] I would say that Prabodh Chandra Bagchi was a notable exception: In order to seek for the wonder that was India he tried to search for it not only within India but also beyond her boundaries.

On his second trip to the East, Sylvain Lévi (28.III.1863–30.X.1935) arrived at Santiniketan in the month of November 1921 at the invitation of Rabindranath Tagore (1861–1941) upon the foundation of the International University on 22 December. Lévi then deeply and richly influenced Bagchi.

This well-known but beautiful story begins here. Following Lévi's earnest advice Prabodh Chandra Bagchi travelled extensively, and was consequently able to bring out much fruitful research. Prabodh's personal affection for his teacher was solidly planted when he accompanied Lévi to Nepal in 1922. It is enviable to see Madame Lévi describe him in her journal.[6]

Sylvain Lévi sent Prabodh Chandra Bagchi to so-called Indianized Southeast Asia. Hanoi was a world-renowned centre for such studies under the eminent directorship of Louis Finot (1864–1935), followed by George Cœdès (1886–1969),[7] and the competent scientific patronage of Sylvain Lévi.[8] Prabodh Chandra Bagchi doubtlessly got acquainted with a number of leading scholars there and became a pioneer in this field in India.

He further visited Japan in order to observe her Buddhist studies and seek for research materials. His master taught him the importance of the materials preserved in Japan and of the studies as well as the living religion observed there. On his first visit to Japan in 1897 Sylvain Lévi discovered much source material of great interest to him.[9] In Tokyo later on Lévi established an intimate contact with his Japanese colleagues. In the meantime the Maison Franco-Japonaise was founded with the generous patronage of the then French Ambassador, as well as the dramatist and poet, Paul Louis Charles Claudel (1868–1955) and his Japanese counterpart the business tycoon Eiichi SHIBUSAWA(澁澤榮一青淵: 1840–1931). In September 1926 Sylvain Lévi arrived in Tokyo to take up an appointment as the founding director of the Maison (1926–1928).[10] Strictly speaking, its establishment was legally approved in March 1924, and it was inaugurated in December 1924. Immediately after his arrival in Japan, Sylvain Lévi began to collect materials for the study of Buddhism in Japan. This must have become an indispensable guidebook for later students of Buddhism.[11]

Incidentally, around that time a number of distinguished French scholars spent their youth in the East. Among many others it may be noted here that early in 1926 Alfred C. A. Foucher (1865–1952) came to Tokyo. Paul Demiéville (1894–1979) resided in Hanoi (1919–1924), Amoy (1924–1926) and Tokyo (1926–1931). Their base of academic activities was the Maison,[12] from which the first fascicle of an indispensable work Hōbōgirin appeared in 1929 under the direction of Sylvain Lévi and Junjirō TAKAKUSU (高楠顺次郎1866–1945) and the editorship in chief of Paul Demiéville.[13] For any serious scholar in the field of Buddhist studies must no doubt be indebted to its annexed volume. It is not just a table of contents of the *Taishō Issaikyō* (大正新脩大藏經) but is full of useful information of Indo-Sinic as well as Sino-Japanese Buddhist literature.[14]

Needless to say, Sylvain Lévi must have constantly stimulated Prabodh Chandra Bagchi through his elaborate and elegant writings. Lévi had made a distinguished contribution not only in academic works but also for the benefit of the general public and students. And it was exactly around this period that

Lévi brought out a collection of six essayistic but serious articles on India and its outer world in book form.[15] This book includes an address delivered in English at the University of Dacca on 4 February 1922. I wonder if Bagchi had a chance to hear it.[16]

Bagchi and China

Soon after his return home from Paris he brought out an ambitious book on the relation between India and China. At the very beginning of the "Foreword" to this book,[17] he quotes his teacher's word seriously. Since I believe that it is the starting point of his studies, I would like to quote it here in full:

> "In concluding one of his thought-provoking essays of *L'Inde et le Monde*, Professor Sylvain Lévi says, `In the great movement of exchange, which constitutes from time immemorial, the organic life of the whole of mankind, India has largely given as she has largely received. We may, being carried away by our prejudice, exalt or deprecate her role; but her role she has played like the rest of the world with the rest of the world. If nature and laws have tried their best to isolate her, thereby her part has only become a specially important one; each group, race or nation in its acts as in its thoughts, in its conscience as in its instincts, is related to the whole of humanity".
>
> "But we Indians, ignore too much that India has played her role *like* the rest of the world *with* the rest of the world. The isolation in which India is living to-day, shut up from the rest of Asia and her general movements, is a forced isolation of her evil days. She has got to break once more the colossal barriers around her and to come in close touch with the outside world on a basis of equality. ... ...". (Bagchi, *op.cit.*, p. 1).

Bagchi absorbed a great deal of French scholarship. He was always an ardent and beloved teacher at home. As I have demonstrated it in my recent book on Eugene Burnouf, humanism is the keyword to understand the French scholarship in Buddhist studies, or Asian studies as a whole. Throughout his book Sylavin Lévi carries out his idea with humanism. Bagchi cited Lévi's words in his translation. The original runs at the end of Chapter I "L'Inde et le Monde" of his renowned book:

> " ... Dans cet immense mouvement d'échanges qui constitue de temps immémorial la vie organique de l'espèce humaine, l'Inde a largernent donné comme elle a largement reçu. On peut, au gré des passions, exalter ou déprécier son rôle; mais son rôle, elle l'a joué comme le reste

du monde, avec le reste du monde. Si la nature et les lois ensemble ont tout fait pour l'isoler, son cas n'en prend qu'une valeur plus décisive: chaque groupe, race on nation est dans ses acres comme dans sa pensée, dans sa conscience comme dans ses instincts, solidaire de toute l'espèce humaine". (Lévi, *op.cit.*, p. 21).

Later on Bagchi seems to have elaborately revised and enlarged his book in question in 1945[18] and 1950/1951.[19] Bagchi loved things Chinese. He dedicated this book "To Friends in China – To show that we are not forgetful. The road is long, so do not mind the smallness of the present. We wish you may accept it": 示市不空心/路遠莫怪其少/願領 (*op.cit.*, p. iii).

Incidentally, it is of great interest that a Chinese grand savant Chi Hsien-lin (季羨林: 06.VIII.1911-) mastered many classical languages and achieved western methodology during his stay at Göttingen from September 1935 to October 1945. He returned to his home country in the spring of 1946 via Switzerland, France, Vietnam and Hong Kong and in autumn of the same year he was appointed to the chair of Oriental languages at the University of Peking. Since then he has contributed a great deal in the field of Indo-European, Indological and Buddhist studies. He is a scholar who has developed a fresh approach to the related fields of study in China. Chi Hsien-lin has absorbed much on German methodology and digested it onto his soil He has then promoted the digestion of his many students.

At the same time he has always shown his keen interest in the cultural relations between China and India. Chi has brought out a number of important works on the relevant topics. It is impossible to describe him and his achievements in brief.[20] He treats every topic meticulously in linguistic and historical perspective.[21] It is fortunate that all of his important papers have appeared in a series of various collections. In 1982 Chi brought out a collection of his philological works,[22] which contains his hitherto unpublished dissertation on the conjugation of the finite verb in the *Mahāvastu-Avadāna* submitted to the University of Göttingen in 1941. During this period he spelt his name as Dschi Hiän-lin.[23] It is followed by a number of his collected papers, many of them being in duplicate.[24]

It may not be an accidental coincidence that Prabodh Chandra Bagchi was guest professor at the University of Peking in 1947–1948 (as will be mentioned below). Chi loves things Indian. He has often visited India and made careful but affectionate observations.[25] Being a well-known writer in prose and poetry, Chi has written hundreds of essays.[26]

Sylvain Lévi had always tried to make the humanistic approach in the nucleus of his writing. I believe that this has been the essential tradition of French scholarship in Indian and Buddhist studies since the foundation of

Buddhist philology and of research into the cultural history of Buddhism by Eugene Burnouf (12.VIII.1801–28.V.1852).

Bagchi and French Scholarship

Bagchi can not have ignored Lévi's wide knowledge of Indo-Asian linguistics.[27] As mentioned above, during his first tour to Japan in 1897–1898 Lévi uncovered a number of important works. Among them were two Indo-Sinic dictionaries compiled in China and now lost there, but preserved only in Japan in blockprint. Prabodh Chandra Bagchi edited them with utmost care.[28] However, printing wood blocks have often been sold and bought by dealers. And characters can sometimes be inlaid in the printing wood. A blockprint may be slightly different from others. It is not exactly clear to me which printing Bagchi had really used.[29] It is now eagerly hoped that a new critical edition will be prepared with more materials available now.[30]

In any case, he then dedicated the volumes to the memory of his teacher at Calcutta, Sir Asutosh Mookherjee (1864–1924), as the first Indian organizer of scientific works: "À la memoire / de / SIR AUSTOSH MOOKERJEE / le / premier organisateur / des travaux / scientifiques dans l'Inde" (Bagchi, *op.cit.*, II, p. (v)).[31] Indeed, it was Sir Asutosh, who had sent him to Visva-Bharati, where he met his beloved lifelong master Sylvain Lévi. All those who have teachers or who are teachers of others cherish Sylvain Lévi's name. In fact, Bagchi calls him "mon cher Guru Monsieur Sylvain Lévi".

Prabodh Chandra Bagchi's wide range of research work was brushed up under the efficient guidance of Sylvain Lévi in Paris for the period between 1923 and 1926. It was also in Paris, where Prabodh was fortunate enough to learn a great deal from various eminent scholars such as Antoine Meillet (1866–1936), Paul Pelliot (1878–1945), Jules Bloch (1880–1953), Henri Maspero (1883–1945) among many others. In connection with his work beyond the Indian boundaries Bagchi must have been influenced by Henri Cordier (1849–1925)[32] as well as René Grousset (1885–1952).[33] It was there, I believe, that he firmly attained the western methodology. In carrying out his research work he carefully consulted the first and second source materials written in both eastern and western languages either classical or modern. This is evident from reading his publications.

No one would deny Henri Cordier's remarkable contribution to Asian geography and history as well as his bibliographical works. It may therefore be interesting to know of his whole private library collection, which is now kept in the famed library named Shid Bunko at Keio University in Tokyo (since 1975). It was formerly in the possession of Lord Moritatsu HOSOKAWA (細川護立: 1883–1970) of Kumamoto, who bought it at an auction during his stay in Europe. A scholar's library collection tells many stories of scientific researches by itself. It is a library of about 5,000 books.[34]

After the death of René Grousset a grand exhibition was organized in his honour in collaboration with a great number of scholars, collectors and museums throughout the world. Japanese specialists also lent their helping hands. Its wide range of coverage in Eurasia itself shows a vivid account of his scholarship and familiarity among the people.[35]

In Paris Bagchi had fostered friendships with others who were there, even from the farthest east. Immediately after his return to India Bagchi began to bring out his detailed work on the Chinese Buddhist canon. He inaugurated the new series in Calcutta.[36] Incidentally, I cannot but help feeling I am living in a completely different age, when I think of those days in which Stanislas Julien (1799–1873) was producing a number of important works out of the canonical literature in Chinese without having a complete set of the Tripiṭaka!

His rich international background often explains the quality of his research work. The book of outstanding value published immediately before his death is another example. The core of this work is a series of lectures he delivered in Calcutta as Hem Chandra Basu Mallik Professor of Indian History from 1949 to 1951. It is a work based upon a wide range of his well documented knowledge. He turns his keen eyes and his profound and fresh insight, as always, to the relation of these studies to India, as the title gives eloquent proof.[37] It is a pity, therefore, that Prabodh Chandra Bagchi has given no detailed reference to his arguments. Once again Sylvain Lévi must have been his initiator in this respect. The Guru had shown him the path to the goal.[38]

Among many others Sylvain Lévi knew about the importance of Jain studies from Chinese source materials. It may well be worthwhile to mention here that Lévi seems to have encouraged Bagchi to take up Jain studies from this angle. Lévi writes about it in one of his many letters addressed to a famed Jain scholar.[39]

Sino-Indian Scholarly Friendship

He was not just a scholar who worked on ancient India and China, but also a bridge between the ancient world and the modern. In connection with his studies on Sino-Indian relations from historical perspectives, mention must be made of his appointment as the first visiting professor of Indian history and culture at the University of Peking. The Government of India accredited this position from 1947 to the next year. There he was intimately acquainted with the then President of Peking University, Dr. Hu Shih 胡適 (1891–1962), one of the most prominent scholars at the time. It was in that university that a number of young and promising scholars of Indology were seriously working immediately after the World War II. In this connection it is indeed fortunate to see Jan Yün-hua at McMaster University in Hamilton, who has brought out a stimulating article (in Chinese).[40]

If one carefully compares the works both of Sylvain Lévi and Prabodh Chandra Bagchi, it is clear that the influence may not just be one-way.[41] But it is really beautiful and admirable to see how much Prabodh Chandra looked up to Lévi as his great role. Though briefly, he expresses his sentiment in his obituary.[42]

After joining Visva-Bharati in 1945 he fostered a number of disciplines and disciples. He was elected Vice-Chancellor in 1954, when everyone had expected him to facilitate the work of students pursuing Chinese and Japanese studies in particular. His untimely death is still lamented by all serious scholars throughout the world.

If Bagchi had lived longer, he might have corrected the direction of what is called a "restoration" of Indic texts from their corresponding Chinese and/or Tibetan versions. I am very opposed to such projects.[43]

Afterword in Short

In short, I have tried to place special emphasis upon the importance of international scientific intercourse and mutual understandings among academics. Bagchi was undoubtedly an illustrious example in this regard. Therefore, I deeply lament for his premature death. It is the duty of the following generations to further promote his profound achievements in striving towards the goal of greater human knowledge. It is after all the globalization of the real humanities, not the cultural monopolization under the multiplicity of civilizations.

Finally, Professor Kalyan Kumar Sarkar at Windsor in Canada, one of the most distinguished among Prabodh Chandra Bagchi's students, was the author of a nice booklet offering a warm, if rather brief description of his teacher.[44] He afterwards also wrote a tribute to his teacher containing a condensed description of works by Bagchi.[45] In this connection it may be worth quoting some short obituaries of Prabodh Chandra Bagchi.[46]

Addenda

After having published this paper I realized that I had placed a little too much stress on the international relations. Bagchi must naturally have had a good academic climate in pursuit of his research work at home, particularly at the Viśva-Bhāratī. A variety of scenes in the good old days is found in a booklet published on its 50th anniversary: *Santiniketan 1901–1951* (23 December 1951;

reprinted on the 70th anniversary on 23 December 1971, and later in September 1986) (Calcutta: Visva-Bharati, 1986), (ii), 35 p., 63 pI. (after p. 18).[47]

Further in this connection some earlier works in the relevant fields of study may have had an educative influence on Bagchi, sce e.g. Probhat Kumar Mukherjee, *Indian Literature Abroad (China)* (=*Calcutta Oriental Series*, No. 22, E.14) (Calcutta: Calcutta Oriental Press, 1928), (ii), iii, 98 p.

Notes

1 See Louis Renou, "Sylvain Lévi et son oeuvre scientifique", *Memorial Sylvain Lévi* (Paris: Paul Hartmann, 1937), p. XX.XV1. This article was originally published in the *Journal Asiatique*, CCXXVIII (1936), p. 1–59. – cf. *infra* n. 41. One may now consult Gauranga Gopal Sengupta, *Indology and its Eminent Western Savants (Collection of Biographies of Western Indologists)*. With a foreword by the late A. L. Basham (Calcutta: Punthi-Pustak, 1996), esp. p. 213–215.

2 Cf. Akira YUYAMA, *Eugène Burnouf: The Background to his Research into the Lotus Sutra (= Bibliotheca Philologica et Philosophica Buddhica, III)* (Tokyo: International Research Institute for Advanced Buddhology, Soka University, 2000), xiv, 192 pages: see esp. p. 40f.: §5.2.0 end, also p. 23f.: §3.4.1 end.

– Since the appearance of my book on Burnouf I have been feeling rather ashamed at having committed too many typos in addition to my careless omission of a number of works in the "Reference" section. 1 was rushing to bring it out in fixed time and had thus no time left to revise the composition. Although this seems like crying over spilt milk, I am sincerely hoping to write a short revisional paper within a few years, if at all possible. In the meantime, more information of a relevant topic may be available on request, if any.

3 See Suniti Kumar Chatterji, "In Memoriam – Prabodh Chandra Bagchi (1898–1956)", *Indian Linguistics – Bagchi Memorial Volume,* by Members of the Faculty of the Schools of Linguistics, Deccan College, Poona, jointly with Linguistic Society of India (Published by the Linguistic Society of India, 1957), p. 1–11, 1 frontisp. (photo) (written Calcutta, 20.VII.1957). – cf. next note.

4 Prabodh Chandra Bagchi, *Indological Studies: A Collection of Essays* (Santiniketan: Visva Bharati Research Publications Committee, 1982), xxi, 523 p., 1 portr.-frontisp. ["Index", p. 501–523]. -In it is reprinted Chatterji's tribute, p. ix–xxi.

5 V. Raghavan, *Indological Studies in India* (Delhi-Patna-Varanasi: Motilal Banarsidass, 1964), p.32.

6 D. Sylvain-Lévi, *Dans l'Inde (de Ceylon au Népal)* (Paris: F. Rieder et Cie, 1926), esp. p. 114 et suiv. Later on in her diary she refers to him familiarly as Prabodh and mentions that he was going to follow his master to study for two years in Europe after one year in Hanoi (*ibid.*, p. 168).

Both M. et Mme Sylvain Lévi must have enjoyed their trip to the East. A rare photo of the couple in Indian costume taken in 1922 at Santiniketan is found in a booklet: *Université de Paris – Institut de Civilisation Indienne 1933–1935, p. 22.*

7 Cf. George Cœdès, *Histoire Ancienne des États Hindouisés d'Ertrême-Orient* (Hanoi: Imprimerie d'Extrême-Orient, 1944), VIII, 366 p. (incl. 2 tables & 5 cartes); Nouvelle édition revue et mise à jour par G. Cœdès (Paris: Boccard, 1964), 494 p., tables & cartes; G. Cœdès, *The Indianized States of Southeast Asia*, edited by Walter F. Vella & translated by Susan

Brown Cowing (Canberra: Australian National University Press, 1975), xxi, 403 p., maps & tables.

Also G. Cœdès, *Les peuples de la péninsule indochinoise: histoire – civilisation* (= *Collection Sigma*, II) (Paris: Dunod, 1962), 228 p., 1 carte, XVI pl.; G. Cœdès, *The Making of South East Asia*, translated by H. M. Wright (London: Routledge & Kegan Paul, 1966, repr. 1967 / Paperback ed.: Berkeley-Los Angeles-London: University of California Press, 1983), xvii, 268 p.

Cf. Jean Filliozat, "Notice sur la vie et les travaux de M. George Cœdès", *Bulletin de l'École Française d'Etrême-Orient*, LVII (1970), p. 1–24, 1 portr.-frontisp. ["Publications", p. 10–241.

8 Cf. e.g. G. Cœdès, "In Memoriam", *Bulletin de l'Ecole Française d'Etrême-Orient*, XXXV (1936), p. 507–515 [= Extrait du BEFEO, 9 p.]; Victor Goloubew, "Louis Finot / Sylvain Lévi et l'Indochine", *ibid.*, p. 515–550 (et P1. LXXIX) / p. 551–574 (et Pl. L) XX) [= Extrait, p. 9–44 / p. 45–681.

9 See "Rapport de M. Sylvain Lévi sur sa mission dans l'Inde et au Japon", *Comptes rendus de l'Académie des Inscriptions et Belles-Lettres* (Paris 1899), p. 71–92 = *Mémorial Sylvain Lévi* (Paris: Paul Hartmann, 1937), p. 237–270.

10 See *Bulletin de la Maison Franco-Japonaise*, VIII, 2–4 (Année 1936) (Paris: Paul Geuthner Tokyo: Mitsukoshi, 1937), Première partie, p. 17–62: "Sylvain Lévi et son œuvre"; *Hommage à Sylvain Lévi pour le centenaire de sa naissance* (Paris: E. de Boccard, 1964).

11 Sylvain Lévi, "Matériaux japonais pour l'étude du bouddhisme", *Bulletin de la Maison Franco-Japonaise*, Série française, No. 1 (Tokyo 1927), p. 1–63 (whole number); a portion of this article "Inventaire des sectes bouddhiques japonaises" (p. 25–54) is to be found in: *Mémorial Sylvain Lévi*, p. 319–340.

12 Paul Demiéville, "Nécrologie – Alfred Foucher (1865–1952), René Grousset (18851952), Jules Bloch (1880–1953)", T`oung Pao, série II, vol. XLII (1954), p. 406–411, 411–415, 415–417. -see p. 407 on Foucher and the inauguration of the Maison.

13 法寶義林/*Hôbôgirin: Dictionnaire encyclopédique du bouddhisme d'après les sources chinoises et japonaises*, publié sous le haut patronage de l'Académie Impériale du Japon, I: *A-Bombai* (Tokyo: Maison Franco-Japonaise, 1929), 96 p. (incl. 41 figs.), VIII pl. + "Supplément au premier fascicule", I, XV p.

14 *Fascicule annexe: Tables du Taishô Issaikyô* (1932), (I), II, 202 p.; Édition révisée et augmentée par Hubert Durt et Anna Seidel (Paris-Tokyo 1978), (v), 372 p.

15 Cf. e.g. Sylvain Lévi, *L'Inde et le Monde* (Paris: Librairie Ancienne Honoré Champion: Librairie de la Société de l'Histoire de France et de la Société des Anciens Textes, 1926), 177 p. – cf. "L'œuvre comp let de Sylvain LÉVI", *Bibiographie bouddhique*, VII–VIII: 19341936 (1937), p. 27b: No. 276.

16 Lévi, "Eastern humanism", *op.cit.*, p. 155–175.

17 Prabodh Chandra Bagchi, *India and China* (= *Greater India Society Bulletin*, II) (Calcutta: Abinash Chandra Sarkar at the Prabasi Press, January-February 1927), 42 p.

18 Unfortunately, I have not yet been able to see his *India and China* (Calcutta: China Press Ltd., 1945), 240 p. – cf. Nalinaksha Dutt, *Indian Historical Quarterly*, XXI (1945), p. 151f.

19 Prabodh Chandra Bagchi, *India and China. A Thousand Years of Cultural Relations*. 2nd ed., revised and enlarged (Bombay: Hind Kitabs, 1950 / New York: Philosophical Society, 1951), viii, 234 p., 1 folded map (frontisp.).

20 A detailed biographical sketch and a list of his publications can be found in: 季羡林教授八十華誕紀念論文集/*Papers in Honour of Prof. Dr. Ji Xianlin on the* Occasion *of His 80th Birthday*, I (南昌: 江西人民出版社, 1990): 季錚, "季羡林教授年譜與譯著目錄",

p. 1–7 (年譜: up to 1990), p. 8–35 (譯著目錄: 1929–1991); 錢文忠, "季羨林教授學術", p. 37–43.

An Arabist Tsai Tê-kuei by name has recently published a voluminous biographical work on Chi Hsien-lin: 蔡德貴, 季羨林傳 (太原: 山西古藉出版社, 1998), ii, 13, 836 p., 6-page frontisp. (including many photos in colour).

21 To my knowledge at hand, his first collected papers on the relevant topics appeared in 1957: 季羨林, 中印文化關係論叢 (北京: 人民出版社, 1957), (iii), 202 p. Since then quite a few were published, i.e. in 1982, 1990, 1991.

22 印度古代語言論集 . *A Selected Papers on the Languages of Ancient India • Ausgewählte kleine Schriften zur altindischen Philologie* (北京: 中國社會科學出版社, 1982), (vii), 438 p.

23 Dschi Hiän-lin, "Die Konjugation des finiten Verbums in den Gāthas des Mahāvastu", *op.cit.*, p. 1–132 [originally: III + 118 pages]. – cf. J. W. de Jong, *Bibliographic bouddhique*, XXIV-XXVII: 1950–1954 (Paris 1958), No. 476: "Thèse de Göttingen non-imprimée".

Cf. A. Yuyama, "A Bibliography of the *Mahāvaseu-Avadāna", Indo-lranian Journal*, XI (The Hague 1968), p. 16: §B.1. Further Klaus Ludwig Janert, Verzeichnis *indienkundlicher Hochschulschriften : Deutschland - Österreich* -Schweiz (Wiesbaden: Otto Harrassowitz, 1961), esp. p. 60: No. 865 *Dschi, Hiän-lin (Shiann-lin Jih)*.

24 S 季羨林學術論著自選集 (北京: 北京師范學院出版社, 1991), (vi), 2 , 1 4 , 675 p., 1 portr.frontisp./季羨林佛教學術論文集 (=中華佛學研究所論叢, IV) (臺北: 東初出版社, 1995), (i), 8, 2, 2, 512 p. (photo on cover/title pages)/中國社會科學院學者文選 • *Selected Works of the Scholars in the Chinese Academy of Social Sciences*: 季羨林集 (北京: 中國社會科學出版社, 2000), (v), 2, 2, 403 p.

25 See e.g. a nice pocketbook: 季羨林, 天竺心影 (天津: 百花文藝出版社, 1980), (ii), 2, 126 p.

26 His interesting essays are to be found in: 季羨林學術文化隨筆 (= 二十世紀中國學術文化隨筆大系) (北京: 中國青年出版社, 1996), VI, 300 p. And his complete works in prose appeared recently in four volumes: 季羨林散文全編 (河北省高碑店: 中國廣播電視出版社, 1999).

27 Cf. e.g. Jules Bloch, *Sylvain Lévi et la linguistique indienne. Leçon inaugurals lue au Collège de France le 13 avril 1937* (Paris: Adrien-Maisonneuve, 1927), 30 p. – Bloch read his inaugural lecture at the time when he succeeded to the chair of Sanskrit language and literature held by Lévi until his death (1894–1935).

28 Prabodh Chandra Bagchi, *Deur lexiques sanskrit-chinois*, I-II (= Sino-Indica: Publications de l'Université de Calcutta, II–III) (Paris: Librairie Orientaliste Paul Geuthner, 1929–1937), (iii), 336 p.; (v), ii, 337–544 p.

29 Bagchi, *op.cit.*, II (1937), p. 339 cum n. 1. Cf. "Rapport de M. Sylvain Lévi sur sa mission dans l'Inde et au Japon", *Mémorial Sylvain Lévi* (1937), p. 267.

30 A. Yuyama, "Toward a New Edition of the Fan yü Tsa-ming of Li-yen", *Wisdom, Compassion, and the Search for Understanding: The Buddhist Studies Legacy of Gadjin M. Nagao*, edited by Jonathan A. Silk (= Studies in the Buddhist Tradition, edited by Luis O. Gómez at the University of Michigan, Ann Arbor) (Honolulu: University of Hawai`i Press, 2000), p. 397–411.

31 On Sir Asutosh see e.g. A. P. Das Gupta, *Asutosh Mukherjee (= National Biography Series)* (New Delhi: National Book Trust, 1973), (xii), 179 p.

Cf. further Jay Gopal Banerjee, "Sir Asutosh Mookerjee: His Life and Work", *Sir Asutosh Memorial Volume, I* (Published by J. N. Samaddap, Patna, 1926), p. iii–xiv.

32 Cf. e.g. *Bibliographic des Œuvres de Henri Cordier, Membre de l'Institut, publiée à 1'occasion du 75e anniversaire de sa nairsance* (Paris: Paul Geuthner, 1924), VIII, 151 p., 1 portrait-fronstisp.

33 Cf. e.g. *La vie et l'œuvre de René Grousset* (= *France-Asie: Revue mensuelle de culture et de synthèse franco-asiatique*, 8e année: 88–89 / tome IX: Sept.-oct. 1953), VII, 761–934 p., 1 portr. frontisp. et 1 facsimilé page.

34 コルディエ 文庫分類目錄 / *A Classified Catalogue of Books of the Henri Cordier Collection* (慶應義塾大學附屬研究所．斯道文庫 Shido-Bunko: Institute of Oriental Classics, Keio University, Tokyo), (i), 16, 1, 147 p., 2-plate frontisp. (portrait & photos of books).

35 Ville de Paris – Musée Cernuschi: *La découverte de 1'Asie – Hommage à René Grousset: L'exposition: Découverte de l'Asie a été organisée par la Ville de Paris pour rendre hommage à l' œuvre de celui qui a le plus contribué à faire connaître en Occident les cultures asiatiques à René Grousset de l'Académie Française, Conservateur en Chef du Musée Guimet, Conservateur du Musée Cernuschi 1885–1952*....... (1954), X, 157 p., XXXII planches (plus 8-page corrigenda et addenda).

36 Prabodh Chandra Bagchi, *Le canon bouddhique en Chine: Les traducteurs et les traductions*, I–II(= *Sino-Indica: Publications de l'Université de Calcutta*, I et IV) (Paris: Paul Geuthner, 1927–1938), (iii), LII, 436 p.; (v), 437–744 p.

37 Prabodh Chandra Bagchi, *India and Central Asia* (Calcutta: National Council of Education, Bengal / Printed at Santiniketan, 1955), (vii), 185 p., 1 folded map.

38 See e.g. Sylvain Lévi, "Central Asian Studies", *Journal of the Royal Asiatic Society*, October 1914, Article No. XXVII, p. 953–963 (abstract of his paper read 16 June 1914). Bagchi may have missed this in his otherwise useful comprehensive "Bibliography", *op.cit.*, p. 162–163.

39 *Letters to Vijayendra Suri*. Published with an introduction by Raghu Vira (Bombay: Yashodharma Mandir – London: Arthur Probsthain, 1960), p. 151: "...Jainism requires a well trained Chinese Scholar. I hope that my new student P. C. Bagchi who is sailing back to India next June and who is good in Chinese and Tibetan will be of help on that side....".

40 Jan Yün-hua (冉雲華), "胡適與印度友人師覺月/Dr. Hu Shih and His Indian Friend - Dr. P.C. Bagchi", *Chung-Hwa Buddhist Journal* (中華佛學學報), No. 6 (Taipei, July 1993), p. 263–278 ('English summary' on p. 278). Jan has added a useful list: 'A Bibliography of Dr. P. C. Bagchi's Works' on p. 272–277. - Jan seems to have taken it from Sarkar (cf. *infra* n. 44). The works written by Bagchi in Bengali have regrettably been omitted.

41 For Lévi's publications see Maurice Maschino et Nadine Stchoupak, "Rétrospective: L'œuvre complet de Sylvain Lévi", *Bibliographie bouddhique*, VII-VIII (1934–1936) (Paris: Adrien-Maisonneuve, 1937), p. 1–64. - cf. also *supra* n. 11

42 Prabodh Chandra Bagehi, "Obituary Notice – Sylvain Lévi", *Indian Historical Quarterly*, XII, 1 (March 1936), p. 177–186 ('List of Works', p. 180–186).

43 Cf. A. Yuyama, "Restoration – Translation – Emendation: Along the Way to Revisit the *Vimalakīrti-nirdeśa* Cited by Kamalaśila in his *Bhāvanakrama III*", *Festschrift Sodō MORI* (Hamamatsu, in press).

44 *Prabodh Chandra Bagchi*, published with a Foreword by Lila Majumdar (on 22 December 1956) (Printed by Ranajit Kumar Dutta at Nabasakti Press in Calcutta), 25 pages: "Dr. P. C. Bagchi - A Short Sketch", p. 3–9; "Dr. P. C. Bagchi and Research Studies in Visva-Bharati", p. 10–14; "Important Events in Dr. P. C. Bagchi's Life (1898–1956)", p. 15f.; "A Bibliography of Dr. P. C. Bagchi's Works", p. 15–25. – cf. *supra* n. 40.

45 Kalyan Kumar Sarkar, "Hommage au Professeur Prabodh Chandra Bagchi", *France-Asie: Revue mensuelle de culture et de synthèse franco-asiatique*, 13e Année: n° 144 / Tome XV (Saigon 1958), p. 207–209. - Incidentally, it may interest some colleagues to see a

subtitle "Pour le 2500' anniversaire du <<Parinirvana>> du Bouddha" in the list of contents of this issue.

46 V. Raghavan in the *Journal of Oriental Research,* XXV: 1955–1956 (Madras-Mylapore: Kuppuswami Sastri Research Institute, 1957), p. 97; and anonymously in *The Modern Review,* LXXXXIX, 3 (Calcutta 1956), p. 186. *Annals of the Bhandarkar Oriental Research Institute,* edited by R. N. Dandekar, XXXVI: 1955 (Poona 1956), p. 381.

47 I have recently noted yet another publication, which drew my attention a lime too late to see it: *Visva Bharati – Santiniketan, 1901–2000* (Calcutta: Publications Department, Visva-Bharati, 2000), 57 p., ills.

INDEX

Professor Bagchi used different systems to transcribe Chinese words and phrases in his essays. We did not attempt to standardise them in the text because it often required consulting original sources and editions not easily accessible. Instead, we have tried to provide, in brackets, the Hanyu Pinyin equivalent/correction for some of the words and phrases included in this Index. Where possible we have also added the relevant Chinese characters.